Moses and Civilization

Moses and Civilization

The Meaning Behind Freud's Myth

Robert A. Paul

Yale University Press   New Haven and London

Published with assistance from
the Mary Cady Tew Memorial Fund.

Designed by Sonia L. Scanlon.
Set in Berkeley type by Rainsford Type,
Danbury, Connecticut.
Printed in the United States of America by
BookCrafters, Inc., Chelsea, Michigan.

Library of Congress Cataloging-in-Publication Data
Paul, Robert A.
Moses and civilization : the meaning behind Freud's myth
/ Robert A. Paul
p.   cm.
Includes bibliographical references and index.
ISBN 0-300-06428-4 (alk. paper)
1. Psychoanalysis and religion. 2. Freud, Sigmund, 1856–
1939—Religion. 3. Moses (Biblical leader) 4. Bible O.T.
Pentateuch.—Criticism, interpretation, etc.   I. Title.
BF175.4.R44P38   1996
200'.1'9—dc20   95-23585
CIP

A catalogue record for this book is available from
the British Library.

The paper in this book meets the guidelines for
permanence and durability of the Committee on
Production Guidelines for Book Longevity of the
Council on Library Resources.

10   9   8   7   6   5   4   3   2   1

For Leslee

Contents

Moses and Civilization

1

Beyond Freud's Moses

I

This book represents my effort to further the understanding of Western civilization begun by Freud in his "cultural books," especially *Totem and Taboo, Civilization and Its Discontents,* and *Moses and Monotheism.* These works contain an insight of great depth and power to which we have remained blind because Freud himself did not correctly understand what he had observed and so presented his theory to the world in ways that made it easy to dismiss or refute—and thus, to neglect and ignore. By rectifying certain missteps Freud made in the development of his argument, I hope to reawaken interest in the great mythic matrix he identified within which our civilization has evolved, stamping it with its distinctive character.

I need not undertake a detailed exegesis of Freud's theory of civilization (by which term he meant Western civilization, as was the fashion when he wrote).[1] The heart of that theory I take to be this single fruitful—but misleading—insight: our civilization, and especially its moral and religious aspects (upon which other aspects may be said to depend), can be understood by using the analogy of a case of obsessional neurosis in an individual. Freud announces his theme in his first foray into cultural criticism, the 1907 essay "Obsessive Actions and Religious Practices"; it informs the entire text of *Totem and Taboo* and is equally present (if less explicitly so) in *Civilization and Its Discontents;* it receives its final, most explicit exposition in Freud's last major work, *Moses and Monotheism.*[2]

There, Freud summarized the theory thus:

> Early trauma—defence—latency—outbreak of neurotic illness—partial return of the repressed. Such is the formula we have laid down for the development of a neurosis. The reader is now invited to take the step of supposing that something occurred in the life of the human species similar to what occurs in the life of individuals: of supposing, that is, that here too events occurred of a sexually aggressive nature, which left behind them permanent consequences but were for the most part fended

off and forgotten, and which after a long latency came into effect
and created phenomena similar to symptoms in their structure
and purpose. (1939, 80)

Just as in the person with an obsessional neurosis all the thoughts,
images, feelings, and dreams encountered during free association form a
spinning galaxy around a central unconscious fantasy built upon the repressed and defensively distorted memory of a childhood trauma or traumatic situation, so, Freud believes, the fervently but irrationally held beliefs
and practices of any religion take their meaning from the repressed collective memory of a founding historical traumatic event.

That event, which Freud first proposed in the final chapter of *Totem
and Taboo,* is the deed that marked the end of our living in the state of
nature and gave rise to "civilization": namely, the murder of the primal
father by his rebellious sons.[3] According to Freud, humans originally lived
in an elementary social unit he called the "primal horde." In this group, a
senior dominant male ruled those females he could control as his consorts,
along with their immature offspring. As the daughters became sexually mature, the dominant male, or "primal father," added them to his harem. But
when his sons matured—and thus posed a threat to his exclusive sexual
access to the females—he either drove them out, castrated them, or fought
them to the death. When the primal father was eventually dethroned, the
victorious junior male would simply take his place, and the system would
reproduce itself.

The traumatic deed upon which the history of civilization depends,
according to Freud, was the rebellion of a band of brothers, united in their
hatred of the primal father's sexual monopoly and his authoritarian rule
who, emboldened, perhaps, by the invention of some new weapon, decided
to put an end to the system of the primal horde. They killed their oppressor
and ate him, intending thus magically to gain his strength while destroying
his hated domination. But a struggle for succession threatened, as each
brother hoped or plotted to attain the dominant position. What forestalled
the return of the hated system was the ambivalence the brothers had felt
toward the primal father. Although they had hated him, they had also loved
him and depended on him for protection, not only from external aggressors
but from anarchy within the group. Having expressed their hatred by their
murderous deed, they now, because of their affection for him, felt guilty.
They therefore established a covenant whereby each renounced the goal for

which all had rebelled, namely, sexual access to the females. At the same time they forswore murder within the group.

With this pact, the primal horde came to an end, and a new social system emerged—the one upon which our civilization is based—that rested on prohibitions against incest and murder specifically instituted to avoid the reemergence of the primal horde. The memory of the murder of the father now became a source of guilt for the brothers and their descendants. First as a fantasied "totem animal," then as the deities and heroes of subsequent stages of civilization, and finally as the monotheistic paternal God of the Judeo-Christian tradition, the memory of the primal father returned as the repressed, enforcing the ever-stricter rules of self-discipline that turned humans from creatures of the savanna into the unhappy denizens of the contemporary cosmopolitan world.

For Freud, the Judeo-Christian religious tradition so central to Western civilization and its intellectual, moral, and sociopolitical history plays a special role in this evolutionary tale. He came to believe that the Israelites had in fact murdered Moses and thus reenacted the primal murder that founded their own civilization. Having then repressed the memory of this crime, they fell prey to a collective obsessional neurosis, namely, Judaism itself, with its apparently trivial or pointless rules, ordinances, ceremonies, prohibitions, and self-accusations. Christianity, so Freud argues, arose when a Jew, Saul of Tarsus (Saint Paul), intuitively realized that the neurotic sense of guilt prevalent in the civilized world was the result of the seemingly forgotten—but unconsciously remembered—murder of Moses and, behind that, the murder of the primal father. Paul founded a successful and dynamic cult that spoke to a universal condition by proposing that if one consciously admits one's guilt and atones for it through the sacrificial death of Jesus, one can be freed of both anxiety and the compulsion to submit to the rigorous demands of Judaism. Although the Israelites alone killed Moses, everyone bears the guilt for the original crime—the killing of the primal father—hence, for Freud, Christianity had the potential of becoming a universal religion.

No one, of course, believes this story of Freud's. Without even addressing the question of the dubious historical and ethnographic "facts," the use of a thoroughly outmoded cultural evolutionism, and the apparent implication that future generations acquire the repressed complexes of their ancestors by some sort of direct inheritance, we can reject the central analogy itself as untenable: a civilization just is *not* like a person. It does not have a childhood, a latency, an adolescence, or a maturity; it does not have a collective "mind" or subjectivity, and it cannot in any meaningful way be understood as the sort of entity that could have a neurosis. The people who constitute a civilization may certainly have neuroses, even similar or typical ones; and they surely have memories—including repressed ones—as well. There are even collective memories, in the sense that records of past events may lie in public, accessible places: books, for example; But to speak of a civilization as if it were a living organism with a developmental cycle that, in its present "adulthood," could exhibit the symptoms of a neurosis because of the repressed memory of a trauma experienced in its earlier "child-hood"—this just won't fly.

II

Yet despite the (to us) self-evident inadequacy of Freud's argument as I have summarized it cursorily here, there yet remains something intuitively at-tractive and even persuasive about his analogy. There is, first, the intensely compulsory quality that religious practices often possess, which makes them impervious to alteration or refutation by rational argument, even though they often seem to have no rationale other than the feeling that one must perform them or risk unbearable punishment, guilt, or anxiety. There is also the observation, borne out by recent research, that the mental opera-tions used in the construction of obsessional and compulsive symptoms are not simply similar but identical to ones used in the construction of rituals the world over.[4]

Another consideration is that the symbolism of many religious beliefs and practices from diverse cultures, especially those of the Judeo-Christian tradition, are consistent with the sorts of fantasies encountered in the anal-ysis of people with either Obsessive-Compulsive Personality Disorder or elements of the disorder in their character.

And finally, a good case can be made that the obsessive-compulsive personality, and especially its manifestation in the normal or high-functioning range, is a typical and distinctive character type central to West-ern civilization. When one considers the bureaucracies upon which the West has come to depend, whether in government, business, or military affairs; the professions to which they give rise, such as law or finance; the enterprises of science, technology, mathematics, engineering; or all forms of literate scholarship, management, and record keeping; one cannot imag-

ine them functioning effectively without the voluntary participation of people for whom such activities are experienced as appropriate and fulfilling
in some way, and who are motivated not only to acquiesce to the organization of their lives by such structures but actively to maintain and reproduce these cultural and social institutions.

In the subdiscipline of psychological anthropology we seek, among
other things, to understand the correspondence and interaction between
phenomena at the collective, sociocultural level, on the one hand, and those
at the individual level, on the other. Cultural systems have features that
cannot be reduced to the individual level, it is true; but individuals are also
something other than mere pawns whereby cultural forces and dynamics
play out their autonomous scripts. Cultures and social structures exist only
as long as the individuals who constitute them actively pursue certain activities out of motives and in pursuit of goals that are meaningful first and
foremost to *them* as purposive, desiring, strategizing persons. If a culture,
however defined (Western Judeo-Christian civilization, for example), can
be differentiated from any other social group in any meaningful way, it
must follow that the people who produce, maintain, and reproduce it are
acting on a complex of desires, goals, and strategies that are distinctive in
their overall patterning from those of people in other cultural settings.

The challenge in psychological anthropology is to understand how
cultural symbols, social institutions, and individual actors interact to produce the various observed phenomena. For writers with a psychoanalytic
orientation one part of that task is to show how cultural symbol systems
and individual psychodynamic constellations form and inform one another
in a dialectical, mutually constitutive process.[5]

How, then, can the connection between Freud's theory of culture and
a valid understanding of Western civilization be pursued without entailing
the flaws that rendered Freud's own attempt unsuccessful?

III

To retrace Freud's path of reasoning, and to avoid the wrong turns he made,
I shall begin where I think he himself may have begun. A patient, like one
Freud might have seen (though such patients are rarely treated in analysis
today), suffering from a full-fledged obsessional neurosis, would present as
symptoms an array of practices, verbal formulas, and/or unwanted thoughts
that he or she considered irrational but that he or she could not get rid of

by willful effort or rational argument. For Freud, this complex of symptoms could be rendered intelligible by understanding them as compromise formations in which the impulses connected with an unconscious fantasy struggled with defensive measures intended to ward off the forbidden or anxiety-producing impulses and to keep them from reaching conscious awareness.

The unconscious fantasy, in turn, would be comprehensible as an unconscious memory, defensively distorted to some greater or lesser degree, of an event (or set of events) from childhood that was so overwhelming, overstimulating, painful, or otherwise unmanageable by the psyche that it constituted a trauma. Through analysis, the patient and the analyst could reconstruct a version of the original trauma. Conscious knowledge of the trauma, Freud believed, if properly worked through in analysis and in the transference, would result in a diminution of the traumatic memory's power to produce irrational and compulsory symptoms.

An example from Freud's early writings on obsessional neurosis provides a good illustration of the way a symptom complex can be explained by the discovery, or, as the case may be, reconstruction, of a childhood trauma. Here, the patient, an eleven-year-old boy, feels compelled to perform a complex ceremonial before going to bed: "He did not go to sleep until he had told his mother in the minutest detail all the experiences he had had during the day; there must be no bits of paper or other rubbish on the carpet . . . ; his bed had to be pushed right up against the wall, three chairs had to be placed in front of it, and the pillows had to lie in a particular way. In order to go to sleep he was obliged first to kick both his legs out a certain number of times and lie on his side" (1896, 172n).

This set of practices seems arbitrary and irrational, yet it is clearly also experienced as compulsory by the boy suffering from the neurosis. The solution is found when Freud either elicits or reconstructs a memory (it is not clear which) of a traumatic event: the boy had been sexually abused by a servant girl as a small child. When a more recent event rearoused the traumatic memory, the compulsion both to repeat and to ward off the trauma consciously expressed itself in the apparently bizarre but actually quite meaningful obsessional ceremonial:

> The chairs were placed in front of the bed and the bed pushed to the wall in order that nobody else should be able to get at the bed; the pillows were arranged in a particular way so that they

should be different from how they were on that evening; the movements with his legs were to kick away the person who was lying on him; sleeping on his side was because in the scene he had been lying on his back; his circumstantial confession to his mother was because, in obedience to a prohibition by his seductress, he had been silent to his mother about this and other sexual experiences; and finally, the reason for his keeping his bedroom floor clean was that neglect to do so had been the chief reproach that he had so far to hear from his mother. (172–173n)

I contend that Freud's perception of the analogy between Judeo-Christian religion and obsessional neurosis began from his judgment that the performance on a regular basis of religious rituals and practices by the great mass of his otherwise "rational," "civilized" contemporaries stands in need of explanation. Why are the particular rituals and practices of Judaism and Catholicism (the religions of his own environment) adhered to with such solemnity, scrupulousness, and compulsion?

His method of answering this question is the same as the one he uses to understand the obsessional ceremonial of an individual: to identify a repressed fantasy and to reconstruct the repressed trauma that has given rise to it.[6] In his Austrian milieu, the most prominent religious ritual would certainly be the Catholic Eucharist, participated in every week by multitudes and sponsored by the theocratic regime of the Hapsburg Emperor. Freud, I propose, worked backward from the contemporary ritual to envision what the trauma must have been, as this passage from *Totem and Taboo* indicates:

> If . . . Christ redeemed mankind from the burden of original sin by the sacrifice of his own life, *we are driven to conclude* that the sin was a murder. The law of the talion, which is so deeply rooted in human feelings, lays it down that a murder can only be expiated by the sacrifice of another life: self-sacrifice *points back* to blood guilt. And if this sacrifice of a life brought about an atonement with God the Father, the crime to be expiated can only have been the murder of the father. (1913b, 154, my emphasis)

The italicized portions of this passage give evidence that Freud is here interpreting a present-day ritual along psychoanalytic lines to reconstruct a past traumatic event, the repressed collective memory of which he assumes motivates the ritual and the beliefs that surround it.

A passage from *Civilization and Its Discontents* supports my view that it was by such an inferential, reconstructive procedure that Freud built up his picture of the events of his hypothesized primal murder: "From the manner in which, in Christianity . . . redemption is achieved—by the sacrificial death of a single person, who in this manner takes upon himself the guilt that is common to everyone—*we have been able to infer* what the first occasion may have been on which this primal guilt, which was also the beginning of civilization, was acquired" (1930, 136, my emphasis).

Freud is perhaps most candid about the reconstructive method he uses for his hypothesis of the primal horde and its bloody finale in this passage from "Thoughts for the Times on War and Death":

> In my book *Totem and Taboo* . . . I have, following clues by Robertson Smith, Atkinson, and Charles Darwin, *tried to guess* the nature of this primal guilt, and I believe, too, that the Christian doctrine of today *enables us to deduce it*. If the Son of God was obliged to sacrifice his life to redeem mankind from original sin, then by the law of the talion, the requital of like by like, that sin must have been a killing, a murder. . . . And [if?] the original sin was an offense against God the Father, the primal crime of mankind must have been a parricide, the killing of the primal father of the primitive human horde, whose mnemic image was later transfigured into a deity. (1915b, 292–293, my emphasis)

A nice bit of evidence supporting my view that the story of the primal crime is a reconstruction based on an interpretation of the Mass is Freud's rather blithe remark, in *Totem and Taboo,* that after the brothers had killed the primal father, "cannibal savages as they were, it goes without saying that they devoured their victim as well as killing him" (1913b, 142). I doubt most of us would agree that this particular detail "goes without saying." But we can see how it might have seemed obvious to Freud, were he working backward from a ritual in which the body and blood of the sacrificed savior are supposed to be consumed as part of the talionic repayment for the original deed: if in the ritual a "son" is eaten, then it follows that at an earlier time, by the law of the talion, the son(s) must have eaten the father.

In the theory of hysteria Freud put forward together with Josef Breuer (Breuer and Freud 1895), so-called auxiliary scenes are events that later in life in some way recall the original traumatic scene, like the unspecified event in the case of the eleven-year-old with the sleeping ceremonial that brought back to consciousness, in the form of the neurotic symptom, the original traumatic episode of sexual abuse. In Freud's reconstruction of the Judeo-Christian tradition, the hypothesized assassination of Moses by the Israelites came to play the role of an auxiliary scene, an incident so reminiscent of the original trauma as to constitute the occasion for the development by "civilization" of a neurotic symptom complex—in this case, the Judeo-Christian religious tradition itself.

Thus far, I have tried to demonstrate that Freud's theory about the primal deed giving rise to civilization is not merely an arbitrary flight of fantasy but follows from a particular method (reconstruction), based on a particular ceremony (the Catholic Mass), resting on a particular theoretical supposition (that the ceremonies central to the life of a civilization can be interpreted in the same way that we interpret the symptomatic obsessions and compulsions of a neurotic individual). How might one support or validate such a theory? The obvious way would be to seek independent corroborating evidence that the reconstructed traumatic event did in fact take place, as "predicted" on the basis of the reconstruction. In the case of *Moses and Monotheism* and its hypothesis about Judeo-Christian religion, one might argue that historical evidence of the murder of Moses would constitute such supporting evidence. Indeed, Freud claimed to have based his decision to write *Moses and Monotheism* on the fact that an independent scholar, Ernst Sellin (1922), purported to find just such evidence in the book of the prophet Hosea.[7]

It follows, then, that much of the skepticism with which Freud's hypothesis of the primal murder—and of its recurrence in the case of Moses— has been greeted arises from the fact that Sellin's theory is widely rejected as a historical conjecture and that no evidence can be imagined, let alone produced, attesting to the original murder that is supposed to have ended the regime of the primal horde and instituted the history of civilized society.

We are led to conclude, then, that what renders Freud's theory indefensible is its grounding in the attempt to reconstruct actual historical events. Not only have these events not been discovered by independent research but even if they had been, they would still leave us with two insoluble problems in Freud's formulation. The first is that we would be forced to make an invalid analogy between the developmental cycle of an individual and the history of a civilization. Second, we would have to believe that later generations, even down to the present day, are powerfully motivated by the repressed memory, not of something that happened to them in their own early childhoods but of something that happened eons ago, something that has led a continued, undiminished but latent existence in the collective psyche by some mechanism that we can hardly imagine within the confines of our contemporary views of mental and cultural life.

IV

But while Freud often spoke of his story of the primal crime as if it represented either an actual historical fact or else a typical occurrence that was repeated over and over in the formative stages of human society, on other occasions he spoke of his reconstruction as a "just-so story," a "scientific myth," or simply a plain old "myth."[8] The difference is critical, but Freud did not capitalize on it, wedded as he appears to have been to his belief that he could find the historical truth that underlies religious belief and practice. But since his supposed "historical truths" are nothing other than his own reconstructions, no one but he, in the absence of corroborating evidence, could have or has had much faith in them.[9]

A myth, however, is not something that happened in the past; it is a story about something that is *supposed to have* happened in the past. The myth, far from being a phenomenon lost in the mists of archaic time, is a phenomenon of the present, for the myth works and remains active and alive by means of the ongoing retellings, enactments, performances, and rituals that actualize it at any given time.

When I refer to something as a myth, I do not mean the word in the pejorative sense of ordinary English, as a "false story" or a "fictional, prettified history," as opposed to "fact" or "reality." I use *myth* in the far stronger sense of a narrative that accounts for the creation of the present order of things at the most comprehensive level. The power of myth does not depend on whether it tells a true story about ancient history but rather upon whether it is capable of providing an authoritative foundation for the continual construction, maintenance, and reproduction of an ongoing social order. A narrative that performs this role is by definition a myth, and is "sacred" insofar as all things seem to take meaning in relation to its authority, while that authority does not appear to derive from anywhere in the present human world. On the contrary, this world is made possible only by the myth itself. The myth relates the story of the origin of the present world and implies how to orient oneself toward this world, as constructed by its master signifiers.[10]

If, then, we reexamine Freud's mode of reasoning, ignoring the issue of whether he offers an accurate reconstruction of the historical past and recognizing instead that we are dealing with a myth, we may ask a question related to but different from the one Freud asks, one that is far more fruitful and involves us in no unsupportable assumptions. That is, if we look at the Christian Mass and its related beliefs and practices as enactments of a great mythic narrative, then we may ask whether we can interpret the ritual, and the story of the Passion it dramatizes, as the fruition of an earlier deed— not, however, an event that has occurred earlier in *history* but rather an event that occurs earlier *in the mythic narrative itself.* Could it be, in other words, that if we are led, as Freud was, to reconstruct a primordial patricide to account for the expiatory ritual sacrifice of a son, that such a patricide forms an earlier episode of the *myth?* If that were so, then we could test our hypothesis by simply looking back in the story to see whether there is any episode corresponding to Freud's myth of the primal crime.

We could, for example, restate Freud's assumption that Moses was murdered by his fractious followers not as a historical fact but as a mythic tradition. If, that is, Sellin is right and there are traces of such a tradition in the book of Hosea, then one need not argue that the event really happened, only that the episode forms part of the story. But support for Sellin's hypothesis is too weak for us to sustain it with any enthusiasm, and so we may abandon this line of reasoning.

Since the Passion story upon which the Mass is based is found in what is called the New Testament by Christians, it stands to reason that the place to look for a precursor in the form of a primal crime is the Old Testament. But our initial expectations are not high. Indeed, it is an oft-repeated point in critical evaluations of Freud's theory in *Moses and Monotheism* that the Hebraic canon, unlike the Hellenic one, does not contain a central patricide: there is, it is said, no Jewish Oedipus.[11] And this appears to be so: Cain killed his brother, as we are often reminded, and Abraham would have killed his son, Isaac, in obedience to God had not the Lord provided a ram as a substitute.[12] But all the patriarchs lived to ripe old ages (although Jacob, it is true, was nearly given heart failure by his son Joseph's various adventures). Of Moses's father we hear next to nothing, and Moses himself, whatever Hosea might have thought, is clearly portrayed for us in Deuteronomy as dying a natural death at the venerable age of 120.

Even I, while musing in this way, was about to give up on the whole idea when there came a realization that, once I thought of it, seemed so obvious, so powerful, and so right that I was persuaded to write this book and place that observation before the public. In short: the whole narrative of the Torah—the first and, in my view, the foundational segment of the entire Hebrew and Christian canon—taken in its entirety, is nothing other than the story of the primal crime. The so-called Pentateuch, the five books of Moses, which forms the heart of Jewish worship and provides the foundation for the Christian tradition as well, is, I now realize, the story of the primal horde, of the rebellious deed that overthrows that system, and, especially, of the aftermath of that deed, namely, the foundation of Judeo-Christian civilization. The Bible story matches Freud's with such uncanny precision that once one realizes what is going on, one sees both Freud's myth and the Bible in an entirely new way.

V

In broad outline, Freud's story of the primal rebellion comprises three separate moments: the era of the regime of the primal horde, the rebellion by the band of brothers, and the establishment of the new order founded on the prohibition against incest and murder, accompanied by the deification of the slain father/tyrant. My analysis of the Torah narrative likewise requires three divisions, corresponding to the old regime, the rebellion, and the establishment of the new regime. It is crucial, therefore, to identify the moment of rebellion itself, since the rest of the analysis follows from that choice.

There can be no question that the only figure in the Torah equal to the titanic role he is to play in the myth is Moses. He is the first and greatest of the prophets, and it is to him that God reveals the Law that rules the Jews (and the Christians) to this day. It is in Moses's Torah that the 613 commandments are to be found, and it is his Torah alone that is continually read aloud in the synagogues of world Jewry. Freud was thus quite right to suspect that Moses would have to be the precursor of Christ in the Passion story and so would have to be implicated in a reconstruction of the founding moment of Judeo-Christian civilization. One can imagine that once Freud had arrived deductively at the hypothesis that there must have been a primal patricide, Sellin's hypothesis of the murder of Moses, together with the other sources that suggested the same idea, would have seemed to be corroboration that his conjecture was well-founded.[13]

My understanding of the myth also implicates Moses, but not as the

victim of the primal patricide. In my view, rather, it is Moses himself who
is the perpetrator of the primal deed. That deed is the rebellion against the
pharaoh of Egypt and the liberation of the Israelites from Egyptian bondage.

The deed having been identified, the rest follows: the regime of the
primal horde corresponds to the era of Israelite bondage in Egypt under
Pharaoh, while the aftermath of the rebellion—and it was this realization
that initially showed me I was on the right track—is indeed the establishment of a new social, moral, and religious order: that is, the revelation of
the Law at Mount Sinai.

This analysis divides the Torah into three parts but at first glance does
not seem to exhaust it. After all, the bondage in Egypt does not even begin
until the opening of Exodus, and the revelation at Sinai comes in the twentieth chapter of the same book. This seems to leave all of Genesis unac-
counted for beforehand, and the remainder of Exodus as well as Leviticus,
Numbers, and Deuteronomy left over.

The latter point seems to me easily addressed. While it is true that the
literal moments atop Sinai occupy only part of Exodus, the remainder of
the Torah is largely given over to the enunciation of laws, ordinances, and
prohibitions, many of which are still in effect, that establish social norms,
a moral order, and the method for the performance of religious actions,
including worship, how to construct the tabernacle, sacrificial ritual, and
annual festivals. True, the three later books contain a continuing narrative
of the wanderings of the Israelites under Moses in the wilderness, but there
is less wealth of incident than occurs in just a few chapters of narratives
like the stories of the patriarchs in Genesis. I therefore propose to regard
the last three of the five books of the Torah as continuations and elaborations of the third moment of the Freudian scenario: that is, the establishment of a new, "civilized" form of life to replace the brutal regime of the
primal father. Such "story" as remains is encompassed by the lifespan of
Moses and largely concerns the establishment and maintenance of his authority.

As for Genesis, my reading of the Torah narrative as a unified whole
suggests that the first book of the Torah plays the role of overture to the
central narrative, which occurs in Egypt. Like the long genealogical pro-
logues in many other mythic traditions, Genesis starts at the beginning,
with the creation of the world, and goes on to spell out how it has come
about that there is a people called the Israelites, how they came to be in
Egypt, and how there came to be a man named Moses who would play the

role of culture hero. In many other mythic traditions, the culture hero is not the creator of the cosmos but a descendant of the first beings. The culture hero plays the crucial role of establishing the order of things as they are today. This is, as I look at it, the role assigned in the Judeo-Christian myth to Moses, who, in the pre-Sinaitic world enunciates by his divinely inspired words the new parameters of earthly existence.

A second purpose of Genesis, as I see it, is to provide a treasury of mythic stories that, by ringing various changes on a few central underlying themes, makes visible the matrix of terms and relations out of which the central overarching myth is to be constructed. Thus, for example, the theme of fraternal strife is repetitively played out between Cain and Abel, Isaac and Ishmael, Jacob and Esau, and Joseph and his brothers. This theme will be addressed and the conflict "resolved" in the Egyptian story, when the previously competitive brothers are able to band together in opposition to the father. This is exemplified in the Moses narrative by the fact that Moses is portrayed as acting in unison with his older brother, Aaron, rather than in competition with him, despite the clear evidence of tension between them.[14]

In addition, we can see that whereas in Freud's myth, the oppressive regime of the primal horde is regarded as the condition of humans living in the original state of nature, in the Torah narrative the fall into civilization occurs later. Before the rise of the cruel pharaoh who enslaves the Israelites, intergenerational conflict is described as manageable. And, indeed, in the original society of the Israelites—that is, the twelve sons of Jacob (called Israel) and their families—a happy ending concludes the book of Genesis. Conflict and estrangement between the father and his sons, and between the brothers, are overcome, the family is elevated to a position of power and prosperity in Egypt through the success of Joseph, and even Pharaoh himself regards Joseph and his clan with respect and affection. It is, I believe, this state of harmony, before the fall into the Freudian primal-horde situation, to which various utopian movements have hoped to restore civilization. The reading of Torah through Freud therefore allows us to modify his formulation on the basis of what we find in the myth.

Finally, I must stress that while I believe that my reading of the Torah is in large measure essentially valid and correct, it by no means invalidates other readings. Rather, it brings to light a hitherto-unremarked dimension of the protean text. There is plenty in Genesis, as well as in the rest of the Torah, that is there for reasons other than relevance to this particular narrative structure, and, indeed, there are even aspects that are inconsistent with it.

VI

Let us now return to my contention that Freud's myth is an explicit attempt to apply the schema of the history of an obsessional neurosis to civilization. It is true that, as I argued, Freud's analogy is inappropriate when applied to the history of a civilization. But this objection is obviated by my own formulation, according to which Freud's narrative corresponds not to the history of civilization, but to an identifiable *myth* about the history of civilization.

It follows, therefore, that if the two myths are the same in structure and the Freudian myth has the structure of an obsessional neurosis, then the Torah narrative, too, must have the structure of an obsessional neurosis. And this is indeed the case. A story in a book can obviously describe or portray the dynamics of an obsessional neurosis, or of the Obsessive-Compulsive Personality Disorder, in a legitimate way that cannot be ascribed to a historical *process*.

But the Torah is no ordinary book that people read to themselves by the fireside. It is a performative text. It is not just *about* a myth; it *is a myth*. And as such it does what myths do: it creates a cosmos within which a form of life takes place and acquires meaning for those under its influence. My analysis provides an insight, then, into how it comes about that a civilization in which the Torah story is one of the great master narratives—as I think no one could reasonably deny is so for the Judeo-Christian tradition—values, requires, and produces in its members a character type with the psychodynamics typical of the healthy end of the obsessive-compulsive scale—a personality type I shall call the "conscientious personality."[15]

Obsessional neurosis is one of the two syndromes that Freud originally identified as "transference neuroses," the other being hysteria. Both of these Freud understood as representing characteristic defensive styles responding to conflicts from the oedipal period of life. If the scenario expressed in his myth of the primal rebellion is a schema typical of an obsessional neurosis, it must be inherently oedipal. One may view Freud's story of the primal deed as the individual Oedipus complex writ large on a social and historical scale. Or one can see the individual Oedipus complex itself as the instantiation in the particular case of the broader mythic scenario informing the cultural system. In either case the implication is that there is a common structural pattern underlying the Oedipus complex, the myth of the primal rebellion, and, I would add, the foundational myth of Judeo-Christian civilization.

While it can be assumed that the oedipal phase of development, far from being a pathological syndrome or particular to any time or place, is an attribute of human life in general, the different ways it is structured, formulated, modeled, and resolved vary both among individuals and in different historical and cultural settings.[16] The Western Oedipus complex, with its characteristic way of handling the ambivalence between the generations, is at least in some part shaped by the religious myth. In a dialectical process, the cultural myth obtains its energy from its correspondence with the deepest wishes, conflicts, and anxieties of the individuals under its sway. The individuals are themselves formed by the cultural myth in such a way that their inchoate impulses, fears, and fantasies are given a definite, publicly valorized shape and meaning.

The mythic narrative of Moses thus plays a central role in the reproduction of a cultural system that has motivational force for the actors who comprise it, by arousing and organizing their own strongest desires and anxieties. At the same time we can understand how this myth achieves its forceful and even compulsory appeal, for it speaks to fundamental human conflicts, wishes, and fears.[17]

2

The Primal Horde

I regard Freud's myth of the primal horde as being an analysis, if perhaps unwitting, of the central narrative around which the Judeo-Christian tradition is organized.[1] If we recognize this, we can use the analysis to understand the structure and dynamics of our civilization insofar as it has developed within the mythic cosmos underwritten by the biblical myth. As we have seen, I shall use the myth as a tool for cultural analysis, not, as Freud did, as either a reconstructed historical fact or a naturalistic account of humans in the precultural state of nature. Freud's theory, which, as Claude Lévi-Strauss rightly observed, is yet another version of the myth itself, can serve us by presenting a sort of stripped-down, generic version of the myth that allows us to see its contours and dynamics clearly.[2]

As we have seen, according to Freud, humans at one time lived in a state of nature, which a single great event—the successful rebellion against the primal father by the band of brothers—brought to an end. Society, religion, and morality came into being as restrictions and inhibitions of the free and unregulated expression of individual volition in the interest of establishing a lasting orderly collective existence. Freud took his image of primordial human society from no less an authority than Charles Darwin, who put forward the following hypothesis in his *Descent of Man:* "The most probable view is that primaeval man aboriginally lived in small communities, each with as many wives as he could support and obtain, whom he would have jealously guarded against all other men. Or he may have lived with several wives by himself like the Gorilla. . . . The younger males, being thus expelled and wandering about, would, when at last successful in finding a partner, prevent too close inbreeding within the limits of the family" (cited in Freud 1913b, 125).

I should mention that Freud used the term *horde* to refer to a small family group composed of a single adult male, his female consort or consorts, and their juvenile offspring. As Freud's translator James Strachey points out, this has led to confusion because the word *horde* usually connotes a large, unorganized group of people (Freud 1913b, 125n). Darwin and Freud intended to conjure up quite the opposite image. It would sound less odd to refer to what Freud called the primal horde by some more neutral and contemporary phrase like the "elementary social unit," but I shall retain the original to make clear that I have in mind Freud's specific formulation.

In *Totem and Taboo,* Freud characterizes existence in the primal horde in this single sentence: "All that we find there [in Darwin's primal horde] is a violent and jealous father who keeps all the females for himself and drives away his sons as they grow up" (1913b, 141). He elaborates in "Group Psychology and the Analysis of the Ego": the primal father's "intellectual acts were strong and independent even in isolation, and his will needed no reinforcement from others. . . . He loved no one but himself, or other people only insofar as they served his needs. . . . He, at the very beginning of the history of mankind, was the 'superman' whom Nietzsche only expected from the future" (1921, 123).

In this essay, Freud goes on to distinguish between two different kinds of psychology, the one for the group and the one for the individual (the lone individual in primeval society being the primal father). The father, who is "of a masterful nature, absolutely narcissistic, self-confident" (123–124), is characterized by individual psychology, while the sons exemplify group psychology. This latter phenomenon is the result of the sexual privation the father imposes on the sons. Unable to give full expression to their own impulses, especially the sexual, the sons use their unspent and aim-inhibited libido to bond with one another and form a social coalition: the primal father "forced them, so to speak, into group psychology. His sexual jealousy and intolerance became in the last resort the causes of group psychology" (124).

Although the father loves no one but himself, the brothers are able to love one another in an ongoing "social" rather than purely impulse-driven way, through a transformation that the narcissism of each, being unable to find uninhibited expression, must undergo. That is, each son loves his brother because he sees in him a reflection of his own narcissistically loved ideal self-image. This is possible, so Freud argues, only because the brothers really are similar because each has taken for his own "ego ideal" the admired and envied father.

Not yet having coined the term or the concept *superego* at the time of this essay, Freud nonetheless clearly anticipates the idea when he writes "The primal father is the group ideal, which governs the ego in place of the ego ideal" (127). In other words, before civilization, the individual had no internalized superego of his own.[3] The coherence of the group, such as it is, is made possible by the common identification of each son with his brothers and with the father, whose absolute authority derives from the circumstance that he himself is completely free of either object-ties or an ego ideal (or "superego" figure) other than himself.

In *Moses and Monotheism* Freud offers a somewhat more fleshed-out picture of life with the primal father: "The strong man was lord and father of the entire horde and unrestricted in his power, which he exercized with violence. All the females were his property—wives and daughters of his own horde and some, perhaps, robbed from other hordes. The lot of the sons was a hard one; if they roused their father's jealousy they were killed or castrated or driven out" (1939, 81). Here the females of the group enter the picture, and they are all portrayed as the property of the father, regardless of whether they are his flesh and blood—his "daughters"—or not.

While it is by no means my intention to treat the primal horde naturalistically, as a depiction of any human or protohuman society that has ever existed, yet it is worth briefly noting that the sort of "harem" social organization described here is by no means as far-fetched a depiction of at least some forms of primate social life as it is sometimes thought. Compare the Darwin-Freud model with this recent description of

> the "harem" system of the hamadryas and gelada baboons, and to some extent the gorillas, for example. Here a male gathers, by various means, a harem of about six females to himself and guards these constantly. He either becomes an "apprentice" to a dominant male, tags along with him, and eventually takes over his females. Or he gathers young females, "fathers" them, and rears them to adulthood. Or he takes over the harem of another male after a fight. Or some combination of the above. (Fox 1993, 216)[4]

II

Freud's remark that the strong man of the horde is "lord and father" of the others may serve as the basis for observing that Freud's description of the horde actually brings together two quite different discourses that are often thought to be incompatible, namely, a Darwinian and a Hegelian. That the senior male is the "father" of the others emphasizes the Darwinian dimension of the schema, according to which the structure is based on the politics of reproduction: the father is that male who can subdue rivals into submission by force, exclude them from reproductive access to the females, and dominate the females in order to impregnate as many as possible and thus disseminate his genes widely.[5]

To the distinction between the sexes required for sexual reproduction is added another distinction—the one between junior and senior males. Senior males, in the Darwinian scenario, are those able to seize, hold, and defend the position of dominant male in a group. Junior males are those excluded from sexual or at least primary reproductive access to the females by virtue of the superior force of the senior male. Their strategy is to bide their time, either by "apprenticing" themselves submissively to the senior male, leaving the horde until they can produce their own harem by collecting infant "daughters" and raising them to be consorts, or successfully challenging the senior male to a fight for dominant status.

This scenario is triadic, containing three distinct and recognizable statuses: female, senior male, and junior male. It is also asymmetrical: the males are subdivided into senior and junior ranks, while the females are treated as a single category. Since this represents a Darwinian scenario, a Darwinian explanation can be offered. For the female, whose reproductive life and potential reproductive capacity is highly constrained by temporal limits, it is in her best reproductive interest to have as many babies as possible. It does not decisively influence the number of her pregnancies whether she has one or many mates, but it is in her interest to mate with the most dominant male(s) on the theory that his genes, passed on to her own sons, will make them potential candidates for successful accession to senior status and will thus help disseminate her own genes widely.

By contrast, it is in the males' interest to impregnate as many females as they can, while limiting their long-term consorts to that number of females and offspring they can protect from the predations of rival males. A male can go through many fertile years without reproducing and still have a competitively successful reproductive career by waiting till seasoning, maturity, strength, cunning, and alliances allow him to ascend to senior status and reproduce with his own harem. Sexual selection by the females for the most likely reproductive candidates among the males creates a competition among the males in which the losers may either be excluded (that is, "castrated") or forced to wait in the status of junior males until their moment of succession arrives (if it ever does).

In schematic form, the triadic structure of this dimension of the primal horde reveals itself as isomorphic with that of the male oedipal situation, in which there is no inhibiting consideration about "incest," and the junior male, or son, is in competition with the senior male, or father, for the woman who may be either his mother or consort or both, depending on the outcome. (Here Freud's use of the schema actually violates Darwinian principles, since for Darwin, even in nature, steps would be undertaken to avoid incest, or "too close inbreeding.")

III

The Hegelian scheme, by contrast, is dyadic, being composed of two statuses, lord and bondsman (or master and slave). From this point of view, the senior male stands in the relation of lord to the others in the group, regardless of sex, by virtue of his authority over or domination of them.

The senior male is lord of the females of the harem because he coerces sexual compliance from them by superior strength and the threat of violence. For their part, the females have an ambivalent attitude toward the senior male. They resent being dominated. Yet, as we have seen from the Darwinian point of view, they serve their own reproductive interests by bearing offspring sired by the most dominant male.

Between junior males and senior males, the situation more blatantly concerns power. In Hegel's myth of the lord and bondsman, the founding political distinction between dominant and subordinate statuses emerges not from the realm of competitive sexual reproduction but from the domain of the struggle for freedom and recognition between individuals.[6] For Hegel, individuals (here let us say males, though of course a version also occurs between females as well as between individuals of both sexes) struggle with each other for the recognition by the other of themselves as autonomous, willful, desiring, choice-making consciousnesses. When these adversaries confront one another, they may enter into a struggle for dominance, which ultimately becomes a struggle to the death.

The decisive outcome of this duel is that one adversary proves willing to risk death, thus demonstrating that he places a higher value on recognition as a free consciousness by the other than on his organic existence. The other, choosing life over glory, submits to the one willing to risk all, out of his own will to self-preservation. Thus master and slave come into being in relation to each other. The one willing to risk death becomes a free, self-sufficient consciousness who negates the independent existence of his adversaries, as well as of the objects of his desire: the former he vanquishes and forces to submit, the latter he consumes on the spot. The slave, who preferred self-preservation, lives dependent on others: on the master, to whom his own will is subject, and also on the objects of his desire, which, because he cannot fully attain them, retain their existence independent of him and thus force him to enter into a relationship with them.

The terms of the inequality for Hegel emerge not in the world of sex, love, and reproduction but in work, the other half of the Freudian pair of "love and work." The master does not have to work to preserve his life, because his work is done for him by the slave. But the slave, for whom things in the world remain external to his consciousness, has to work on the materials provided by nature to render them usable.

I do not have the leisure here to explore further the relevance to Freudian theory of the Hegelian model, but it should be clear from my brief sketch how nicely it parallels Freud's depiction of the status differential between senior and junior males in the horde. The senior male is narcissistic, dominating, and negating of the otherness of others, while the junior males and the females are forced out of their narcissism, as it were, and so made to enter into relationships with each other and with the world.

For Freud, as for Hegel, it is the slave who has the last laugh, for the narcissistic isolation of the master proves a historical and evolutionary dead end, and an ungratifying one. The recognition he sought, and for which he risked his life, eludes him, because he has reduced the other to a slave whose recognition is without value since it is only a reflection of the master's domination of him. It is the slaves who are able to overcome their subordinate position, for they have developed true object relations. They have been forced by work to submit to the reality principle and have become able to envision a future state in which the distinction between lord and bondsman is eliminated, and in which each person grants mutual recognition.

When the band of brothers finally rebels and put an end to the primal father, they find that they cannot establish this free society of equal and mutually recognizing individuals without a compromise, which in Freud's formulation is founded on the renunciation of the incestuously desired women of the horde. Since no one is to be absolute master in the new society, each brother must deny his impulse to make himself a harem master similar to the deposed tyrant. For Freud, as for Lévi-Strauss, the origin of the new society rests on the prohibition on mating and sexual desire within the horde or kinship unit. This entails the exchange of women between men of different hordes with one another and thus the birth of mutuality and of a society larger than the elementary kin unit, knit together by the requirement of intermarriage with other hordes.[7]

Of course, freedom in the Freudian scenario is available only to the newly liberated males. Even after the death of the primal father, the women remain the property of the men and are objects to be disposed of by those men. Now, however, instead of accumulating the women in a harem, the men use them as exchange items to cement alliances with men who would otherwise be their rivals and enemies. In Freud's schema, as in the story of the Pentateuch that embodies it, the master-slave relationship is done away with between men, only to be retained and reinforced between men and women. For this reason both the Freudian and the biblical traditions may appear both liberating and oppressive: they enunciate an ideal of mutual recognition while ignoring or violating it in the realm of relationships between the sexes.

IV

The Freudian scenario retains this unequal sexual dimension because Freud insists that the project of liberation and the establishment of a society of equals implied in the Hegelian scheme is complicated by, and must contend with the reality of, the Darwinian model, in which the highest goal is not liberation or fulfillment or a just society but reproductive success. The intrinsic conflict Freud saw between sexuality and the ego is better viewed, I think, as a conflict between a life plan built around strategies for reproductive success and thus ultimately directed by the interests not of the individual but of the genes—and a life plan built on the best interests of individuals living in a society with others of their kind. Freud himself recognized this and made it the basis of his first distinction between two great classes of instincts, the ego instincts and the libido: "We accept the popular distinction between egoistic instincts and a sexual instinct; for such a distinction seems to agree with the biological conception that the individual has a double orientation, aiming on the one hand at self-preservation and on the other at the preservation of the species" (1911, 74).

Freud's scenario of the primal horde encompasses both the Darwinian and the Hegelian scenarios and preserves the tension between them. The

Darwinian triadic structure of senior male–junior male–female can collapse into the dyadic master-slave relationship. The senior male can play the role of master, in which case the females are either assimilated to the junior males as a collectivity of junior persons or ignored altogether as nonpersons. Or the senior males and junior males can be assimilated, retaining the master-slave relationship between men and women, either by assimilating the two classes of males to each other or by the exclusion of one of the classes. Before the rebellion the junior males are marginalized, while afterward the senior male has been eliminated. A third logical possibility by which the triad can collapse into a dyad would be for the female and the senior male to ally against the junior male. This is the situation of the classical "primal scene," at which the junior male becomes aware of his marginalization by the sexual alliance between his parents.

In the biblical narrative, as in the Freudian scheme, we also discover a creative tension between the values determined by considerations of descent, kinship, and sexual reproduction and those determined by the effort to create a just society of autonomous equals, one that reconciles the desires and needs of each individual with the requirements of collective social life. On its surface, the story of Moses is explicitly in the Hegelian political mode: it concerns the liberation of an enslaved people from a dominating master and the establishment of a more just social order. But the submerged Darwinian and oedipal aspects of the schema unobtrusively yet unmistakably permeate the text as well, just as the manifest content of the free-associative process of a patient in analysis reveals itself to be structured not only by its explicit concerns but also by the paradigm of an underlying unconscious fantasy.

V

The paradigm of the primal horde, in my analysis, is a conceptual schema that enables us to analyze the myth it generates. In the logic of the myth, civilization is a system that has resulted from the transcendence of a certain state—in Freud's myth the state of nature, in the biblical myth the pre-Sinaitic era. That state itself stands in an antithetical relation to the moral cosmos brought into being by the formative deed of the culture hero (or heroes)—the rebellious sons in Freud's story, Moses in the Torah narrative. Civilization represents a transformation, and a negation, of the underlying paradigm, which contains within itself the seeds of further evolutionary development.

As we have seen, stripped to its fundamental elements, the primal-horde paradigm consists of three statuses: female, senior male, and junior male. Conceptually, it is as if a primal human unity were first divided into two by the distinction between male and female and then the male division were further divided into junior and senior. The features distinguishing male from female are those involved in the process of sexual reproduction. The features signifying junior and senior are derived along two different dimensions: senior males, by definition, mate with the females, and senior males exercise power or authority directly over junior males (and females) in a dominance-submission relationship. The derivation of the three terms from their original unity is illustrated in figure 1a. The three dyads that together comprise the primal triad are illustrated in figure 1b, while the whole structure is illustrated in figure 1c.

It is a significant feature of the primal-horde model that the prohibition on "incest," or inbreeding among close genetic relatives, is present only by its absence. This must be so if it is the case, as Freud's model requires and as I shall show the biblical story also entails, that the founding deed of civilization is the imposition of the incest taboo itself.

What Lévi-Strauss defines as the "atom of kinship" is the model of the precultural primal horde as I have described it—subjected, however, to a single additional distinction: that is, the difference between consanguineal and affinal relations, or in plainer English, between siblings, defined as those who *cannot* "marry" (or mate legitimately), and spouses, defined as those who *can*. In Lévi-Strauss's diagram of what he considers the fundamental unit of kinship, the senior males are now distinguished by whether they marry the female.[8]

Thus three separate male statuses exist in this more fully transformed model, namely, the brother, husband, and son of the still-undifferentiated female. The different roles that women may play—sister, wife, and mother—are all present in the diagram, even though there is only one woman, by virtue of the fact that each woman stands in all three relationships to the three different categories of men (see figure 2).

(I probably need to stress yet again that I by no means intend to suggest that our protohominid ancestors, or our nonhuman primate relatives, lived or live in a state of unregulated breeding in which incestuous

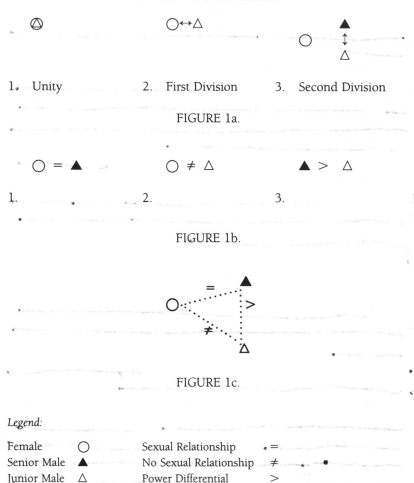

1. Unity   2. First Division   3. Second Division

FIGURE 1a.

1.   2.   3.

FIGURE 1b.

FIGURE 1c.

Legend:

Female	○	Sexual Relationship	=
Senior Male	▲	No Sexual Relationship	≠
Junior Male	△	Power Differential	>

and nonincestuous unions alike are freely undertaken. This is empirically not the case for any nonhuman primates. I am only describing the conceptual basis of the myth on which our civilization is based.)

As Lévi-Strauss shows in his discussion of his fundamental unit of kinship, there is yet another distinction to be added to it: the dyadic relations comprising the unit may be characterized as positive or negative. Thus, as he demonstrates, in some societies, such as those of various peoples of the Caucasus, the relationship of a man with his mother's brother will generally be positive and mutually supportive, while the one with his father is marked by hostility and distance. In other societies, such as that of the Trobriand Islands, for example, the situation is reversed, and a man feels

Third Division

Lévi-Strauss's Atom of Kinship

Legend:

Female	○	Marriage		=
Senior Male	▲	Sibling Relationship		———
Junior Male	△	Relationship of Filiation		

FIGURE 2

close affection for his father but fear and respect for his mother's brother. Similarly, relationships between brother and sister may be intimate and affectionate, as in the Caucasus, while those between husband and wife are tense, avoidant, or difficult; or vice versa, as in the Trobriands, where marital relations are warm and informal, but opposite-sex siblings are subject to stringent taboos and avoidance rules.

These considerations point back to another aspect of Freud's assumptions about the primal horde: the relationships within it are marked by ambivalence. This is especially relevant for us in the case of the senior male–junior male dyad. Ambivalence here is not to be thought of as a weak or half-hearted balanced neutrality but rather as the simultaneous presence of powerful currents of love and hate within the same relationship. For Freud, such ambivalence is typical of all strong love relationships; significantly, he deems it particularly prominent in the etiology of obsessional neurosis.

As we have seen, in the primal horde, according to Freud, there is oppression, domination, and rebellious hostility between the generations of males, yet there is also love, need, and affection. The sons need the protection of the father, they admire him and need his paternal guidance, and they have filial affection for him. The father not only views his sons jealously as potential rivals but loves them as parents love their children. From the point of view of reproductive success, their genetic fitness enhances his own, so it is in his interest to see them breed. This ambivalence powers the developmental process of the primal events according to the myth. For after the sons have expressed and spent their hatred of the father by killing him, they are overcome by remorse, and they miss him enough to re-create him in the form of a deity.

In the more elaborated schema represented by Lévi-Strauss's diagram of a post-rebellion civilized society based on the incest taboo and wife exchange, the two sides of the ambivalence are no longer present to the same degree in a single relationship but are divided between different dyads. Thus, as we saw in the Trobriand model, a son has a close and affectionate relationship with his father, contrasting with a formal, distant, authority-dominated relationship with his mother's brother; while among the Caucasian peoples a son has an affectionate relationship with his mother's brother and a tension-filled relationship with his father. But both cases equally represent differing surface outcomes of the decomposition of an underlying junior male–senior male relationship marked by ambivalent strains of love and hate. This structural process may be compared to the psychoanalytic concept of splitting, whereby in fantasy an ambivalently loved parent may be conceptually regarded as being two people, the good parent and the bad parent.[9]

Splitting is perhaps most plainly observed in fairy tales. Thus, for example, in "Cinderella," the maternal role is represented by two oppositely charged characters, the persecuting cruel stepmother and the wish-granting Fairy Godmother.

VI

To further illustrate how these processes of decomposition (or splitting) are represented in myths, we may turn briefly to the story of Oedipus. We think of the classic oedipal situation as being triadic: two parents and a child (and for our present purposes, a male child). The mythic Oedipus kills his father and marries his mother. As many observers have pointed out, the father in this story, Laius, is a heartless tyrant who tries to kill

Oedipus at birth and so can be said to have asked for what he had coming to him. In this respect, Laius enacts the role of the dominating and jealous senior male of the horde.

But the murderous rivalry between generations of males is only one half of the ambivalence. Where is the other? Here we must recall that Oedipus is depicted in the myth as having two families: his Theban family, consisting of his biological parents, Laius and Jocasta, and his second family, the adoptive family in Corinth (which he believes is his only family), consisting of Polybus and Merope. This Corinthian family is benign and loving, and Oedipus leaves them only out of concern for their well-being: he wants to avoid bringing upon them what the Delphic prophecy has foretold. Thus Oedipus has both a good father and a bad father: Polybus and Laius. But although there are now three males in the story, they can be understood as transformations of the two-male structure. Simply, in this particular myth the senior role is divided along the axis of good-bad (or loving-hostile) and represented by two different characters.

This example also shows that terms like *father* and *son* are complex and composite. Not only can fathers be both persecuting and loving, but the role of "father" may be considered to have one significance as the biological progenitor, another as the legal guardian, another as the social *pater*, yet another as the senior male who teaches, or nurtures, and so on. In the myth of Oedipus we might ask, Who is the real father, Laius who sired yet hated him or Polybus who adopted and loved him? The question is pointless. For this reason, I shall use the terms *senior male* and *junior male*, leaving as a matter for observation and analysis how any particular myth divides the various roles and features.

It is my assumption that in the great mythic complexes built on the paradigm of the primal-horde schema, a good deal of such splitting and other forms of decomposition takes place, whereby single roles or relationships are represented by multiple characters, each embodying a different aspect of the complex whole. What remains constant, however, is that all these characters are decompositions of the three fundamental statuses.

Roland Barthes, whose book *On Racine* (1983) comes as close as any to being a prototype of the sort of structural and psychoanalytic analysis I am engaged in here, writes in a similar vein of the Racinian corpus:

If we make one essential tragedy out of eleven, if we arrange in a kind of exemplary constellation this tribe of some fifty tragic characters who inhabit Racinian tragedy, we shall discover the figures and the actions of the primeval horde: the father, unconditional master of the sons' lives . . . ; the women, simultaneously mothers, sisters, and mistresses, always coveted, rarely obtained . . . ; the brothers, always enemies because they are quarreling over the inheritance of a father who is not quite dead and who returns to punish them . . . ; lastly, the son, mortally torn between terror of the father and the necessity of destroying him. . . . Incest, rivalry among the brothers, murder of the father, overthrow of the sons—these are the fundamental actions of the Racinian theatre. (1983, 9)

(The "brothers" and the "son" in Barthes's schema can of course be further reduced to the single status of "junior males" in my formulation.)

VII

The myth of Oedipus and the myth of Moses are closely linked, not only thematically but also as different expressions of what is no doubt a common underlying Eastern Mediterranean mythic paradigm. Of more relevance for our purposes even than the myth of Oedipus, however, is another mythic complex with the same underlying structure, one that played a major role in the civilization from whose soil sprang in part both the Hebraic and the Greek worlds: Egypt. It is no accident that the key narrative of the Torah, and hence of the Bible and of the Judeo-Christian tradition as a whole, takes place in Egypt, whose great cultural influence permeated and shaped the various cultures around it for centuries.

Edmund Leach, whose structural analysis of the story of Moses (1983) has influenced my own thinking greatly, argues that the Egyptian pharaohs were both the dominant political figures in the region for much of its history and the cultural models for kingship throughout the Middle-Eastern world: "The religious ideology surrounding the real Pharaoh . . . embodies, in a highly condensed form, a particular structure of religious ideas. Permuted forms of this same structure appear as episodes in the Bible . . . [as] *transformations* of the Egyptian version" (1983, 39). Thus, according to Leach the religious ideas undergirding the institutions of the Egyptian pharaohs formed as well the mythic prototypes upon which biblical traditions built. As is well known, the religious ideas to which Leach refers represented the pharaohs against the backdrop of a great mythic cosmology centered around the story of Isis, Osiris, and Horus.[10] Each pharaoh was thought to be an incarnation of the god Horus, while the deceased father and predecessor of the living pharaoh was identified with Horus's father, Osiris. Osiris married his sister, Isis, and the principal wife of each pharaoh incarnated this goddess. Isis was thus both the sister and wife of the Osiris, the dead father who now ruled the underworld. In relation to the living pharaoh (as Horus), Isis was not only wife and sister but also mother.

Leach refers to this mythic model and the practices founded on it as "positional succession based on sibling incest" (1983, 39) and he proposes as the "basic formula" for this system the following: "If God the Father and God the Son are consubstantial coeternal, then the 'mother of God' is also a 'spouse of God' and the mother is spouse to her own son. . . . The relationship between the male aspect of [the deity] and the female aspect of [the deity] may . . . be viewed either as mother/son, or wife/husband, or daughter/father, or sister/brother. The Osiris, Isis, Horus mythology combines all these possibilities" (40). This analysis demonstrates with what efficiency the myth works: a single female character can, in the context of this triadic scheme, fill four different statuses and stand in four different kinds of kin relationship to male others.

Leach's analysis also makes clear that the Isis-Osiris-Horus triad is identical in every respect but one with the primal-horde schema as I have been developing it here. There is first a division of the deity into two, a male and a female aspect, represented by an incestuously married brother and sister (or, rather, a pair for whom the distinction between sibling and spouse is not operative). The male aspect of the deity is then further subdivided by generation, with a senior aspect, or "father," and a junior aspect, or "son."

The crucial difference between this myth and the primal-horde schema is that in the Egyptian system it is the *junior* male, Horus, as the living pharaoh, who is actually married to the female, while the dead father, Osiris, who was graphically castrated in a central episode of the myth, is packed off to the underworld. This is an elementary transformation of the horde pattern and can be interpreted to mean that the pharaoh is depicted as an oedipal victor: that is, as a son who has succeeded his father and become senior male. By virtue of having accomplished this momentous feat, the son is seen as fit to rule over his fellows. The pharaonic model can thus be seen as what happens when the junior male emerges victorious from a struggle for succession, as opposed to what happens when a junior male rebels to end the system of succession itself, as Moses does.

But in examining this scenario, whereby a deed—the castration and murder of the senior male—leads from a primal-horde situation to a transformation of it, whereby the generations exchange places, we notice that a crucial aspect has been glossed over: it is not Horus who killed and castrated his father. Indeed, as I look at the matter, for Horus to do so would disqualify him as a legitimate heir because it would make him a regicide, patricide, and usurper as well as an oedipal hero. After all, even Oedipus, when he discovered that the usurper and patricide was himself, could no longer continue as king of Thebes but had to castrate himself symbolically by blinding himself and banish himself from the throne and the city in talionic punishment for the crime by which he had become king.[11]

Yet if the best way for a junior male to succeed to senior status is to overcome his predecessor and kill or castrate him just as the senior male was wont, according to Freud's model, to do to his potential junior rivals, and if, at the same time, killing your father and/or the king is a crime punishable by death and/or castration, how can a junior male ever manage to succeed to the dominant position without also committing an unpardonable crime? The pharaonic myth exemplifies one of the more common techniques myths employ to overcome the problem, namely, the decomposition of the ambivalent relationship between father and son to which I referred earlier.

In a process of splitting, the Isis-Osiris myth transforms itself by generating another central character, Seth, who is Osiris's evil younger brother. It is Seth who castrates and kills Osiris and usurps his throne. And it is he who then persecutes Horus, in the sections of the myth known as the contention of Seth and Horus. In the course of this battle, Horus and Seth inflict grievous harm on each other: Horus castrates Seth, and Seth puts out one of Horus's eyes.

This transformation of the basic structure achieves the efficient result of doubling both senior and junior male by means of the addition of a single character. In relation to Osiris, Seth is a junior male, not only because he is younger but because Osiris as king ranks over him. Furthermore, it is suggested in the story that Osiris takes Seth's wife-sister, Nephthys, for his own consort, thus enacting the dimension of the paradigm whereby the senior male enjoys the women of the group at the junior male's expense.

Seth the cuckold thus doubles Horus: Horus is the good, legitimate son of Osiris, while Seth is the rebellious, traitorous aspect of the same junior male.

At the same time, Seth as the usurping king who now persecutes the legitimate heir, Horus, is an evil twin of the senior male. While Osiris is the good and legitimate senior male, father, and king, Seth is the jealous persecutor who tries to kill the good junior male. Thus Seth may be said to mediate between Osiris and Horus, being junior to the one and senior to the other, and to resolve the dilemmas inherent in the ambivalent relationship between senior and junior male. It is *he,* not Horus, who commits the crime of castrating and killing the senior male/primal father/pharaoh; in contending with *him,* Horus is not being treasonous but on the contrary avenging the murder of the legitimate senior male.

Exactly the same structural move may be recognized in any number of stories in our tradition that exemplify the same structural paradigm. A good example is found in the story of *Hamlet,* where Claudius, the wicked younger brother of good king Hamlet Senior, plays the role of the usurping oedipal junior male by killing the senior male and marrying his wife. At the same time he also plays the role of the infanticidal, persecuting senior male vis-à-vis Hamlet (Junior) himself.

The myth of Moses, as I shall show, is also a playing-out of transformations implicit in the basic triadic schema of the primal horde. This can be demonstrated in formal analysis; in addition, there is a clear historical and cultural relation between the myths of the Levant, as well as those of Greece, and Egyptian mythic prototypes, which the setting of the Exodus story in Egypt underscores.

VIII

Before I leave the topic of the primal-horde paradigm in general, as a formal structure and as a cultural reality in the region of the Eastern Mediterranean, and move to specific consideration of the Torah narrative, I would like to address one further aspect of the primal horde as a cultural conceptual model. Is there any basis, in the real material social life of the people among whom the paradigm is operative and central, for conceiving of life in this particular way? Is there, in short, any model ready to hand in the real world that might serve as a source domain for the metaphorical construction of social life according to the model of the primal horde?[12]

While the Bible was certainly composed by and for town dwellers of some sophistication, the stories themselves dwell to a remarkable extent on the lives and doings of pastoral nomads, or shepherds. Abraham, Isaac, and Jacob, the patriarchs of the Israelite people whose stories occupy the bulk of the book of Genesis, are all depicted as *gerim,* wandering herdsmen who are welcomed by the settled agriculturalists as they pass through with their flocks. Agriculturalists often offer pasture to nomadic herders in return for the grazing by the animals of the stubble in their fields, for the manure provided by the animals, and for the various animal products for which they can trade with the shepherds.

Moses, too, though he began life as a courtier in Egypt, received his divine summons while tending the flocks of his father-in-law, the Midianite shepherd Jethro. David rose to the royal throne from the status of shepherd boy, and of course the presence of shepherd symbolism in the Psalms, the Christian Bible, and elsewhere in the Bible is well known. Why all these sheep? Certainly there were pastoral nomads then as now in the region when the biblical texts were written and compiled, but then as now they were a minority, peripheral to the town life that produced the written Bible.

I suggest that the primal-horde schema exists as an explicit cultural model in the consciousness of those who breed and tend herd animals. Many of the uses to which such animals are put are not fatal to the animal: they can be milked or shorn while still alive, and they can be put to hard labor, such as pulling wheeled vehicles or plows. But for other purposes the animal must be killed: to be eaten, for example, or to be stripped of its hide for leather. The herdsman wishes to get the maximum economic value from his animals in the form of usable products and work. At the same time he wishes to conserve his flock and ensure that it reproduces and if possible grows larger, thus giving him more economic resources.[13]

The flock, now no longer living in a state of nature but rather in a domesticated condition, is subservient to the will of the shepherd, who, while he may have affection and respect for his animals—and even grant them some degree of recognition as genuine Hegelian others—is ultimately serving his own interests. He therefore treats his animals as means rather than as ends, subjecting them to artificial rather than natural selection.

His strategy will usually be some variation of this common pattern: he does not kill any of the females, but rather uses them as breeders. He does, however, kill some or even many males. He maximizes his own interest by choosing as stud males those who possess the fertility and other qualities he wishes to see multiplied among his animals and puts to his own use the remainder of the males. In this way, the herd is divided into three statuses: females, males who breed (or senior males), and males who do not breed (junior males), whose fate is to be castrated (either to make them fat for eating or tractable for work), enslaved, or killed for food.

There is a tendency on our part to forget that even a "good" shepherd not only cares for but also kills and eats at least some of his charges. Roberto Calasso puts it nicely: "As Victor Hugo said, 'the gospel makes God a shepherd. The Trappists make him a butcher.' But shepherds, who protect their flocks, also slaughter them little by little" (1994, 217).

Thus while the patriarch of a primal horde could not, in the real world, make it a practice to castrate, kill, or eat his sons, as Freud's model suggests, the shepherd can and does behave in just this way to his own horde/herd of animals. We might say, then, that the status of Freud's primal father has been divided between the herdsman and his stud males. The stud males take care of reproduction while the herdsman plays the role of authority. There are thus four characters in this schema, achieved by a decomposition of the senior male role. The structural dyad of the females and the stud males serves the goals of the genes. The dyad of the herdsman and the junior males maximizes the interests of the herdsman, who plays master to the junior male's slaves.

By separating out a double, who is still his subordinate, to carry out the reproductive function, the herdsman is able to exploit the process of sexual reproduction for his own economic benefit. He uses the reproductive capacities of the herd animals to produce a product, the junior males, who become his slaves, his food, and his wealth. Under the system of natural selection, the function of self-preservation is ultimately subordinate to the highest goal, reproduction. But we see that in the case of animal domestication, sexual reproduction of the domesticated animal is subordinated to the self-preservation of the herdsman.

It is possible to argue, I think, that the state, as this form of social organization originated in the city-states of the Near East, applied to the rule of some humans by others the model of animal domestication (which had indeed originated not long before, speaking in evolutionary time, in that very region, at least as far as sheep and goats were concerned). If one stratum of humans—the rulers of the state and the town dwellers who served their interests—could conceptualize their relation to those agricultural producers whom they ruled and upon whose labor and reproductive capacity they depended for their own maintenance on the model of the herdsman to his flock, then it is easy to see how the primal-horde model could be transferred from the relationships between humans and animals to those between rulers and ruled.

The division of the senior male role into the dyad of herdsman and stud animal, which separates the power axis from the axis of sexual reproduction and the function of self-preservation from that of reproduction of the genome, provides a basis and a model for the separation of the "spiritual" and the "carnal" that plays a distinctive role in the development of Judeo-Christian civilization, with its concomitant devaluation of sexuality and reproduction as "merely" animal.[14]

The model of the primal horde, then, is clearly present in the cultural matrix out of which the Hebrew mythic narrative arose in the form of the Egyptian pharaonic myth, and a clear instance of it in the real world was present in the social and economic lives of the people of the era of the composition of the Torah narratives. These two arguments come together and become one; indeed, "Pharaoh was expected to show infinite solicitude for his people: it was not for nothing that he compared himself with a shepherd, and carried a shepherd's crook as part of his regalia" (Cohn 1993, 15). And as I have shown, if the pharaoh is a shepherd, then he is both a benevolent pastor to his people and a cannibalistic butcher. The profuse imagery drawn from the pastoral realm throughout the Bible is an indicator of the presence and centrality of the primal-horde conceptual scheme as it is actually represented in the model of the herding of animals, and Egypt represented this form of society.

3

Israel in Egypt

The book of Genesis is a genealogical chronicle, enlivened with tales and anecdotes about the various characters encountered along the way. It begins with the creation of the world and of the first couple and ends with the coming into being of a people called the Israelites. *Israel* was the name assumed by the patriarch Jacob after he wrestled with an angel; the Israelites were, at first, only a family group composed of Israel, his twelve sons, their respective wives and children, and his daughter, Dinah. The twelve brothers, who are the eponymous ancestors of the twelve "tribes," or clans, of the Israelite people, are Reuben, Simeon, Levi, Judah, Issachar, and Zebulun, the sons of Israel's senior wife, Leah; Gad and Asher, the sons of Leah's maidservant Zilpah; Joseph and Benjamin, the sons of Israel's second wife, Leah's younger sister Rachel; and Dan and Naphthali, the sons of Rachel's maidservant Bilhah. Exodus 1:5 tells us that this group numbered seventy people in all when they settled in Egypt, including the wives, families, and servants of the brothers.

It is important to note that this is the first group in the narrative that constitutes a sizable society, but it still consists only of a father and his grown children; it does not yet constitute a people or an ethnic group. This unified family group prospers when one of them, Joseph, finds royal favor in Egypt, and the others join him there. Their welcome status in Egypt changes drastically, however, when a new pharaoh arises, one who does not know Joseph; he subjects the Israelites to persecution and slavery.

The burden of my argument here is that the pre-Sinaitic epoch in the Torah narrative can be understood as a depiction of society before the transforming event that establishes civilized life as we now know it. But since the Israelites do not even come into existence as a group until the generation of the thirteen children of Israel, it is only they who are suitable, among the characters in Genesis, to exemplify the state of society before civilization because only they are a group large enough to be a society. Therefore, we may say that in the myth the Israelite siblings are the first society. They thus also constitute the prototype of society before the founding of civilized life on the basis of the covenant of Sinai.

If we examine the society of Israelites with this in mind, we can distinguish two aspects of their collective experience, a good and a bad. The good part of the story chronicles the rescue of Joseph from his envious brothers, his rise to the position of viceroy to the pharaoh himself, and his happy reunion, after many colorful incidents, with his brothers and father. Thus ends the book of Genesis. The bad part follows immediately, in the opening pages of Exodus. Joseph has died, and a new, wicked pharaoh arises who shares none of his predecessor's kind feelings toward the descendants of Israel. Only in this later period does the society formed by the Israelites in Egypt correspond to Freud's description of the primal horde.

But since we are not bound by the limits of Freud's vision, we can enlarge the scope of the mythological precivilized society by supposing that the good and bad periods are reverse transformations of each other along the affective dimension. They themselves, in other words, form a split representation of an underlying pattern characterized by ambivalent relationships within the group, decomposed and depicted as two historical moments, one succeeding the other.

Jacob/Israel, unlike Freud's primal father, is a benign patriarch, who neither persecutes nor tyrannizes his children, and who not only reproduces successfully himself but also allows his sons to become fathers as well. He does, it is true, accumulate a harem of four consorts, but it never occurs to him to try to prevent his sons from doing the same.

Nor is he without provocation to jealousy from the junior males. The oldest son, Reuben, violates his father's bed, sleeping with one of his father's consorts, Bilhah, the mother of Reuben's own half-brothers Dan and Naphthali: "While Israel stayed in that land [Migdal-eder], Reuben went and lay with Bilhah, his father's concubine; and Israel found out" (Gen. 35:22).[1] This, one would have imagined, would be just the sort of thing designed to drive the primal father into a murderous, castrating fury, according to Freud's picture. But Jacob/Israel does not respond at all until he is lying on his deathbed much later in the narrative, and even then his only punishment of Reuben amounts to little more than a slap on the wrist: "Reuben, you are my first-born. . . . Unstable as the water, you shall excel no longer; For when you mounted your father's bed, You brought disgrace" (Gen. 49:3–4). In other words, Israel takes away from Reuben the privileges of the first-born—a rebuff, certainly, but not drastic. Thus we may characterize

Israel as a mild father who promotes the reproductive and sexual success of his children and is not inclined to see them as rivals.]

The era of good feelings in Egypt is presided over by the pharaoh whom Joseph serves as grand vizier. He may be interpreted as a further decomposition by doubling and aggrandizement of the image of the benign, tolerant patriarch under whom people thrive: an idealized version of the patriarch Jacob/Israel, in other words. The intertwining of the pharaoh's household with that of the Israelites that is so crucial to the story of Moses begins with Israel's favored son, Joseph. Joseph's relationship to his pharaoh epitomizes the good horde, in which junior and senior males are in harmonious union. We may contrast this situation with the later relationship between Moses and *his* pharaoh(s). The two cases are mirror images, produced by a splitting into a good and bad half of the ambivalent relationships between junior and senior males inherent in the primal horde structure. Joseph and Moses, the main protagonists, can be seen as reverse duplicates of each other.

For his part, Joseph has risen so high in the Egyptian court that he figuratively, and almost literally, becomes senior to Pharaoh himself. As Joseph remarks to his brothers, "So it was not you who sent me here, but God; and He has made me a *father to Pharaoh,* lord of all his household, and ruler over the whole land of Egypt" (Gen. 45:8, my emphasis). A midrash on this passage makes Joseph's "fatherhood" of and seniority to Pharaoh still plainer: "As Joseph's dealings were kind and gentle with his brethren, so was he a helper and counsellor of the Egyptians, and when Pharaoh departed this life . . . the king's last wish was that he [Joseph] *might be a father unto his son and successor Magron.* . . . Joseph was made actual ruler of the land, and though he was only viceroy in Egypt, he ruled over lands outside of Egypt as far as the Euphrates" (Ginzberg 1911, 2:169, my emphasis).

Thus not only is Joseph a father to the pharaoh in a figurative sense, as his sage adviser; but in the midrash he is actually the father of the young pharaoh Magron, becoming Magron's adopted father after the pharaoh dies. Magron is junior to Joseph in every respect, including age and generation, power, and socially recognized kinship. So, for purposes of the myth, Joseph is the father of Pharaoh. At the same time, Joseph's "good" pharaoh is portrayed as one who does not prohibit, indeed, actively supports, the accession to fatherhood and seniority of the males junior to him, here represented by Joseph; in this respect, Pharaoh duplicates Jacob/Israel.

(Incidentally, the assertion that Joseph was ruler, not viceroy, of the lands between Egypt and the Euphrates makes him ipso facto king of the land of Canaan, thus legitimizing the later Israelite occupation of that region.)

It can also be argued that Joseph stands in a relation of lordship to all of Egypt, while the Israelites will be in bondage to the pharaoh in the time of Moses. A problematic passage, Genesis 47:20–22, describes how Joseph, by controlling the food supply during a famine, makes Egypt indebted to him: the people, having first given him their money and livestock in return for supplies from the royal granaries, now give him their land as well. Genesis 47:21 seems to say that after the land passed over to Pharaoh through his agent Joseph, Joseph "removed the population town by town." This reading does not make much sense in context: Where would he remove them to, and why? But a slight emendation of the Masoritic text, supported by readings from the Samaritan Pentateuch and the Septuagint, has led many commentators to prefer the reading "he reduced them to servitude."[2]

We may thus characterize Joseph as father to the pharaoh, lord of the land of Egypt, and helper to his brothers and the Egyptians. By reversing these various features into the negative, we obtain an accurate picture of the situation in the subsequent era, the time of Moses and the pharaoh who does not know Joseph. Moses, Joseph's mirror image, is son to the pharaoh, he and his people are bondsmen to Egypt, and he is the victim of a pharaoh who, far from being a helper, is an oppressor of the Hebrews.

II

This analysis suggests that the Moses-Pharaoh narrative is to be understood as a transformation of the Joseph-Pharaoh story, both having been produced by splitting the father/son figures along the axis of positive and negative affective relationships. Is there further evidence in support of this view, beyond its internal coherence?

An essentially structural analysis, in which we break down a mythic narrative into terms and relations between terms and then examine regularities in the patterning of the larger schemas built from these elements, works when it produces reasonably convincing demonstrations of coherent and systematic order within the domain of the materials under consideration.[3] Each successful demonstration that an episode or feature of the story can be understood as being generated from the elementary set of terms and relations assumed to be at work constitutes further support for (but not, of course, proof of) the adequacy of the working hypothesis about the underlying generative schema. By the same token, irregularities and inconsistent or unexpected results force us to revise our assumptions.

Perhaps we could look elsewhere, outside the range of the materials we have already examined, to see whether the conclusions we have reached are corroborated (or on the other hand contradicted) by what we encounter in new but related textual material.[4] The Bible is such a vast text that we can always look elsewhere in it; this was indeed the underlying assumption behind the production of the form of rabbinic commentary known as midrash. As Daniel Boyarin (1990) shows, these commentaries worked by a technique whereby apparent gaps in one passage might be filled in by arguments, images, or tropes drawn from passages elsewhere in the Bible.

Boyarin also argues, to my mind convincingly, that the midrash may be taken as the "unconscious" of the text, revealing aspects of it that may be overtly absent or suppressed.[5] In the same way, I shall use stories from the midrashic tradition to augment my analyses, treating them almost as if they constituted free associations to the biblical text on the part of the rabbis. The midrashic tales are responses to or further elaborations of themes suggested by the text, often with vivid imagery. In these midrashim one can sometimes see ideas made explicit that from the text itself we can only deduce by structural analysis or symbolic interpretation. When we find such imagery in a midrash corresponding to what we have deduced by means of a structural analytic technique, we can take it as further support for the line of analysis we are developing.

Here I have argued that the key variable in producing the Joseph and Moses stories as versions of each other differing along the axis of good and bad has to do with whether the most senior male to whom the hero is related, the pharaoh, is himself good or bad. We can pinpoint the precise moment in the narrative when the "good" situation, epitomized by the mutually supportive relationship of Joseph and Pharaoh, turns into the "bad" situation, to which Moses will be called to respond. It is Exodus 1:8, in which we learn that "a new king arose over Egypt, who did not know Joseph." This "new" pharaoh enslaves and persecutes the Israelites, in stark contrast to his predecessor.

A midrash on this line asserts, in apparent contradiction to the plain meaning of the text, that this new pharaoh was not a different man but the same man, with a changed attitude toward the house of Israel. After all, so the rabbis argue, Scripture does not say that the old king died, only that a new one arose. Besides, how could it be that the new pharaoh would never have heard of Joseph? Rather, the phrase "who did not know Joseph" should be understood to mean that the pharaoh turned against the memory of Joseph, and against his kinsfolk.

According to the midrash, what happened was this: The Egyptians suggested to the pharaoh that they attack the Israelites. (One could plausibly imagine them saying this if Joseph had indeed reduced them to servitude, confiscated their property, and enriched himself and his family at their expense.) Pharaoh at first angrily rejected their suggestion: " 'You are idiots. To this day we are eating what one might say belongs to them. . . . But for Joseph, we would not have survived [the famine].' " When Pharaoh refused to listen to the people they deposed him for three months, until he said to them, " 'I agree to whatever you wish' " (*Exodus Rabbah,* 9–10; Bialik and Ravnitzky 1992, 8).[6]

Whatever else it may mean, this story serves as substantiation from within the tradition itself of my contention that different characters, such as the good and bad pharaohs, are from a structural point of view decompositions of a single elementary term, the ambivalently regarded senior male. This midrash seems to be asserting, and thus confirming, my own supposition, that there is only one pharaoh, who plays the part of the senior male in the Torah narrative. His different modes of goodness or badness are only variables or features implicit in the schema that may, as the story requires, lead to his being depicted as different individuals with different affective valuations in different narrative episodes.

III

The new pharaoh, the one who does not know Joseph, regardless of whether he is the same person as his apparent predecessor, is clearly an enemy of procreation, at least as far as the Israelites are concerned: " 'Look, the Israelite people are much too numerous for us. Let us deal shrewdly with them, so that they may not increase' " (Exod. 1:9–10). His first move is to oppress them, imposing hard labor upon them. It remains unclear exactly how this is supposed to deal with the population problem: perhaps the Israelites are going to be so exhausted after a hard day building the garrison cities Pithom and Ramses that they will have no energy to procreate.[7] In any event, when, not very surprisingly, this measure has no effect, and the Israelites continue to multiply at an alarming rate, Pharaoh decides on a move that is somewhat shrewder than the first but still not all that clever. He tells the Hebrew midwives, " 'When you deliver the Hebrew women, look at the birthstool; if it is a boy, kill him; if it is a girl, let her live' " (Exod. 1:16).

This tactic at least has the advantage of addressing the issue of reproduction directly, but it fails to take note of the asymmetry between male and female reproductive capacities. Killing the boys and leaving the girls alive would not, in principle, reduce the number of pregnancies and births at all, provided there were at least a few males—or even one—left standing. The better strategy, of course, would be to kill the girls and keep the boys for slave labor. We must conclude, then, that this pharaoh is not only not very shrewd, but downright stupid, or else that his strategy suggests some other narrative purpose, one more consistent with our earlier deductions: namely, to have Pharaoh represent the jealous senior male of the primal horde.

A midrash on this passage takes note of the very problem I have raised. In it, God addresses Pharaoh thus: " 'O wicked one! He who gave you this advice is an idiot! You ought rather to slay the females, for if there are no females, how will the males be able to marry? One woman cannot marry two men, but one man can marry ten or a hundred' " (*Exodus Rabbah,* 19).

As I have suggested, Pharaoh's reasons for his acts do not fit with their consequences, but they are consistent with another, unstated but clearly implicit, motive. Once again, a traditional midrash clarifies the issue: "The Egyptians were as much interested in preserving the female children as in bringing about the death of the male children. For they were very sensual, and were desirous of having as many women as possible at their service" (Ginzberg 1911, 3:251).

Thus, if we go by the consequences of his deeds and not by his stated motives, Pharaoh's purpose is not to control the population but to eliminate the junior males as potential rivals and to monopolize sexual access to the females—or, in other words, to behave like the jealous tyrant of the primal horde. We can, in fact, explain on this basis why Pharaoh tries two apparently inappropriate measures to keep the Israelites from multiplying. Each attempt expresses a different aspect of the male-status asymmetry in the primal horde: when Pharaoh oppresses the Israelites, he is demonstrating the relation of lordship and bondage, whereas when he orders the deaths of the male children, he is representing the aspect of sexual jealousy and the monopolization of sexual and procreative rights.

This passage provides a clear example of how the method I use can uncover detailed sense in a passage that, if read literally, seems inconsistent, arbitrary and irrational—or perhaps composed of disparate fragments. On the surface the passage implies that, fearing the increased numbers of the Israelite immigrants, Pharaoh tries measures that are ineffective and inconsistent, even with each other (if he kills the boys, who will build the cities of Pithom and Ramses?).

But read in the way I propose, the passage communicates the following ideas, which are consistent with each other and with the myth of the primal horde:

- The pharaoh is an enemy of the sexual procreation of others.
- The pharaoh is a tyrannical taskmaster.
- The pharaoh is a jealous infanticidal guardian of his sexual prerogatives, who monopolizes sex and procreation.

One of the important methodological lessons we learn from this analysis is that we must not take too seriously motivations announced directly in the text. What the myth is accomplishing, in fact, is presenting the necessary structural elements and transformations of an underlying unified idea, in this case one best understood in abstract form as the myth of the primal horde. In an attempt to unite these elements into a narrative account, the text weaves them together *as if* they were chronological events and *as if* the actors performed their actions for motives and reasons of their own. But these "reasons" are, as often as not, rationalizations or secondary elaborations designed to give an apparent narrative quality to mythic images that are dictated not by the actors' motives but by the requirements of the underlying structure. Quite often, these secondary elaborations are obviously clumsy; they produce some of the many "problems" the Bible presents when viewed as if it were an attempt at a strong realistic narrative. But, as I am arguing, this is not the most successful or productive way to look at it if one is interested in finding out what it *means*.[8]

But the objection might be raised that, unlike the senior male of the primal horde, Pharaoh is not killing his own sons but rather the sons of a rival patriarch, Jacob/Israel. This is certainly so. And from a naturalistic, Darwinian point of view, he is acting very shrewdly indeed, insofar as he may be viewed as pursuing a strategy of maximum inclusive genetic fitness. The senior male of a primal horde who comes into contact with the offspring of a rival senior male would be wise to do just what Pharaoh did: kill the males as potential reproductive rivals and spare the females to become bearers of his own genetic offspring.

While I agree that the Darwinian explanation has validity, I propose that more is to be gained by not stopping there but by thinking more deeply about how myths work. We have already seen that the text tells us that the Israelites and the pharaohs have become one interwoven family: Joseph the Israelite becomes the father of an Egyptian pharaoh, just as an Egyptian pharaoh will soon become the father of the Israelite Moses. Their fortunes and identities cannot be treated as entirely separate units. True enough, Joseph is the pharaoh's social rather than genetic father, and the same is true of the relationship between Pharaoh and Moses. But this doubling of the family, which the breaking down of the "father," or "senior male," role makes possible, is a good example of decomposition.[9]

I argue that the Israelite family and the pharaoh's family are intertwined in the text to emphasize that they are split representations of a prototypical single family, just as Jacob and Pharaoh, or Joseph's pharaoh and Moses's pharaoh, are the split representation of the good and bad father, who in turn represent different aspects of the senior male. From the point of view of the myth, then, the image of Pharaoh ordering the death of the male Israelite children should be read as a depiction of the "bad" senior male of the "bad" primal horde, representing those aspects of the senior-junior relationship that can be characterized as tyrannical, sexually jealous, and persecuting. In this particular instance, the imagery employed involves senior and junior males who are related not biologically but rather by differences in generation, power, and social status. Biological filiation is only one definition of the senior-junior relationship, and it need not be included in every case, since it is itself one of the variables out of which the myth is constructed.

But for those who still find this analysis unsatisfactory (including myself), I shall pursue the argument further to show that Pharaoh really did kill *his own* male offspring. When he ordered the killing of the male Israelite children, Pharaoh called down upon himself, according to the great ruling principle of the talion—"like for like"—the answering death of his own son.[10] And this indeed occurs explicitly in the text: the last of the ten plagues visited by God upon the Egyptians in Exodus 7–12 is the death of the first-born Egyptian children. Specifically: "The Lord struck down all the first-born of the land of Egypt, from the *first-born of Pharaoh* who sat on the throne to the first-born of the captive who was in the dungeon" (Exod.

12:29, my emphasis). In this way, Pharaoh, in ordering the death of the Hebrew infants, causes the death of his own son.

(It is a complication, but not a major one, that the pharaoh of the plagues is not, as I shall show, the same as the pharaoh who orders the death of the Hebrew boys; but for the present, we may take the character of "Pharaoh" as a mythic unit—something the rabbis themselves were eager to do, as we have already seen.)

To illustrate how this sort of argument for responsibility according to the talionic principle is employed within the tradition itself, let me cite a midrash explaining why the Egyptians, in executing Pharaoh's infanticidal command, decided to drown the Hebrew male children by throwing them in the Nile. They chose this method precisely because they convinced themselves that it would insure them against talionic consequences:

> [The Egyptians] knew that God pays measure for measure, therefore they believed that the drowning of the men children would be the safest means of exterminating the Hebrews, without incurring harm themselves, for the Lord had sworn unto Noah never again to destroy the world by water. Thus, they assumed, they would be exempt from punishment, wherein they were wrong, however. . . . Though the Lord had sworn not to bring a flood upon men, there was nothing in the way of bringing men into a flood. . . . The end of the Egyptians was that they met their death in the billows of the Red Sea. "Measure for measure"—as they drowned the men children of the Israelites, so they were drowned. (Ginzberg 1911, 3:256)

From this story we learn that talionic calculation is explicit, and it is taken seriously: its consequences are observed, traced, and understood. So, by the same principle, when Pharaoh kills the Hebrew children he thereby kills his own genetic male offspring—not to mention the Egyptian first-born throughout the land to whom he stands, as king, in the position of senior male.

In another midrash, the theme of Pharaoh as executioner of his own Egyptian children is made more explicit. According to this tale, when the Egyptian first-born hear of Moses's announcement of what the tenth plague will be, they plead with their fathers to spare them by complying with the Hebrews' request to be liberated. The fathers refuse, saying, " 'It is better for one of every ten of us to die, than the Hebrews should execute their purposes' " (Ginzberg, 1911, 2:365). The first-born turn to Pharaoh with their plea, but he answers them by having them beaten for their presumptuous request. Pharaoh, by thus refusing to spare the doomed first-born (physically abusing them to boot), in effect kills them. The first-born, refusing to submit easily, begin a war with their fathers, in which there are many casualties. The result, then, is that in the wake of Pharaoh's decree, not only the Hebrew boys but also thousands of Egyptian first-born junior males are killed by him and by the other senior males.

The hard-hearted, filicidal calculation of Pharaoh and the Egyptian fathers that the loss of their first-born would decrease the population by only a tenth turns out, in any event, to be cruelly mistaken: "For the Divine decree included not only the first-born sons, but also the first-born daughters, and not only the first-born of marriages then existing, but also the first-born issuing from previous alliances of the fathers and mothers, and as the Egyptians led dissolute lives, it happened not rarely that each of the ten children of one woman was the first-born of its father" (Ginzberg, 1911, 2:365). Thus Pharaoh's infanticidal decree against the Hebrews has the ultimate effect of decimating the children of the Egyptians.

I conclude this section, bringing together a number of the mythic themes I have been examining, with the following midrash, which shows that because Pharaoh's infanticidal order was issued out of insatiable sexual lust, so the talionic revenge for it was also brought about by lust: "What is the meaning of 'I have compared thee, O my love, to a steed in Pharaoh's chariots'? [Song of Songs 1:9.] That the waves of the sea appeared in the form of mares, while [those of] the wicked Egyptians were like stallions full ·of lust that ran after them until they were drowned in the sea, as it says, *The horse and his rider hath he thrown into the sea (Ex. xv, 1)*" (*Exodus Rabbah*, 291–292). We see here that Pharaoh, and the Egyptians generally, originally acted out of sexual desire, like the jealous sire of the primal horde. We have seen that a herdsman (or animal keeper) and his male animals divide the role of senior male between them, the stallion representing the dimension of sexuality, the rider representing the dimension of domination and authority. When the Egyptians and their pharaoh allowed themselves to be ruled by lust in seeking to kill the Israelite boys and spare the women, they thereby brought about their own talionic fate, for their own sexual impulses, symbolized by and embodied in their stallions, refused to be guided by their masters: "The Egyptian said to his horse: 'Yesterday I led thee to give thee water to drink, but thou didst refuse to follow me; and now thou hast come to drown me in the sea' " (292).

One is almost inevitably led, I think, to call to mind Freud's famous description of the relation between the ego and the id: "Thus in its relation to the id it [the ego] is like a man on horseback, who has to hold in check the superior strength of the horse. . . . Often a rider, if he is not to be parted from his horse, is obliged to guide it where it wants to go" (1923, 25). As we see in this case, where the horse wants to go takes the rider, quite frequently, into water over his head. (I might also mention that the typical Western image of the human personality as one in which a soul or mind tries to manage a carnal body is metaphorically drawn from the domain of the herdsman and his beast, only now a man's own body is understood as his stallion.)

IV

As often happens in myth and folklore, the impulse of the jealous senior male to prevent the junior males from reaching sexual maturity is focused on a particular junior male, whose destiny it is, as the senior male perceives it and as it may in fact be, to usurp the senior male's own position. In the biblical text, Pharaoh does not specifically try to kill Moses until the latter is grown and has killed an Egyptian. But the traditions and legends again help us confirm our suspicion that in some degree Pharaoh's infanticidal gesture is directed specifically at the infant Moses.

After the Hebrew midwives have valiantly refused to comply with Pharaoh's command—thus winning themselves a place of eternal honor in the Jewish tradition—Pharaoh, perhaps almost in desperation at his inability to hold the Israelite population in check, gives this peremptory command "to all his people": " 'Every boy that is born you shall throw into the Nile, but let every girl live' " (Exod. 1:22).

In the sentences immediately following, we read that an Israelite couple from the tribe of Levi have a baby (Moses), whom his mother sends down the Nile in a wicker basket caulked with bitumen and pitch. We do not know how many boys were thrown into the Nile. Indeed, the ambiguous wording of Pharaoh's blunt command makes it sound as if everybody, including the Egyptians, was supposed to throw their male babies in the river. But we hear about only one, Moses, who is indeed destined to overthrow Pharaoh's tyrannical rule.

Did Pharaoh foresee this when he ordered the death of the male children? According to a midrash, Pharaoh had a dream in which he saw a man holding a scale. On one side of the scale were all the elders and nobles of Egypt while on the other was a single kid (baby goat). The kid bore down its side of the scale against the combined weight of all the grandees of the Egyptian court. Pharaoh asked for an interpretation of this dream from his diviner, magician, and adviser Balaam.

Balaam plays an important role in the Torah narrative. He is a Mesopotamian seer, whose services are sought out by the Moabite King Balak in Numbers 22–24, to help him get rid of the Israelites who, under Moses's leadership, are passing through Moab on their way to the promised land. The two best-known episodes involving Balaam both describe how his own magic inadvertently turns him into an ally of the Israelites rather than of the Moabite king who hired him. In one case, the ass on which he is riding is miraculously able to see an angel of the Lord who stands in the road and refuses to continue the journey. In the other, when Balak asks him to issue a prophetic curse on the Israelites, Balaam instead involuntarily speaks with the true voice of the Lord and predicts the success and flourishing of the Hebrew people.

Later, in Numbers 31, however, Balaam is identified as having led the Moabite (or Midianite) women to seduce the Israelite men and betray them into worshiping Moabite (or Midianite) idols, which led to the disastrous apostasy at Shittim described in Numbers 25. Balaam came to take on the role of an "eternal adversary" in the legends and lore surrounding the Torah stories. Most frequently, although he is a foreigner, he is portrayed as a powerful magician serving as an adviser or diviner in the court of the pharaoh, together with his two sons, Jannes and Jambres. Usually his divinations are quite accurate.

This is the case in the present instance. Balaam tells Pharaoh that his dream means that a son of Israel will destroy Egypt and free the Israelites. It is Balaam who, when Pharaoh asks how to avert this fate, advises him to have the boy children thrown into the river. Balaam points out, as we have seen, that God promised never again to destroy the world by flood, thus apparently ruling out talionic retribution for the deed of drowning the boys. Balaam then engages in a nice piece of Talmudic thinking: only water will work against the Israelites, he warns, because in the past God has already delivered Abraham from the fire of the Chaldeans, Isaac from the sword of Abraham, and Jacob from the labor imposed on him by Laban.

Balaam's foresight and calculations are good but not perfect: Moses is indeed destined to die by water, but through the effects of the waters of Meribah (as we shall see), not by drowning, as Balaam had assumed (see Ginzberg 1911, 3:256).

As another precaution lest the foredestined child somehow escape death, Pharaoh orders guards to be posted to observe all pregnant Hebrew women in their ninth month. But again he makes a fatal miscalculation: he forgets that it is in the nature of prophets, like Moses, to be born in the sixth month. This, according to a midrash, is the real meaning of the line in Exodus concerning the mother of Moses: "When she saw that he was a fine child, she hid him for three months" (Exod. 2:2). Those three months were the period of time between the actual date of Moses's delivery and the apparent due date when Pharaoh's henchmen would be ready to do away with him.

V

The midrashic commentaries have spared nothing in their efforts to depict the pharaoh of Egypt as an unredeemed, sadistic persecutor, a monster of infanticidal depravity. The Jerusalem Talmud, for example, tells us that God punished Pharaoh for his cruelty to the Hebrews by bringing leprosy upon him and that he suffered terribly and became a source of revulsion to all those around him. But he decides on a plan to cure himself, suggested by none other than the evil vizier Balaam. The cure requires Pharaoh to bathe every day in the blood of a Hebrew child. This particular piece of advice so outrages the one just counselor in Pharaoh's court—Jethro, the future father-in-law of Moses—that he leaves Egypt in disgust and settles in Midian, where he takes up sheepherding.

In the midrash, this Pharaoh, who succumbs to his disease after years of slaughtering a Hebrew child a day in the vain quest for a cure, has a successor who proves even more barbaric. Whenever an Israelite fails to produce his assigned quota of bricks, the officers of this heartless new pharaoh would go "to the women of the children of Israel, and take their infants from them, as many as the number of bricks lacking in the measure, and these babes they put into the building instead of the missing bricks. The task-masters forced each man of the Israelites to put his own child in the building. The father would place his son in the wall, and cover him over with mortar, all the while weeping, his tears running down upon his child"

(Ginzberg, 1911, 2:299). As I shall argue in Chapter 5, the intention of these extreme vilifications is to ward off in advance the guilt that will accrue to Moses for his rebellion against and killing of Pharaoh. Pharaoh is portrayed in such an unspeakable light that there can be no question that Moses's deed was justified. Most of us would probably agree that it was, but the mythic tradition has not granted forgiveness so easily.

VI

As we have seen, myths employ the techniques of decomposition, which produces doublings, reversals, or more drastic transformations of central themes. I believe that one reason for this is to make the structure plain, precisely so that it can be understood and communicated, even if not at a level of explicit conscious awareness. The theme of the filicidal senior male provides us with a nice example of a case of doubling of a theme whose surface variations only partially disguise an underlying unity.

We have seen that the pharaoh plays the role of bad father in the Moses narrative (though not in the Joseph story) and as such he is to be contrasted with Jacob/Israel as well as with Joseph's pharaoh, the good fathers. But let us look for a moment directly at the man whom the Bible identifies not as Moses's social father, his *pater,* but as his actual biological *genitor.* In Exodus 2:1, Moses's parents are identified only as a man from the house of Levi and a daughter of Levi. Later we shall find out a little more about them, but for now all we need to know is that Moses's father is a man named Amram and his mother a woman named Jochabed.

An interesting legend takes Amram as its apparent hero: At the time when Pharaoh's dire edict about the drowning of the male Hebrew children goes forth, Amram, an elder of piety and eminence, is serving (anachronistically) as president of the Sanhedrin, the governing council of the Israelites. His response to the crisis is to propose that all Israelite husbands should live separately from their wives. "[Amram] said: 'we labor in vain' and was the first to divorce his wife. At that, all the others divorced their wives" (Bialik and Ravnitzky 1992, 60).

In other words, in order to avert the anticipated slaughter, Amram decides it is best for the Israelites not to produce a new generation. So while Pharaoh plans to kill the new generation of boys only, after they are born, Amram, more radically still, proposes to prevent not only the boys but all Hebrew children from even coming into existence. That the effect of his ordinance is even more devastating than that of Pharaoh's is not lost on Amram and Jochabed's oldest child, the prophetess Miriam. She upbraids her father thus: " 'Father, your decree is more cruel than Pharaoh's, for Pharaoh decreed only against the males, while you decree against both males and females. . . . Now since Pharaoh is a wicked man, there is doubt whether his decree will or will not be fulfilled; but since you are a righteous man, your decree is sure to be fulfilled' " (60).

Miriam, in thus speaking wisely, plays the part of the rescuer of the Hebrew children, including her younger brother Moses—just as she will rescue Moses after he is born. Her words have their desired effect, and Amram relents. He publicly remarries Jochabed, and, following his lead, all the Israelites remarry their former spouses, whom they had divorced in obedience to his earlier decree. Jochabed, though more than a hundred years old, miraculously becomes soft and lovely; Amram has intercourse with her, and she conceives Moses.

This story, incidentally, is supposed to account for an apparent inconsistency in the biblical text. Exodus 2:1–2 says: "A certain man of the house of Levi went and married a Levite woman. The woman conceived and bore a son." The son in question is Moses, but the passage implies his parents married and Jochabed conceived him right away: in other words, that he is the first-born child. Yet we later hear in the biblical text that Moses has an older sister, Miriam, and later still we become acquainted with his older brother, Aaron, who plays a major role in the Bible narrative. How can this be?

To solve the riddle, the rabbis apparently devised the Amram-Miriam story, which makes Moses's conception the direct result of the marriage of Amram and Jochabed, who at the same time already have two older children, without any scandalous implications and with each character acting from only the most highminded and pious of motives.[11]

The story does manage to create the needed rationalization, but it also illustrates what contortions are required if one assumes that, to have validity or truth, a biblical text ought to conform to the standards of a narrative chronicle of events unfolding in human historical time. The Amram-Miriam story makes more sense not as a bit of history but as a structurally determined duplication of the infanticidal decree of the pharaoh—to which Miriam, indeed, compares it in the midrash. Amram is made to look like the opposite of Pharaoh: he is an Israelite, Pharaoh is Egyptian; he is just and pious, Pharaoh is wicked. The identical role of Miriam as rescuer in both instances provides a clue to their underlying identity: both men are senior males who issue decrees that would have had the effect of destroying Moses, were it not for the intervention of the "woman," Miriam. (In the story of Moses's rescue from the Nile, of course, Miriam is only one of the multiple female rescuers on the scene.)

The important difference between Amram and Pharaoh in the midrash is that Pharaoh is motivated to kill his junior rivals by excessive lust and jealousy, while Amram is motivated by piety and concern for his potential children and for the children of Israel generally. We may say that Pharaoh threatens Moses's life out of excessive devotion to sexuality and fertility, Amram out of excessive asceticism and sterility. These opposites represent the extremes a successful social organization and moral order must mediate and reconcile to produce a viable system for the reproduction of successive generations.[12]

VII

To expand this discussion of the various guises assumed by the filicidal senior male in the biblical myth and the legends spun off from it, let me mention only briefly one of the most spectacular decompositions of this idea—one that is perhaps not clearly visible or comprehensible as such until viewed from the perspective of the primal horde. I refer to the fact that the most senior of all senior males in the biblical myth—God—attempts on several occasions to obliterate his "children," either in the form of life in general, as in Noah's flood, or more specifically his chosen people, the Israelites, for example, by means of the pestilences that decimate them as divine retribution for such lapses into idolatry as the incident with the Golden Calf (Exodus 32) or the apostasy at Shittim (Numbers 25).

Of particular relevance in the present context is the much-disputed passage Exodus 4:24–26, in which, after sending Moses back to Egypt to confront Pharaoh, God himself, so the text seems to say, meets Moses at an encampment along the way and tries to kill him. Zipporah saves the situation by circumcising her first-born son, Gershom, and touching Gershom's(?) legs with the foreskin. No scholarly consensus has been reached about how to interpret this mysterious passage; probably it is what remains of a lost fuller narrative. But whatever its origin or interpretation, its literal meaning is fairly plain: God tries to kill Moses, his chosen representative of the people he has just described in the previous verse as his "first-born."

He is dissuaded by an act of circumcision, suggesting that his attack is not only filicidal but castrating in intent; or, in other words, that even he can play the role of the jealous, persecuting primal father.[13]

Like Amram, but on a grander scale, God is depicted as the antithesis of Pharaoh, representing the beginning and end of all morality as opposed to its opposite or absence. Yet in the circumcision story, too, we find the mythic theme of filicide, which supports the view that the Torah narrative can best be understood within the structure of the primal horde.

VIII

As I mentioned earlier, scholars have frequently noted that while Oedipus provides a paradigm for the Hellenic strain of Western culture, he has no counterpart in the Hebraic strain. Instead, in the Judeo-Christian tradition, of comparable but different significance is the incident known as the *Akedah,* the "binding" of Isaac by his father, Abraham, who was ordered by God to offer Isaac as a sacrifice, as described in Genesis 22. Here, instead of patricidal, the violence is filicidal: Abraham is prepared to kill his only son in obedience to the divine command and is only kept from doing so by the last-minute, miraculous substitution of a ram for Isaac.[14]

My own view is that the Hellenic and Judeo-Christian traditions are more alike than different and that these two stories are no exception. In every tale concerning the succession of a junior male to senior status—a deed that inevitably implies an "oedipal" rebellion—a previous episode of the story portrays a senior male attempting (unsuccessfully, of course) to kill that junior male. The filicidal attempt represents the hostile and jealous side of the ambivalent senior male–junior male relationship, while the survival of the junior male represents the offsetting nurturant and preserving dimension. [15]

As noted earlier, Laius tried to kill Oedipus long before Oedipus killed him. This episode of the story strikes me as being a close parallel to the story of the Akedah: like Abraham, Laius binds Oedipus in response to a divine decree—the Delphic oracle—and prepares to hand him over to death. Oedipus is rescued by a shepherd; Isaac is rescued by a sheep. Of course Isaac does not later kill Abraham, but the story does serve as a structural prelude to the theme of jealous filicide that is so prominent a feature of the story of Moses and Pharaoh and thus anticipates Moses's retaliatory killing of Pharaoh. Pharaoh too, like Laius and like Abraham, plans to kill his would-be successor. And like Oedipus, Moses survives the attack and goes on to succeed by the oedipal deed of killing Pharaoh. For me, then, the Akedah may be understood as yet another decomposition and anticipatory enunciation of the theme of the infanticidal father (or senior male) so central to the entire Torah narrative.

It has become fashionable to berate Freud for having overlooked the filicidal aspect of the Oedipus story—what Georges Devereux identified as the "Laius complex" (1953). This trend seems to me misguided in a number of ways. I must postpone a discussion of most of these for another occasion. For the present, I shall mention only the most relevant objection to it, namely, that it is wrong. Freud can hardly be accused of forgetting about the filicidal dimension of the oedipal situation when we recall that he proposed the scenario of the primal horde as the prototype of the Oedipus complex and that the primal father of that story is no less a filicide (or attempted filicide) than Laius, Abraham, or the wicked pharaoh (or Herod, or Claudius, or Darth Vader). He is indeed the mythic prototype for all of them. For, as we saw, in the primal horde "the lot of his sons was a hard one: if they roused their father's jealousy they were killed or castrated or driven out" (Freud 1939, 81).

4

Incest and Its Vicissitudes

I

We have seen how the situation of the Israelites in Egypt under the rule of the wicked pharaoh can be seen as a depiction in mythic imagery of what Freud described as the regime of the primal father. We shall now look at how the situation described in the Torah narrative before the transformative events of the Exodus and the revelation at Sinai further corresponds to Freud's depiction of the system of the primal horde in presenting a social life before, or without, the regulation of mating or "marriage" by any rules, foremost among which would be the prohibition on incest.

My reading of the text is guided by my supposition that the purpose of myth is to state the rules of existing social organization in such a way that these rules appear to be the outcome of a founding event of unquestionable authority. That is why the 613 commandments prescribed in the Torah are embedded in a mythic narrative in the first place. The founding event—the revelation of the Law at Mount Sinai—takes its overwhelming authority from the events that come before it, most especially the successful rebellion of the Israelites against their Egyptian masters, epitomized in the struggle between Moses and the wicked pharaoh of Exodus. If these events establish a culture as it ideally ought to be, it stands to reason that the situation before them was specifically "precultural," and hence "natural," "wild," or "uncivilized " from the point of view of the "civilized" narrative present.

Since, furthermore, if we accept from Freud and Lévi-Strauss that a key aspect of social life is the regulation of sexuality and mating for reproduction, and thus "marriage," it follows that the precultural era should be represented as one in which the present rules governing sexual union and reproduction were absent. The primal horde, I reiterate, does not represent a real situation; it is the depiction, from the point of view of the social present, of life in the absence of the founding event. Therefore it is bound to appear in some way as the antithesis of the present social order, as a regime characterized by the apparent violation of the present system's most sacred norms and values.

I am the first to admit that the entire book of Genesis—which is what mainly corresponds to the pre-Sinaitic epoch in the Torah narrative—may not at first glance appear to be an explicit depiction of a state of rampant, unregulated sex and complete disregard for considerations of incestuous relationships between sexual partners. On the contrary, the institutions of marriage and kinship that pertain in the social and narrative present of the myth seem overall to be already largely in force in the time before the Israelites' sojourn in Egypt. Let me briefly explain why I think this is so and why it does not constitute, for me, a definitive argument against the interpretation I am putting forward here.

First, it is difficult to depict a social system different from one's own without distorting it, both wittingly and unwittingly, through the lens of the present social conditions under which it is being depicted. At an unwitting level, the influence of the present and thus the pervasive presence of anachronism is nearly inevitable. People are rarely conscious of many of the fundamental rules and values that guide their lives. Therefore, people often depict other times, even very different times, as incorporating unquestioned or "self-evident" aspects of the present. Thus, for example, the rabbis regularly depicted Moses and the patriarchs as engaged in scholarly disputations about passages in the Torah, just as they themselves were. They considered such disputations a central focus of life, and it must have seemed natural to them to depict earlier generations of "Jews" doing the same— without regard for the fact that the Torah had not even come into existence in the time of the patriarchs.[1] In the same way, later painters in the Christian tradition routinely depicted the Nativity or the Annunciation against a Florentine or Netherlandish backdrop.

There is an additional motive for anachronistic elements in the formation and "distortion" of a text. Later Judeo-Christian society, after all, regards the patriarchs as revered ancestors. Actions that do not correspond to present-day moral expectations cast aspersions on the ancestors and so by implication on their descendants. A good illustration of this phenomenon can be found in the ambivalent attitude within the Western philosophical tradition to Plato and Aristotle during the period of Christian supremacy. On the one hand, the two were manifestly great thinkers and the clear forerunners of the intellectual present. But on the other hand, there was no denying that they were—how else to put it?—pagans, and had had the misfortune to have lived before the founding event of Christ's passage on earth. Therefore attempts were made to integrate Christian doctrine with classical philosophy and show them to be mutually coherent: to make it appear that Plato and Aristotle were Christian *avant la lettre*.

By the same token, there can be no doubt that Abraham, say, lived before the revelation of the Law; at the same time, it would certainly not look well to depict the ancestor of the Israelites and thus of the Jews as a wanton violator of every rule in the book. It is inevitable that his portrayal should represent a compromise between the effort to depict the "precultural" world and the effects of seeing the past through the lens of the present.

Yet another reason for apparent discrepancies between the text as it is and my contentions about what it ought to be is one I have mentioned before and can only reiterate here: the Torah text exists for other reasons than the ones I am discussing. My interpretation of the text is certainly one important way of making sense of it, but it cannot have determined everything in the text, which is also responding to numerous other formative influences.

Finally and most important, according to the analogy that Freud makes between the Judeo-Christian tradition and obsessional neurosis, the scenario of the primal horde must correspond to an unconscious fantasy. In an individual, a fantasy—or an unconscious memory elaborated into an unconscious fantasy—derives its power to produce symptoms and defenses that are compulsory and resistant to ordinary efforts to eliminate them from that fact that it is unconscious. The fantasy is denied access to conscious awareness and scrutiny, kept out of the normal circulation of ideas, and thus protected from judgment, criticism, and wearing away through the effects of time and experience. In the same way, if a complex of ideas, like the myth of the primal horde, is to play a powerful and determinative role in the construction of social and cultural institutions such as those of Judeo-Christian civilization, it can only do so if it is unconscious, that is, if it is not manifest or directly observable by conscious awareness.

It is just this circumstance that renders my project of interpretation difficult, not so much to execute as to render plausible to the reader. For on the one hand I must discover a pattern that is sufficiently foundational and pervasive for the organizing role I have assigned it, and on the other, I must do so in a way that shows that pattern to be "unconscious," that is, not available to direct notice. Like the purloined letter, the mythic structure must satisfy the requirements of being both really there and simultaneously invisible, or at least invisible to certain ways of looking. Its presence must be deduced by abstract reasoning and reconstruction, and then it must be sought and found, almost—but not quite—in plain sight.

From this point of view, then, it is *necessary* that the narrative can be read—and is read—in ways that render the mythic infrastructure invisible to ordinary observation. Therefore it is no disproof of my reading that the evidence for the presence of incestuous and unregulated sex and reproduction throughout the pre-Sinaitic era is intermingled with quite another picture entirely, one that does its best to cast such evidence into the shadows even while communicating it.

II

Let us first look at Genesis 6:7. In this passage, early on in the "prehistory" of the Israelites, God has decided that the wickedness of humans is too great to be tolerated and resolves to blot them out. This is the prelude to the great flood, which was survived only by Noah and his family, together with breeding pairs of every living creature. Outdoing both Pharaoh and Amram in filicidal ambition, God makes the following grim resolve: "I will blot out from the earth the men whom I created—men together with beasts, creeping things, and birds of the sky; for I regret that I made them."

We are not told exactly what grieved God so, other than generalized "lawlessness." The preceding passages contain no explicit causal links that would account for what motivates God in his wrath. But we can make an educated guess. If we turn to the opening passages of the chapter, we find these lines: "When men began to increase on earth and daughters were born to them, the divine beings saw how beautiful the daughters of men were and they took wives from among those that pleased them. . . . The Lord said, 'My breath shall not abide in man forever, since he too is flesh; let the days allowed him be one hundred and twenty years.' " (Gen. 6:1–3). Where Plaut (whose translation I am using) has "they took wives from among those that pleased them," a more accurate rendering would specify that they took themselves wives "from among any whom they chose" (*mikol asher baharu*).

I wish to draw attention to the explicit statement in the text that in this period, sexual intercourse was unregulated, and the inhabitants of earth married whomever they chose. Judging by what happens next, we can deduce that this state of affairs enraged God so much that he determined to exterminate life on earth. That his stated intention includes the killing of all living beings, not just people, supports the interpretation that unregulated sex has aroused his fury, because precisely what humans share with the other creatures, especially as the matter is traditionally set up in the Western cultural system, is "animality" or "carnal nature": that is, sexual desire and sexual reproduction. Animals are thought of, in this tradition, as being natural rather than cultural. This in turn is understood to imply that they do not observe the boundaries between acceptable and unacceptable unions, especially the prohibition on incest, which is assumed to characterize human society and the realm of culture.[2]

Several aspects of this passage from Genesis provide links with the story of the Israelites and Moses in Egypt. The tradition explicitly connects Moses's death by water, as well as the deaths of the Egyptians in the Red Sea, with Noah's flood. Like Moses, Noah survives death by drowning, commanded by a persecuting senior male, by floating in an ark (*tevah,* chest or box). Like Pharaoh in Exodus, God is depicted as being concerned precisely with the increase in numbers of a subordinate people: in Pharaoh's case, of the Israelites, in God's, of the dwellers on earth.

Finally, when God decides to fix a limit on the life spans of human beings, he chooses 120 years. This number forms a direct symbolic link to Moses, the biblical character of whom it is explicitly recorded that he lived to the age of 120.

Unlike the pharaoh, however, God eventually provides for the survival of humans and animals alike, and in doing so lays down the basis for a more orderly system of social organization. He peoples the ark with humans and animals according to the obvious alternative to the all-or-nothing approach of the primal horde. That is, he arranges everyone in couples, one mate for each individual. Noah and his wife are saved, along with their three sons and the sons' wives, who will found the three genealogical lines of humanity. The animals, of course, are also paired.

But despite God's precautions, the subsequent chapters of Genesis constitute a veritable catalogue of sexual unions that, by the regulations later established at Sinai, are forbidden, incestuous, or otherwise abominable. No sooner has the ark landed, indeed, than one of Noah's sons, Ham, the ancestor of the Hamitic peoples, commits a grievous sexual impropriety. His father Noah, who has drunk some wine, "became drunk and he uncovered himself within his tent. Ham, the father of Canaan, saw his father's nakedness" (Gen. 9:21–22). This act is in direct contravention of the Sinaitic decree of Leviticus: "Your father's nakedness, that is, the nakedness of your mother, you shall not uncover" (18:7).

In this case, as so often in the biblical text, one can spot the storytellers' aim without much difficulty: the Israelites are about to usurp the lands of the Canaanites (and at the time of writing had long since usurped it). Any mythic lore denigrating the Canaanites and showing them to be descendants of a sexual outlaw would help legitimize the claims of the Israelites to ethical and hence political supremacy.

This is not, however, my concern in the present analysis. The point I wish to emphasize here is that situations are presented in the narration of the events before Sinai which are expressly forbidden by the laws revealed there and thereafter to Moses. But far from wondering at this, or expressing bewilderment that the great patriarchs almost to a man violated what was to become strict Jewish law when it came to sex and marriage, we should take it as confirmation of what I have proposed, namely, that sex and marriage before Sinai were unregulated and dominated by no overarching principles or controls other than the will of the strongest, guided by strategies typical of males competing for forcible control over females and the maximization of their own reproductive fitness.

It was this situation, indeed, that the laws of Sinai were intended to fix; and the text would be vastly more incoherent if what I have described were *not* the case, for there would have been no point to the great covenant if people were already doing what it commanded.

III

I have argued that the social practices depicted in the pre-Sinaitic episodes of the Torah story ought to reflect the antithesis of what becomes normative with the establishment of the Law. Thus, Noah and his son expressly violate one of the commandments regulating sexual propriety found in Leviticus. But this is no isolated incident. On the contrary, the sexual and marital doings of the major figures of the proto-Israelite lineage constitute a veritable catalogue of unions strictly forbidden by the regulations of Leviticus and Deuteronomy. It is as if this prehistory of the Israelite clan had been concocted from episodes arrived at by a systematic negating of the Sinaitic laws.

So, to begin at the beginning, the ancestor of all the Israelites, Abraham (Abram), marries a woman, Sarah (Sarai), who is his half-sister, as he confesses to Abimelech: "And besides, she [Sarah] is in truth my sister, my father's daughter though not my mother's; and she became my wife" (Gen.

20:12). But compare this passage with the following commandment from Leviticus: "The nakedness of your sister—your father's daughter or your mother's . . . do not uncover their nakedness" (1:9). The same rule is reiterated in Deuteronomy: "Cursed be he who lies with his sister, whether daughter of his father or of his mother" (27:22).

Abraham's son, Isaac, marries Rebecca, who is his father's brother's son's daughter, a union that is not specifically prohibited by a Mosaic decree. But in his own encounter with Abimelech in the land of the Philistines, he too passes off his wife as his sister. This deception deliberately forces her to enter an adulterous union with a Philistine to save her husband's life. As Abimelech exclaims when he learns the truth: " 'What have you done to us! One of the people might have lain with your wife, and you would have brought guilt upon us' " (Gen. 26:10). Whether any such thing has in fact happened—Isaac and Rebecca had, after all, been there for some time when their deception was discovered—Isaac certainly has intentionally taken steps that could have resulted in a violation of this commandment: "Do not have carnal relations with your neighbor's wife and defile yourself with her" (Lev. 18:20). Or this one: "If a man is found lying with another man's wife both of them . . . shall die" (Deut. 22:22).

As for Isaac's son Jacob, who became Israel, the ancestor of all the Israelites, "He finished out the [bridal] week with Leah, and then Laban gave him his daughter Rachel to be his wife" (Gen. 29:28). But Jacob's sororal polygamy is specifically banned by the Sinaitic covenant: "Do not marry a woman as a rival to her sister and uncover her nakedness in the other's lifetime" (Lev. 18:18).

Abraham's nephew Lot, meanwhile, has sexual intercourse with his two daughters, and they conceive by him: "Thus the two daughters of Lot came to be with child by their father" (Gen. 19:36). But compare the commandment "None of you shall come near anyone of his own flesh to uncover nakedness" (Lev. 18:6). Lot lives among the Sodomites, who, when Lot was visited by two angels during a stay in their city, shouted out to him: " 'Where are the men who came to you tonight? Bring them out to us, that we may be intimate with them' " (Gen. 19:5). They thus directly violate this later commandment: "Do not lie with a male as one lies with a woman; it is an abhorrence" (Lev. 18:22).

When we turn specifically to the first "Israelites," the twelve sons of Jacob/Israel, we continue to find the same pattern. As we have seen, Reuben, the oldest son of Jacob, sleeps with his father's wife Bilhah, the mother of two of his half-brothers, Dan and Naphtali, thus violating the command-ment "Do not uncover the nakedness of your father's wife" (Lev. 18:8).

Reuben's younger brother Judah, founder of the tribe of Judah and thus of the kingdom of Judaea and hence of the "Jews," unwittingly sleeps with his daughter-in-law Tamar, who disguises herself as a prosti-tute. This violates the law "Do not uncover the nakedness of your daugh-ter-in-law; she is your son's wife, you shall not uncover her nakedness" (Lev. 18:15).

The story of the lone sister of the twelve Israelite brothers, Dinah, is of particular interest here, for while she violates no laws, she herself is violated by Shechem, the son of Hamor, chief of the Hivites. Hamor then makes a request of Dinah's brothers that amounts to as clear an expression of the idea of wife exchange à la Lévi-Strauss as could be imagined: " 'My son Shechem longs for your daughter. Please give her to him in marriage. Intermarry with us: give your daughters to us, and take our daughters for yourselves' " (Gen. 34:8–9). But two of her brothers, Simeon and Levi, take advantage of the Hivite men's weakened state after they have circumcised themselves according to the Israelites' request and kill them all, including Shechem and Hamor. This act may certainly be seen as a direct rejection of the offer of intermarriage made by the Hivites. As such, it supports my contention that wife exchange is a custom that logically emerges only after the covenant that follows upon the primal rebellion.[3]

Thus four of Israel's sons, the four oldest sons of his first wife, Leah, namely, Reuben, Simeon, Levi, and Judah, are depicted as either breakers of what will later become laws governing proper sexual relations or else as enemies of wife exchange. Since wife exchange, according to my present model, is the necessary outcome of the prohibition on incest, Simeon and Levi in opposing it may be understood as proponents of "incest," that is, of retaining sisters within the group rather than giving them out in marriage exchange.

Examined together, the relevant exploits of these brothers give a fair catalogue of behaviors typifying the situation of the primal horde: a junior male sleeps with his father's wife, a senior male sleeps with his son's wife, and a woman's brothers kill the men of a rival horde who want to have sex with her.

One could go further with this exercise, but I think the point is well-enough established: the laws regulating sexual life and marriage promulgated at Mount Sinai stand in a direct relation to the narration of the genealogy of the Israelites before Sinai. What was done before Sinai is prohibited there; what is prohibited at Sinai had been done up until then.

From the point of view of the later, post-Sinaitic world—the point of view, that is, of any reader (or writer) of the text—the state of unregulated marriage would necessarily appear to be one dominated by incest. The concept of incest would not have applied during the period of unregulated sexuality itself, of course, because it represents the violation of a rule that by definition did not exist in an unregulated state of society. But retrospectively, after such rules *are* in force, the *absence* of the rule would be understood as the violation of the *present* rule. Since the present (post-Sinaitic) regulation of sexuality takes as its most fundamental position the abhorrence of sex between closely related people, the pre-Sinaitic, unregulated state would thus appear as one that practiced or condoned incest.

IV

How could there be elements in this or any text that correspond to an unconscious fantasy in an individual psyche? We can picture unconscious ideas in the mind as corresponding, for example, to a set of neural connections that are really there but are cut off from neural pathways to consciousness, perhaps by way of verbal representations. But in a text there is, as it were, no hiding place. Everything is in plain view, and it is hard to picture how a written document could contain significant amounts of information that could be communicated unconsciously while not being directly observable.

One method available to the "textual unconscious" is to disguise the presence of a theme or pattern by breaking it up into pieces and scattering its components around in ways that shift the narrative and emotional focus. This is why it is rarely noticed that Genesis is a catalogue of sexual misdemeanors. Here I want to draw attention to another of the most important hiding places for unconsciously communicated ideas to which a text has recourse: that is, the mind of the reader, who, unlike the text, *does* have the capacity to harbor unconscious thoughts, wishes, fears, and fantasies or to isolate different realms of knowledge from easy interaction with one another.

This strategy, whereby the text activates knowledge in the readers' minds without the readers becoming aware that they know what they know, is well illustrated by the case I now wish to develop, which demonstrates the presence of the incestuous, triadic schema of the primal horde in the Torah narrative. I refer to the lineage of Moses, who as culture hero may be considered not only the founder of the Judeo-Christian society but also an individual whose plight depicts and epitomizes the condition of his people. I submit that for the purposes of this myth, Moses's own family may be thought of as having been decomposed into two: an Egyptian and an Israelite. There is no denying, on the basis of a straightforward and literal reading of the biblical text, that Moses really does have both an Egyptian and an Israelite identity and set of kin relations. And as I demonstrated earlier, the close intertwining of the pharaoh's family and that of the house of Jacob/Israel begins when Joseph becomes Pharaoh's "father" and continues in a reversed mode when Moses becomes a "son" in Pharaoh's family.

I would like now to remind readers of a fact of which they are certainly aware but which is not always brought to mind in the present context. I refer to that fact that the pharaohs were and are well known to practice incest, that is, brothers married their sisters. I have already mentioned the centrality of the myth of Isis, Osiris, and Horus, which begins with Osiris and Isis, brother and sister, becoming lovers while still in their mother's womb. As Edmund Leach has written: "In ancient times, as in modern, one of the best known legends concerning the Egyptian kingship was that the principal wife of Pharaoh was a sister or half-sister. This practice (insofar as it really took place) was modelled on a celebrated mythological formula" (1983, 39).

Leach's parenthetical caveat about whether pharaonic incest really took place need not detain us long. The best evidence indicates that brother sister marriage was not only the norm in the royal house but also that such marriages were preferred for a long period in widespread strata of Egyptian society. Hopkins's classic article (1980) on the subject leaves little room for doubt about the prevalence of this practice in Egyptian society up through the Roman era at least.[4] My argument, however, does not depend on the historical truth of the pharaohs' reputation for incest but on the fact that it is widely known to readers of the Bible, certainly those who lived while there actually were pharaohs on the throne.

Leach, in acknowledging the essential validity of the tradition, makes the point that its importance rests on its being widely known: "*What matters is repute.* . . . The eldest daughter of the Pharaoh's principal wife acquired the title 'God's wife' during childhood. The succeeding Pharaoh, whether or not he was the son of the previous Pharaoh, seems to have married the 'God's wife' " (1983, 59n, my emphasis). As Leach describes the system of succession, the reigning pharaoh's senior daughter was designated his successor, as Isis reborn, now as his daughter, from the womb of Isis in her guise as his sister/wife. The man who was to become pharaoh—usually it was a man, though there were famous cases of female pharaohs—acquired legitimacy by his marriage to the "God's wife." Normally, this man would be the son of the reigning pharaoh, and hence his "God's wife" would be his sister or paternal half-sister.[5]

As Leach continues, brother-sister marriage survived the fall of the pharaohs to flourish in Hellenistic and Roman times, and he adds: "This Ptolemaic revival of the brother-sister marriage patterns . . . would have provided the editors of the biblical texts working at that period with a confirmatory example of what was believed to be traditional Pharaonic behavior" (60n).

All these points were taken for granted by Freud himself, who clearly assumed them to be common knowledge among his readers: "What is represented as insulting our most sacred feelings was a universal custom—we might call it a usage made holy—among the ruling families of the Ancient Egyptians and of other early peoples. It was taken as a matter of course that a Pharaoh should take his sister as his first and principal wife; and the later successors of the Pharaohs, the Greek Ptolemies, did not hesitate to follow that model" (1939, 120–121).

V

The Torah text contains many references to the pharaoh, and insofar as it is true, as I have asserted it to be, that these references may be associated in the reader's mind with the idea of pharaonic incest, then I have shown the likelihood of their being a presumption of the incestuous primal triad in the Torah, in the form of the pharaonic Isis-Osiris-Horus mythic model. What indication is there in the text itself that the connection between pharaohs and incest is actually implied or suggested without being made explicit?

Genesis 12:10–20 describes the sojourn of Abram and Sarai in Egypt during a time of famine in Canaan (they have not yet changed their names to Abraham and Sarah). Abram fears that because Sarai is beautiful, the

Egyptians, thinking her unobtainable by lawful means, will kill him and force her to marry one of them. Therefore, they claim to be brother and sister.

Here is a theme we have already encountered: the Egyptians, driven by insatiable sexual desire—and more specifically Pharaoh, who adds Sarai to his harem—are ready to kill any rival who has sexual rights to a woman and resists handing her over. But on hearing that the man is her brother rather than her husband, or in other words that the two do not have a sexual relationship, the Egyptians simply help themselves to the sister to add to the pharaoh's collection. By giving Sarai as his "sister" to Pharaoh, Abram attains the status of royal brother-in-law and presumably the gifts and favor that go with it.

But now Pharaoh and his household begin to suffer afflictions, and Pharaoh determines, no doubt through his excellent diviners, that his misfortune is the result of an unwitting adulterous union with Sarai. Pharaoh asks Abram, "Why didn't you tell me she was your wife?" and sends them away. Only in a later episode, when a nearly identical situation arises with the Philistine king Abimelech (Gen. 12:20), do we learn that Sarai really is Abram's sister—in other words, that Abram himself has contracted a pharaonic marriage.

Many aspects of this episode contradict my contention that before Sinai there was unregulated mating, an absence of marriage exchange, and no jural or normative distinction between a wife, mate, or sexual partner, on the one hand, and a sister or daughter on the other. After all, here Pharaoh is described as bound by the laws of marriage and the prohibition on adultery and as being someone who *respects,* rather than ignores, the crucial difference between a wife and a sister, since he is willing to seize Abram's sister but not his wife.

At the same time, the overall effect of the passage may *also* have a quite different covert import, insofar as it raises in the readers' minds the following points:

- There is a pharaoh who does not know whether a certain woman is a wife or a sister.
- There is a pharaoh who marries a woman who is married to her own brother.
- There is a man closely associated with the pharaoh who is married to his own sister.[6]

These fragments, I suggest, resemble scattered pieces of a jigsaw puzzle so arranged in the text that we can put them together unconsciously while remaining unaware of doing so consciously. What these fragments taken together do is jog our memories of what we know about pharaohs, as if to say: "You know that pharaohs marry their sisters: recall it now, but do not (necessarily) become aware that you are doing so." By this interpretation the coherence of the explicit narrative conforming to our post-Sinaitic expectations allows us to be distracted or absorbed enough in the surface to remain unmindful of the latent cues and the message they impart about the compelling but forbidden theme of incest.

VI

My argument thus far about Moses's family in the royal house of Egypt is circumstantial and demands certain moves that some readers may not wish to make. In any event, I still have not offered a clear example of the incestuous triad of the primal horde actually being present in the biblical text. I shall now do so.

Having just discussed the background in Genesis of Moses's Egyptian family, let me look now at his Israelite forbears. When they are first introduced in Exodus 2:1, Moses's parents appear without names, identified simply as a "man from the house of Levi" (*ish mibbeit Levi*) and—rather ambiguously, as we shall see—a "daughter of Levi" (*bat Levi*). Only later on, in Exodus 6:20, in the course of a lengthy genealogical discursus on Moses and Aaron, do we discover the names of Moses's parents and their relationship to each other: "Amram took to wife his father's sister Jochabed, and she bore him Aaron and Moses" (Exod. 6:20). From the information in Exodus 6:13–25, we can piece together a more detailed genealogical picture within which to contextualize this striking detail.

Levi is the third of the twelve sons of the patriarch Jacob/Israel. His mother is Jacob's first wife, Leah, the daughter of Laban. Levi has three sons: Gershon, Kohath, and Merari. Kohath has four sons, of whom Amram is the oldest: Amram, Izhar, Bebron, and Uzziel. Amram is thus a grandson of Levi through his father Kohath. Jochabed is bat Levi not in the generic sense, as the phrase is often rendered in English: "a woman of the house of Levi." She is literally the daughter of Levi himself and thus the sister of Gershon, Kohath, and Merari. She marries her nephew, and to him she bears Moses.

We are no longer surprised, I trust, to notice that this marriage is in direct contravention of the laws of Sinai, as these are to be revealed to Amram and Jochabed's own most illustrious male offspring: "Do not uncover the nakedness of your father's sister; she is your father's flesh" (Lev. 18:12). This commandment is repeated in greater detail almost immediately after: "You shall not uncover the nakedness of your mother's sister or of your father's sister" (20:19).

While many of the commandments regarding marriage and sexual relationships are repeated from Leviticus in the later book of Deuteronomy, it is rare for a prohibition to be expressed twice in the table of laws of Leviticus itself. It is not a coincidence, I think, that the marriage of the Lawgiver's own parents is one which is given this redoubled and hence emphasized condemnation.

If we examine the marriage of Moses's parents according to the analytic schema I have laid out, we may describe it as a triad consisting of Kohath, Jochabed, and Amram. Kohath and Jochabed are brother and sister in the sense of being biological offspring of the same father (we hear nothing about their mother or respective mothers). Amram is the son of Kohath—again we know nothing about who his mother is. The triad thus recapitulates the elementary structure of the primal horde: males of a junior and a senior genealogical generation, and a single woman who is an undifferentiated "wife-sister."

In Freud's proposed triad of the primal horde, it is the male who is senior by generation who is depicted as the one with sexual access to the female, while the genealogically junior male is excluded from sexual relations. In the case of the marriage of Amram and Jochabed, however, it is the son, Amram, who marries the woman Jochabed, not his father.

We have already encountered this particular transformation of the basic structure of the primal horde: it is identical with the situation in the myth of Isis, Osiris, and Horus. The son Horus, incarnated in the living pharaoh, marries the sister/wife/mother Isis, while his dead father, Osiris, is relegated to the Underworld in an asexual condition. Amram, then, like Pharaoh/Horus, is depicted as a successful oedipal victor, who has reversed the genealogical order and outcompeted his "senior" rival for reproductive rights to the woman, Jochabed. From this union will spring a son who is destined to put an end to the regime of the primal horde forever.

This reduplication of the triadic schema in Moses's two families, Egyptian and Israelite, confirms my assertion that the primal-horde schema, in its Isis-Osiris-Horus transformation, is indeed present in the Torah narrative concerning pre-Sinaitic times. This in turn supports my view that this period, and especially the time of Moses's early life, corresponds to Freud's description of the primal horde as a regime dominated by an infanticidal and jealous tyrant and sexual exploiter, in whose realm mating is unregulated, incestuous, and responsive to no law other than the exclusion by the victor of the loser in the competition for dominance and sexual access to the female(s) of the horde.

The tradition of the midrash offers further support. As Louis Ginzberg points out, the passages in which the Israelites in the wilderness bemoan the loss of the fleshpots of Egypt can hardly mean that the slave masters fed the Hebrews on dainties. Rather, their complaint, ostensibly about the food, had a different meaning: "The true state of affairs was that they had a lurking dissatisfaction with the yoke of the law. . . . In Egypt they had lived undisturbed by laws, and it was this unrestrained life that they desired back. Especially hard for them were the new laws on marriage, for in Egypt they had been accustomed to marry those closely related by blood, from whom they were now obliged to separate" (Ginzberg 1911, 3:246–47).

The tradition also includes a midrash with specific reference to Moses's own family situation that fits my arguments here. According to this story, the two men, Eldad and Medad, who prophesy in the camp, as reported in Numbers 11:26–29, are the half-brothers of Moses: "When the marriage laws were revealed [at Sinai], all those who had been married to relatives by blood had to be divorced from them, so that Amram, too, had to be separated from his wife Jochabed, who was his aunt, and he married another woman. From this union sprang Eldad, 'not of an aunt' and Medad, 'in place of an aunt,' so called by Amram to explain by these names why he had divorced his first wife, his aunt" (Ginzberg 1911, 3:253). It seems clear, then, that as Freud's myth of the primal horde leads us to expect, Israel in Egypt was in a condition of unregulated marriage and incestuous unions were the norm. Moses's mission was to put an end to that and institute exogamous marriage exchange.

5

Young Man Moses

Freud's scenario of the primal horde requires us to accept that eventually the senior male would be succeeded by a junior male. Freud assumed that the usual state of affairs in those precivilized times would have been that the youngest son, who would be the mother's favorite and who would not reach sexual maturity until his father was already past his prime, would probably inherit the horde and the status of senior male. But it is implied that any junior male could on occasion unseat a senior male in a struggle for dominance. These conflicts, whereby the primal horde would reproduce its structure while changing personnel, would not, however, constitute real revolutions by the junior male(s) because they would leave the social system intact.

What makes the revolt of the junior males in Freud's myth distinctive is that the junior males, having formed an alliance that accomplishes what no individual can, are prevented by the very conditions of their alliance from re-creating the primal-horde system once they have overthrown their oppressor. If they are to remain a society of partners rather than adversaries they must agree to alter the conditions of power, finding some way to establish and enforce a system whereby each is willing to forgo unchallenged rule in the interest of a fair distribution of power and of the instruments and perquisites of power.

The new social system, then, is marked by the necessity of preserving the alliance that led to the victory in the first place. Since it was shared opposition to the tyranny of the primal father that induced the brothers to unite, the era after his death requires some other principle or factor to maintain the commitment of each brother to the new, more equitable system. In Freud's myth, the mechanism the brothers use to cement and regularize their alliance is an artificially created replica of the father, not in the form of a single willful mortal individual such as any of them might aspire to become but as a universally valid law or logos associated with no particular individual or faction, which would apply to each individual. This law, to operate with sufficient compulsion to overcome the ambition, narcissism, envy, aggression, and will to domination of any individual, must be enforced. The purpose is served, in the myth, by the image of a divine being, vastly more powerful than any mortal, who enforces the law with the jealous ferocity of the primal father, in the interests not of his own narcissism but of the group itself.

How is this trick accomplished? What hold could such an artificially created fantasy have over the members of the group that would compel each to be ruled by it, at the expense of the pursuit of his own self-interest, genetic or otherwise? It was this problem that Freud's analogy with an obsessional neurosis was designed to solve: if the memory of the original murder of the primal father remained repressed in the collective unconscious mind of each person in each generation, the unconscious guilt generated by the traumatic memory would have the same compulsory force that one observes in the case of the inhibitions and self-imposed rules and rituals of a person with an obsessive-compulsive neurosis. The only problem with this theory, as I have noted, is that it makes untenable assumptions about collective memories enduring across generations in the unconscious and operating in a civilization the same way a traumatic repressed memory does in an individual.

One aim of this book is to show how the concept of unconscious guilt can be put to the service of an understanding of how the compelling authority of the law arises, using our knowledge of the psychodynamics of obsessional neurosis, without Freud's insupportable assumptions. The myth embedded in the Torah narrative, and the rituals and practices surrounding it, can be seen to mobilize the narcissism, aggression, envy, and ambition of each individual and then transform those impulses into the internal self-regulating agency through which each individual comes to experience the myth as true and its authority as ineluctable.

Here, I wish to focus on an important point that has emerged from these considerations, namely, that what distinguishes civilization from the primal horde is the enduring alliance of the brothers and that this alliance entails and is sustained by shared guilt. What is this guilt, and what are some of its implications?

II

One does not imagine that the primal father experienced any guilt when he defeated a rival, castrated a challenger, or dominated a female. Nor do we suppose that a junior male felt any when he attacked a senior male in an effort to challenge his rule and rob his harem or when he stole immature females from another horde and reared them to serve as his consorts. If a junior male succeeded in killing a senior male and taking over his place in the horde, his only fear would be that the same thing would eventually happen to him at the hands of a younger and stronger rival. Certainly, he felt no compunction about killing a competitor, and once the other was dead, he could safely forget him. How can we characterize the difference between this situation and that of the united brothers who, having killed their father in Freud's myth, were subject to sufficient remorse and guilt to impose upon themselves the rules of civilized society?

For Freud, drawing upon the anthropological theorists of his day, what followed the primal crime was not only the religion of totemism but also the practice of exogamy, that is, of marrying someone from a different kinship unit, whether a family, lineage, clan, or house. Exogamy and incest are reciprocals: if there is a prohibition on marrying within the kinship group, one necessarily marries outside it and thus enters into spouse exchange. Lévi-Strauss, indeed, argued that totemism was itself a metaphoric representation, using animal species as signs, of the relationships among the different subgroups constituting a society and that these relationships were to be characterized as systems of exchange or, more generally, as resting on the principle of reciprocity.[1]

It is impossible to overestimate the importance this principle has had for the anthropological understanding of the nature of society since the classic formulation of Marcel Mauss in his book *The Gift* (1967 [1925]). In societies without a market economy in the modern sense, the exchange of goods, services, and—as Lévi-Strauss stressed—women (or spouses) is embedded in a social principle characterized by the dual obligation to give and to receive. Exchange or reciprocity between individuals or groups in society is not primarily a strictly utilitarian or "economic" activity powered by the quest for wealth or profit or by the need for an item one does not possess, as in barter (in which one gives what one has to obtain something one does not have). Rather, reciprocity is itself an irreducible moral imperative and a good in and of itself, since it is the principle that assures the integrity of society as some kind of unity or alliance. Its fundamental rule is that everyone must participate in the exchange system and that correct participation means to give commensurately with what one has received and by the same token to receive commensurately with what one has given.

Reciprocity as a social principle is thus the exact opposite of the market principle, whose aim is to produce differences in value and encourage each party to seek profit or advantage by exchange. The governing principle of reciprocity is that a gift and its reciprocal counter-gift should be the same; often they are expected to be identical.[2] The effect of the principle of reciprocity is that while people may not simply pursue their own interests and must interact with others, the system is fair, nonetheless, in the sense that ideally everyone can end up "even." At an individual level, participation in society on this basis leads each person to develop a sense of when she or he has given more than she or he has received or vice versa. If one person attempts to accumulate more than a fair share, the rest can unite to implement such sanctions as shame or dishonor. Although each person may still be motivated to behave selfishly, the most effective compromise is for each to participate fairly. When the system works, individuals are apt to see one another's selfish behavior as a threat to the integrity of the system and to uphold the general principle on the basis of their own interest in the continued effectiveness of the principle itself.

The subjective sense that accompanies participation in a system of reciprocity is that of owing or of being owed. There is a sense of obligation, duty, debt, responsibility, which implies a motivation to give or receive according to the demands of reciprocity. If one gives a gift to another, one feels a sense of expectancy until it is returned; if one has received but not given, one feels a sense of debt.[3]

The principle of reciprocity, transformed into the negative, results in a principle of retributive justice: if one is injured, one is owed the opportunity to inflict an equal injury in return. This is the law of the talion, which is as elementary an aspect of human social organization as is the positive rule of the gift.[4] As Adam Kuper writes, "It is a chilling thought, perhaps, but the same logic governs the friendly, ceremonial exchange of the [Trobriand] Kula cycle and the relentless exchanges of the feud. Both are driven by the principle of reciprocity, which is the nearest thing to a universally recognized canon of justice. One has a right to even the score, to get even" (1994, 225–226).

We can situate this principle in our myth by saying that what distinguished the society formed by the brothers after their successful rebellion was that, in order to maintain the alliance that had led to their success, they agreed to be ruled by a principle of reciprocity, epitomized by the prohibition on incest that required them to exchange women exogamously. Instead of each narcissistically pursuing his own self-aggrandizement without regard to the others except as potential competitors, the brothers established a society of mutually indebted and interdependent individuals, where each experienced a sense of obligation to the others and to the system itself. If one finds oneself in a situation of having received more than one has given or of having injured another without having oneself been injured, one can describe this state as "guilt." It consists of an expectation of retribution, either from the offended individual, or from those acting on the individual's behalf, or from the system itself, seen as an objective cosmic principle, working to even the score independent of human agency. (The Hindu and Buddhist doctrine of karma is a good example of this principle understood as pervading the cosmos, extending over infinite time, and operating without benefit of an overseeing high god.)

Later I shall explore how this sense of guilt takes shape in individuals and influences their willing participation in the system. For now I wish to stress that guilt is inherent in a social system ruled by the principle of reciprocity, and that it is this rule that distinguishes the society of the brothers in Freud's myth after the rebellion from the primal horde. This perspective enables me to reformulate Freud's observation that after killing and eating their father, the brothers felt a guilt strong enough to enforce their social contract based on the prohibition on incest. Before the rebellion, there was no such thing as guilt. The brothers acted unanimously, each motivated by the single purpose of getting what he desired for himself and, with the help of his fellows, eliminating the obstacle to it. After the rebellion the brothers felt guilty, because they then became a society ruled by reciprocity. Killing, no matter of whom, became a crime that merited an equal, retributive punishment.

Since myths are made up in the context of a present social system, they too will take for granted the pervasive law of reciprocity. For this reason, in a myth that serves as the charter for a system of laws based on a principle of justice, the founding deed itself demands just retribution by virtue of the law it brings into effect. The cosmogonic deed of the culture hero, insofar as it is a disruption of the previous order, not only brings the law into existence but also thereby condemns itself with that same law. This means that Moses, for example, after leading the revolt against Pharaoh and replacing his tyranny with a regime ruled by a principle of absolute and universal justice administered by an omnipotent deity, must be held accountable for his deed—an eye for an eye, a life for a life.

I cannot emphasize enough that this guilt, which is at the heart of the system, is unconscious, in the sense that while a person in the system may feel a sense of malaise or discontent (Freud's *Unbehagen*), or even a generalized sense of guilt, he or she does not know what he or she feels guilty about. The same is true of people with obsessional defenses, who feel guilty but are consciously unaware of the source of the guilt, having effectively displaced it. It seems to me self-evident that a sense of guilt, sin, or fault has been operative throughout the Judeo-Christian system at least since the time of the prophets. My task is to identify the unconscious fantasy from which that guilt arises.[5]

In the legends that sprang up surrounding the lost years of Moses's life before he slew the overseer, a number of themes are developed that revolve around the idea of Moses's deed as an oedipal displacement of a senior male. But since such an act is expressly forbidden by the law Moses later reveals, the logic of the myth requires that he be justified in some way. The preferred method of justifying an oedipal murder, in both individual fantasy and cultural myth, is by invoking the talion: "I killed him because he tried to kill me first." Such indeed is the device employed in the story of Oedipus. Of course, it must be shown that the attempt made on the culture hero's life by the senior male fails: the hero either survives on his own or is rescued. This attempted murder serves two simultaneous purposes in the mythic logic: it demonstrates that the "crime" of the junior male is really a justifiable talionic punishment of the senior male, and it shows that the junior male has already (nearly) suffered the appropriate retribution for it, namely to be killed himself, thus evening the balance and exonerating him in advance.[6] As with so many other dilemmas, the myth can try to solve the problem of the guilt of the hero by means of decomposition. I showed this operation at work, for example, in the case of the character Seth in the Osiris myth. Nonetheless, it is my contention, based on the myth itself and its evident effects, that the overthrow and killing of the wicked pharaoh, no matter how justified, required an exact retaliation according to the law of reciprocity that was initiated in its wake. Vicarious atonement through symbolic decomposition could not avail. Because Moses never actually underwent this punishment, the debt against the cosmic order was still outstanding.

Having set the problem up in this way, we can ourselves generate the solution: someone equivalent or superior to Moses—a "prophet like Moses"—has to undergo actual death as talionic repayment for the death of the primal father. Then, despite having been killed, that same person must go on to survive, having by his death erased the universal guilt for the primal crime. To accomplish this the myth will have to resort to a rather blatant violation of the reality principle. The execution and miraculous resurrection of Jesus fulfills these conditions. That is why, working backward from the story of the Passion, Freud could reconstruct the myth of the primal crime—which, as I am in the process of showing, is the story of Moses. By the same token I, working forward, can *pre*construct the myth of Jesus from the story of Moses.

III

We have already seen how the pharaoh—the one who does not know Joseph—is portrayed as bent on infanticide. When his order to have the male children killed is foiled by the heroic Hebrew midwives, he issues another filicidal order: " 'Every boy that is born you shall throw into the Nile' " (Exod. 1:22). When Moses is born, Jochabed does something that can be understood as representing both sides of the ambivalence in the maternal relationship. As I have suggested, we might expect women in the primal-horde scenario to feel divided loyalty, being both allied with and submissive to the senior male while resenting his dominance and siding with his junior rival and destined replacement, the youngest son. (Rebecca's alliance with Jacob in outmaneuvering Esau for Isaac's blessing is an example of this pattern.)

Here, Jochabed simultaneously complies with Pharaoh's command, by doing what he says and putting her son in the Nile, and defies his intent by placing Moses in an ark, which allows him to survive the attempted infanticide in which she herself is partially complicit.[7] Jochabed, then, enacts both affective roles, being a persecuting and a rescuing parent at the same time.

From this point on in the narrative, the decomposition runs along sexual lines: the pharaoh embodies pure persecutory hostility toward Moses, while the women play the parts of rescuers or nurturers. Pharaoh's daughter defies her father's command: knowing that the infant Moses is a Hebrew, she nevertheless rescues him from the Nile, going so far as to adopt him. In this way Moses acquires a second family, that of the Egyptian royal household, and thus continues the relationship begun when Joseph became the father of the earlier pharaoh.

Miriam, Moses's older sister, plays an equally important part in Moses's rescue story, watching over the proceedings and arranging for Pharaoh's daughter to hire as Moses's wet nurse none other than his birth mother, Jochabed. In this way, Moses has two nurturant mothers as well as a protective older sister. I surmise that this is the myth's way of telling us that Moses was the favorite of his mother—indeed, he is thrice maternally favored. (Emphasizing this theme, the midrashic tradition has assumed that the midwives who rescued the Hebrew boys from Pharaoh's first attempt at infanticide were really Jochabed and Miriam themselves.)

In this instance, analysis shows that the decomposition of counter-oedipal ambivalence of the parents toward the child has been achieved without the addition of new or mediating characters. Two members of the paradigmatic triad, the female and the senior male, have been assigned, respectively, the positive and the negative aspect of the relationship to the junior male. At the same time, the myth has achieved the important decomposition of Moses's family, making him simultaneously both an Egyptian prince in the royal house and an Israelite from the house of Levi.

(The question of whether Moses was *really* an Egyptian or an Israelite, which so exercised Freud and his critics, does not concern me, since my analysis remains within the confines of the myth and makes no assumptions about who or what Moses might have been in historical terms—a matter about which, in any event, no independent information exists.[8] For the purposes of the story, Moses is really both an Egyptian and a Hebrew, just as Oedipus was really both a Theban and a Corinthian.)

IV

Although the Bible tells us nothing about Moses in the years between his rescue and adoption by Pharaoh's daughter and his killing of the Egyptian overseer, which occurs after he grows up, tradition and legend have filled in some of the gaps. According to one particularly well-known story—repeated, for example, by Josephus in his *Jewish Antiquities*—one day, when Moses is three years old, he is at dinner at Pharaoh's table, seated on his mother's lap (we are not told which mother, though I suppose it doesn't really matter). He reaches over, takes the crown from Pharaoh's head and places it on his own.

Alarmed, Pharaoh demands of his seers the meaning of this portentous gesture. The wicked adviser and perennial adversary of the Israelites, Balaam, claims that the young Hebrew boy has his heart set on attaining the kingdom of Egypt. He reminds Pharaoh how Abraham, Isaac, Jacob, and the sons of Jacob all practiced deceit to overthrow or foil a superior or elder rival. To forestall the possibility of Moses growing up to usurp the Egyptian crown, Balaam recommends that the boy be put to death. Pharaoh is inclined to agree but decides to consult the rest of his counselors before acting.

The sages of the Egyptian court are summoned forthwith, and among them the angel Gabriel appears, disguised as one of their number. He suggests that Moses's gesture may have only been the meaningless play of a toddler, with no malicious intent or ominous significance. He proposes a test to discover whether Moses is precocious enough to have meant something in his grab for the crown. An onyx stone and a glowing coal are placed before Moses. The ember is brighter and shinier, but it is worthless, and dangerous besides, while the gem, though less obviously glittering, is vastly more valuable. If Moses reaches for the onyx, it will prove that he is indeed preternaturally wise and thus guilty of the intention Balaam has imputed to him. If he reaches for the coal, it will prove he is just an ordinary child attracted to shiny things. Moses, who, of course, is preternaturally wise and is destined to overthrow the pharaoh, starts to reach for the onyx. But Gabriel, with celestial power, guides Moses's hand to the glowing coal. When Moses touches it, he burns his hand and, instinctively touching his burnt hand to his mouth, burns his mouth as well. In addition to saving Moses's life, this gesture explains how Moses becomes, as he describes himself in Exodus 4:10, "slow of speech and tongue."⁹

(The scriptural basis for the imagery employed in this midrash comes from Isaiah, who writes: "Then flew unto me one of the seraphim, with a glowing stone in his hand, which he had taken with the tongs from off the altar; and he touched my mouth with it, and said: Lo, this hath touched thy lips; and thine iniquity is taken away, and thy sin expiated" [6:6–7].)

In this story, it is not the Hebrew boys in general but Moses in particular who is the object of an infanticidal attempt by Pharaoh. Moses's destiny as the junior male who will unseat the senior male is recognized, and, as if to forestall blame and retribution for this deed, Pharaoh is shown trying to kill him. As I have suggested, this story accomplishes the dual purpose of justifying Moses's later rebellion and at the same time balancing it with a retaliatory death which, however, Moses of necessity survives. Moses's physical disability, his "speech defect," is to be understood as the scar left by a failed infanticidal attack, like Oedipus's wounded feet. I have elsewhere argued that such genital mutilations as circumcision likewise signify that the bearer has survived a castrating attack.[10] (The scene of the night attack on Moses by God in Exodus 4:24–26 is, I think, consistent with this view, whatever its exact meaning.)

In the midrash, the senior male's ambivalence is decomposed by means of the split between the bad adviser, Balaam, who wishes to kill Moses, and the good adviser, Gabriel, who rescues him. (The mother's presence in this story is mentioned, but we are not told what she does. One is left to imagine whether, when Pharaoh is on the verge of killing Moses, she hands him over without protest, or clutches him to her bosom crying, "You'll have to kill me first," or does something else altogether.)

This story serves to diminish Moses's guilt for the oedipal intent he clearly harbors not only by vilifying the senior male—and providing Moses with an expiatory brush with death—but also by insisting on the complicity in the deed of the good senior male, God himself, here represented by Gabriel. It will become clear from the later development of the myth, however, that none of these efforts at atonement is fully effective.

V

The only thing we know from the biblical narrative about Moses's life before his sojourn in Midian, besides his birth and rescue, is that he kills an Egyptian overseer. (The victim is traditionally understood as a taskmaster over the Hebrew slaves, although in the Torah text itself he is identified only as "an Egyptian.") The story is told with the succinct narrative style so typical of much of the Hebrew Bible to which Erich Auerbach directed our attention in his classic *Mimesis* (1974 [1946]). The tale is therefore easier to quote than it would be to paraphrase: "When Moses had grown up, he went out to his kinfolk and witnessed their toil. He saw an Egyptian beating a Hebrew, one of his kinsmen. He turned this way and that and, seeing no one about, he struck down the Egyptian and buried him in the sand. When he went out the next day, he found two Hebrews fighting; so he said to the offender, 'Why do you strike your fellow?' He retorted, 'Who made you chief and ruler over us? Do you mean to kill me as you killed the Egyptian?' Moses, was frightened, and thought: Then the matter is known!" (Exod. 2:11–14).

Although the Bible story is spare, tradition has elaborated upon it, most notably in a midrash that identifies the Hebrew whom Moses rescues from being beaten as Dathan. Dathan makes an interesting choice for this sympathetic role since he will later emerge as a ringleader of the grumblers and rebels against Moses during the wanderings in the wilderness. In the present midrash Dathan is identified as the husband of a woman named Shlomit, daughter of Dibri. Shlomit's beauty has caught the eye of an Egyptian overseer, who sends Dathan off to work before daybreak. Protected by the darkness, the overseer enters Dathan's house and has intercourse with Shlomit, who thinks he is her husband. Dathan returns in time to see the Egyptian slipping away from the house. Realizing that Shlomit's husband has caught him in the act of adultery, the Egyptian begins to beat Dathan; the latter is only saved when Moses happens upon the scene and intercedes by killing the brutal taskmaster.

The triad consisting of the taskmaster, Shlomit, and Dathan recapitulates the paradigmatic structure of the primal-horde schema: the overseer is the master to Dathan's slave, and, although the junior Dathan is married to the woman, Shlomit, the master or senior male obviously feels free to arrogate to himself the right to have sex with her, as any senior male in the primal horde would do. When Dathan tries to assert his own sexual priority, the senior male beats him and would presumably have killed him had Moses not stepped in.

Instead of the role of persecutor being decomposed, as in the story of the onyx and the coal, in this story it is the character of the junior male that is split, between Dathan, the victim of the aggression of the senior male, and Moses, the killer of the senior male. Moses is moved to his deed because he witnesses the injustice of the oppression of Dathan by the overseer, which can thus be seen as a justifiable retaliation by one Hebrew to avenge the attempted murder of his "kinsman." Rather than surviving his own attempted murder and going on to kill his attacker, in this story Dathan suffers the assault, while his double Moses acts on his behalf and rescues him (instead of being the rescued one, which is his more usual role in these stories).

The junior male is portrayed as an observer in the first part of the story. One could read this as representing the psychology of what Arlow (1980) described as the "revenge motive in the primal scene." As "Dathan," the young junior male discovers the sexuality of his parents, which he interprets as a violation of "his" woman (mother) by a sadistic tyrant who will now attack and kill him. "Moses" is then the split-off representation of the consciousness that "sees" the scene and of the self that strikes back in what feels at the time like justified self-defense and rage.

But justifiable as it may at first appear, viewed from within the context of the Law or, in psychological terms, after the establishment of the superego, the killing of the senior male results in guilt. This is clear here from the fact that no sooner has Moses's deed become known—despite his precaution of looking this way and that—than Pharaoh hears of it and seeks to kill Moses. (Because Moses took care not to be seen, the implication is that only Dathan knew what had happened and therefore that he himself was one of the quarreling Israelites who mocked Moses the next day and thus presumably let the Egyptians know of the incident. This explains why Dathan the grumbler is called upon in the midrash to play the role of the overseer's victim, adding ingratitude to his later crimes against Moses.)

Under the principle of reciprocity, and by the law of the talion, just as Moses was justified in retaliating by killing the Egyptian when he realized that the latter was going to kill his kinsman the Hebrew, so too does it follow that Pharaoh should try to kill Moses for having killed the Egyptian. This is the concrete representation of Moses's "guilt": he now lives under threat of impending death for having killed a man. Just as Moses entered the story as the double and avenger of Dathan, now Pharaoh appears as double and avenger of the slain Egyptian. The killing of an oppressor, no matter how it can be rationalized, under the rule of reciprocity inescapably demands another death. By the same principle, when Moses later kills Pharaoh, he will not be free of a master but will on the contrary acquire a yet-more-ineluctable avenger, the jealous God who vouches for the Law that he has revealed to Moses. By that Law, the same deed God required of Moses, and which Moses was right to commit at the time, also demands commensurate "justice."

VI

Leviticus 24:1–2 relates the following story: "There came out among the Israelites one whose mother was Israelite and whose father was Egyptian. And a fight broke out in the camp between that half Israelite and a certain Israelite. The son of the Israelite woman pronounced the Name in blasphemy, and he was brought to Moses—now his mother's name was Shlomit daughter of Dibri of the tribe of Dan—and he was placed in custody." This fight between two Israelites (or at least part-Israelites) during which one is disrespectful of authority parallels the fight that occurred the day after Moses killed the overseer. In that fight, too, which according to tradition involved the future traitors Dathan and Abiram, one of the men sarcastically asked Moses, when he tried to break it up, whether he intended to kill them as he had killed the Egyptian, thereby making the murder known. Partly on the basis of this connection, the composers of the midrashic tradition have assumed that Dathan was the beaten Israelite and have made him the husband of Shlomit, daughter of Dibri. This connection is all the easier because of the fact that in Leviticus it is claimed that she has a son who is half-Egyptian. This in turn would lead to the theory that the blasphemer's conception must have occurred in the way described in the midrash about the killing of the overseer, that is, when the Egyptian took advantage of Shlomit under cover of darkness.

Moses, who at the later point in the story described in Leviticus has, ironically, indeed become the chief and ruler of the Israelites, just as Dathan had snarled during the fight in Exodus 2:14, orders the blasphemer put to death, but he does not stop there: "Anyone who blasphemes his God shall bear his guilt; if he also pronounces the name YHWH, he shall be put to death. . . . If a man kills any human being, he shall be put to death. One who kills a beast shall make restitution for it: life for life. If anyone maims his fellow, as he has done so shall it be done to him: fracture for fracture, eye for eye, tooth for tooth. . . . You shall have one standard for stranger and citizen alike" (Lev. 24:15–22).

Through the juxtaposition of the story of the blaspheming son of Shlomit by the Egyptian overseer and the enunciation of the law of the talion, the principle operative in the story of the killing of the overseer is made explicit. It is in my view no coincidence that the edict "life for life" is issued in direct response to an infraction committed by a man whose own father, according to the midrash, Moses himself killed many years earlier. In a doubling similar to that of Dathan and Moses in the earlier tale, the blasphemer is made to suffer the displaced talionic punishment that Moses himself incurred by killing the blasphemer's father. But in this case Moses, instead of acting as his double's rescuer, plays the role of his punisher, avenging, as it were, the father's death by finding guilt in and killing his victim's real son. In this episode, then, read in this way, Moses again deflects the death he has coming to him for his, from another point of view, praiseworthy deeds.

VII

A quite different attempt to contextualize the killing of the overseer by way of apologia for Moses may be found in a story related by Artapanus. Artapanus was a Hellenized Jew from Alexandria, a fragment of whose lost defense of the Jews against their detractors is preserved in the writings of the church father Eusabius.[11] In Artapanus's account, Pharaoh has a daughter named Meroe, who adopts a Hebrew child because she is barren; this is Moses. After he grows up he is loved and respected by the people because of his many virtues and attainments, which include introducing the arts of irrigation, writing, and other features of civilization into Egypt. (The story thus rhetorically equates Moses with Osiris, the more usual Egyptian culture hero.)

Meroe's husband, Chenephres, Moses's (adoptive) father, is jealous of Moses and plots against him. He commissions Moses as a general in the Egyptian army in a campaign against Nubia but secretly arranges matters so that Moses will lead only a troop of conscripted farm boys, inexperienced in war. Like David sending Uriah to war so as to get rid of him, as narrated in chapter 11 of 2 Samuel, Chenephres intends Moses to die in battle. But Moses conducts a successful campaign, lasting ten years. He builds a great camp-city near Hermopolis and from there lays siege to Nubia. He conducts the siege so honorably that the Nubians themselves are impressed and decide to adopt from Moses the custom of circumcision.

Having failed to eliminate Moses by a stratagem, Chenephres decides simply to kill him. He hires a Hebrew, Chanethothes by name, to assassinate Moses during the funeral procession for Meroe, Moses's mother, who has died in the meantime. Moses learns of the plot from his brother, Aaron, and kills Chanethothes. It is then, according to Artapanus's account, that he flees to Midian, where his adventures will continue as described in Exodus.

Here again, Moses is depicted as having survived not one but two filicidal attacks on him by his jealous father, conducting himself nobly all the while. There is a split between the good and bad parents, as we also encountered in the birth stories, since Chenephres the father is a persecutor while Meroe the mother is a rescuer, having adopted the otherwise doomed Hebrew boy. But there is also a repetition of the decomposition of the senior male, the evil Chenephres. We observed that in the story of the onyx and the coal the senior male Pharaoh is further decomposed into the bad Balaam and the good Gabriel. In the present story Chene-phres is decomposed into the persecuting Hebrew Chanethothes and the rescuing Hebrew Aaron.

No effort is spared in this story to cast Moses in the best possible light and Chenephres in the worst, as if to argue, "Who wouldn't kill an assassin who plans not only to kill you but to do it at your mother's funeral!" But the very excess of the rhetorical effort to exonerate Moses only indicates how seriously his guilt for killing the overseer (in this case replaced by Chanethothes) is, in fact, taken.

VIII

According to some commentaries, Moses was twenty when he killed the overseer, according to others he was forty. But if Moses died at the age of 120, and if he led the wanderings in the wilderness before that for forty years, then he was eighty at the time of the Exodus. What happened in the intervening years? Was he just minding his father-in-law's sheep in the wilds of Midian all that time? A midrash at least partially answers this question by describing the more than forty years Moses spent in Ethiopia after killing the overseer before arriving in Midian and marrying Zipporah. This tale would account, in a quite elaborate way, for the otherwise mysterious line that begins Numbers 12: "Miriam and Aaron spoke against Moses because of the Cushite [Ethiopian] woman he had married" (Num. 12:1).

The background of the midrashic legend is this: War has broken out between Ethiopia and an unnamed country to the east. The king of Ethiopia, Chichanos, has marched out from his capital city with a great army to attack the enemy. In his absence, he has left the reins of government in the dubious hands of none other than Balaam, together with his sons, Jannes and Jam-bres. Balaam seizes the opportunity to subvert the populace, turning them against the rightful king and declaring himself the new king of Ethiopia. He fortifies the capital to prevent Chichanos's return, raising walls on two sides of the city, digging moats on a third, and protecting the fourth with a swarm of snakes and scorpions.

When Chichanos does at last return from the wars, he is unable to breach the defenses Balaam has erected, so he lays siege to the city for nine years. At this point in the story Moses happens to arrive on the scene, in flight from the pharaoh's wrath over the killing of the overseer. He joins the camp of Chichanos and soon wins the respect and admiration of his fellows. Chichanos chooses this moment to die of some unnamed ailment, and his followers declare Moses their new king, bestowing upon him as his own wife Chichanos's widow, Adoniah, queen of Ethiopia.

As king of Ethiopia, Moses devises a plan to defeat Balaam, who still occupies the capital. He orders his men to collect a flock of storks and to starve them for three days. Then he attacks the side of the city defended by the swarm of snakes and scorpions, letting loose the famished storks to devour the vermin. In this way Moses storms the city, recapturing it for the party of the now deceased Chichanos. Balaam, together with Jannes and Jambres, manages to flee, thanks to Balaam's sorcery, ending up in Egypt, where Balaam becomes an adviser to the pharaoh.

Successfully ensconced on the Ethiopian throne, Moses formally weds Adoniah; but "Moses feared the stern God of his fathers and went not in unto Adoniah nor did he turn his eyes towards her" (Ginzberg 1911, 2:287). He rules wisely for forty years, at which point the queen speaks out, saying that Moses has never consummated their marriage, nor has he worshiped the Ethiopian gods. She proposes that the Ethiopians allow her son by the late King Chichanos, Monarchos by name, to become king, now that he is a man. After some contention back and forth over the issue, Moses decides to leave Ethiopia to the Ethiopians, and Monarchos ascends the throne. Still fearing the pharaoh's wrath, Moses avoids his native Egypt and instead travels to Midian, where the biblical text takes up the tale.

This story beautifully portrays Moses as a victorious and noble oedipal hero without any oedipal guilt: he has displaced the original king and married his widow, without either killing his predecessor or violating the dead king's marriage bed. In the relatively refined sensibility of this tale, none of the major characters is actually killed at all: Chichanos conveniently dies of natural causes to allow Moses to inherit his throne and his wife, and Balaam is merely deposed.

One can, nonetheless, see in this story an elegant playing-out of what, in another context, I proposed as a typical scenario for the succession of a junior male to senior status.[12] This process is by no means easy, under the regime of reciprocity and the talion, since the junior man who succeeds will appear to have benefited from the senior male's demise and thus to be indirectly implicated in the guilt for it. I have suggested that in a typical succession scenario there would be at least four different roles, decomposing the two male characters in the primal-horde triad. There are the rightful king (a good senior male), a junior male who deposes and/or kills him—a bad usurper—a good junior male who kills or deposes the usurper, and finally an innocent heir, who ascends the throne left vacant by the cycle of talionic retribution entailed in the previous set of events. The avenger himself cannot become king, because in killing or deposing the bad usurper, he has become guilty himself, and this typically disqualifies him from profiting from his deed. He is sometimes doubled by a victim who dies on his behalf. If he himself is killed in retaliation he obviously cannot go on to reign unless he is able to survive real death itself, like Jesus.

A good example of this is to be found in *Hamlet,* where the rightful king, Hamlet Senior, is killed by the bad usurper, Claudius, who then marries his widow. The good junior male, Hamlet Junior, avenges his father and kills Claudius, but he too must be killed, by Claudius's accomplice Laertes, in retribution for his deed. This leaves the throne vacant for Fortinbras, who, having been uninvolved in the proceedings in Denmark, is innocent enough to succeed to the throne.

In the Chichanos-Balaam tale, the parallels are clear enough: Chichanos, the rightful king, is deposed (though not killed) by a man junior to him, Balaam. Chichanos dies, and Moses has the crown of Ethiopia and the queen to boot thrust upon him by the Ethiopians themselves. He deposes (but does not kill) Balaam, acting as the avenger of the former good king; but he may not fully reap the benefits of his deed. Although formally married to Adoniah, he remains chaste. And though king of Ethiopia for forty years, he is really only regent until the rightful, innocent heir, Monarchos, comes of age and claims his throne.

The story of the kingship in Ethiopia nicely illustrates the fact that despite, or rather precisely because of, Moses's heroic deeds, he is guilty, by the very ethical code he inaugurates and represents, and so incapable of achieving full senior-male status. Instead he must, as Freud posited in the case of the victorious brothers, renounce the prize for which junior males rebel: absolute power and sexual rights to the woman in the triad. Moses is prevented from claiming that prize, we are told, precisely because of his fear of the "stern God of his fathers." This same stern God will likewise prevent him from enjoying his victory over Pharaoh: having led Moses to the border of the promised land, God allows him to look but not enter and then takes his life.

IX

If Moses did put in a forty-plus-year stint in Ethiopia, one would never guess it from the biblical narrative, which moves here, as it so often does, with lightning speed: "When Pharaoh learned of the matter [the killing of the overseer], he sought to kill Moses; but Moses fled from Pharaoh. He arrived in the land of Midian, and sat down beside a well" (Exod. 2:15). We are thrust with a minimum of transition into Moses's adventures in Midian. At the well where he has just sat down, he protects the seven daughters of Jethro, a Midianite priest, from sheep rustlers, as the women are attempting to water their father's flock. Within a few sentences, Jethro has invited the handsome stranger in and offered him the hand of his daughter Zipporah; Moses marries her, fathers a son, Gershom, and settles into a shepherd's life in Midian.

Jethro—he is variously called Jethro, Reuel, Hobab, and Jether, but I shall refer to him as Jethro for the sake of simplicity—is generally treated as a positive figure in the Judaic tradition. Not only is he Moses's father-in-law and a sage adviser and supporter of the Israelites after the Exodus, but in the midrashim and folk tradition he figures as a "good" (pro-Israelite) adviser to Pharaoh, counterbalancing the wicked Balaam.

In terms of the myth, Jethro, the father of seven daughters, plays a role opposite to that of a jealous sire in the days of the primal horde: instead of keeping the women for his own harem, indifferent to considerations of consanguinity, he willingly gives one away to a junior male, in exchange for the latter's contribution of labor and protection of the women and the sheep. (Jacob, too, had to put in brideservice for his prototypical father-in-law, the wily Laban.) No senior male in his right mind gives away anything, much less a daughter, in the primal horde. The whole idea of "in-laws" implies marriage exchange, the incest prohibition, and exogamy, none of which, according to my argument, come into being until after the imposition of the Law at Sinai and the establishment of the principle of reciprocity.

I am not unduly troubled by such anachronistic applications of post-Sinaitic social norms to pre-Sinaitic times, for reasons I have discussed earlier. But I would, it is true, prefer to find some traces or evidence of the presence of "pre-Sinaitic" elements in the story. First, although Moses has indeed married and become a father, and so reached senior status without an apparent struggle along the Darwinian axis, he is still junior to his father-in-law, for whom he works as a bondsman; he may thus be said to have remained a junior male on the Hegelian dimension and so to have only partially succeeded.

Interestingly, this structural situation is the reverse of that depicted in the story of the kingship in Ethiopia: there Moses becomes king, and thus a senior male on the Hegelian power dimension (at least while Monarchos is still underage), but he does not consummate his marriage with Adoniah and thus never becomes a father, thereby falling short of senior status along the Darwinian dimension. He appears at best only half a senior male.

Much stronger support for my perspective is provided, however, by a midrash that amply confirms my feeling that Jethro, as he is portrayed in the text of Exodus, has given away his daughter far too readily. In this tale Jethro is portrayed as something much more like the desert patriarch I would have expected, behaving toward the stranger who arouses his daughter's interest more like the jealous sire than the accommodating father-in-law. According to this midrash, Jethro has come into possession of a certain wooden rod of great significance. It was created by God on the twilight of the first Sabbath and is inscribed with the unutterable Tetragrammaton, as well as with the names of the ten plagues that are to befall Egypt. God entrusted this rod to Adam, who in turn passed it to his son Enoch. Over the generations it has been in the possession, successively, of Noah, Abraham, Isaac, Jacob, and Joseph. When Joseph died, the rod fell into the hands of Jethro, who, it will be recalled, spent time as an adviser in the Egyptian court, where he was a friend of the Israelites.

Living in self-imposed exile as a shepherd in Midian, Jethro has planted the rod in his garden where, to his amazement, it has taken root and put forth blossoms. Whenever suitors ask him for one of his seven daughters, Jethro puts them to a test: he requires them to try to pull the flowering rod from the ground. In every case they fail, and their punishment is a harsh one, for the rod devours them. Moses has heard of the rod, the test, and the fatal consequences of failure from Zipporah, but he is not deterred. When Jethro makes him try his luck with the rod, he succeeds in pulling it from the ground.

By this sign, Jethro recognizes Moses as the prophet who, as foretold by the Egyptian diviners, would overthrow Egypt. Although he may have been a champion of the Israelites in Pharaoh's court, Jethro apparently balks at abetting the destined destroyer of his homeland: "As soon as the thought struck him [that Moses was the prophet foretold by the diviners], he seized

Moses, and threw him into a pit, in the expectation that he would meet death there" (Ginzberg, 1911, 2:293). But Zipporah secretly brings food to Moses in the pit, and so he is able to stay alive; he remains confined for seven years. At the end of this time, Zipporah reminds her father of the man he had thrown into the pit. She suggests that they uncover him since, if he has died, he will befoul the house with the stench of his corpse while if he is alive, it will prove that he is protected by a special destiny. Jethro agrees, and when he finds Moses alive, he draws him out of the pit, kisses him, and exclaims: " 'Blessed be God, who guarded you for seven years in the pit. I acknowledge that He slayeth and reviveth, that thou art wholly pious, that through thee God will destroy Egypt in time to come, lead His people out of the land, and drown Pharaoh and his whole army in the sea' " (2:294). Following this, presumably, he agrees to the marriage of Moses and Zipporah.

In this story, in contrast to the Bible text, Jethro is depicted as the prototypical senior male of a primal horde: he jealously guards his daughters and puts to death all junior men who seek to marry them, by means of a rod which is at once phallic and cannibalistic. Moses plays his familiar role of the child of destiny subjected to a filicidal attempt by a jealous senior male. In this instance he survives thanks to the nurturance of Zipporah. The story thus has an identical structure to the story of Moses's rescue from the bulrushes: in both cases, the senior male is a murderous persecutor, while his daughter, the female of the story, plays the role of the rescuer. Pharaoh's daughter becomes Moses's mother; Zipporah, his wife. One might take this as confirmation of the equivalence of the two roles in the myth, as in fact they would be within the primal-horde paradigm. Zipporah's rescue consists of feeding Moses, who is in passive captivity—a maternal image. By the same token, Pharaoh's daughter's rescue consists in part of handing Moses back over to his birth mother to be nursed. We may contrast these good images with that of Jethro as the bad senior male vicariously devouring his victims by means of his rod.

Only after a symbolic death and entombment in a pit is Moses able to emerge "revivified," marry the woman, and go on to overthrow the senior male in the person of the pharaoh. This is consistent with my contention that the oedipal hero is required to "die" before achieving victory, both to demonstrate the wickedness of the senior male he displaces and to balance his own destined deed with a compensatory punishment in advance.

The symbolism of the rod and the pit, with their obvious sexual, Frazerian significance, can be situated in a vast network of mythical correlates both within the biblical tradition—Aaron's flowering staff in Numbers 17:23, for example—and in related traditions, such as the myth of Isis and Osiris, with its flowering wooden beam. For the present, I want to concentrate only on one limited but very important thematic chain, whereby Moses in the pit is paralleled both by his chronological mythic precursor, Joseph, and by his later "successor," Jesus.[13]

Joseph is thrown into a pit in a symbolic murder by his brothers. He is rescued and rises to sit at the right hand of Pharaoh as his vizier and even, as we have seen, his "father." Jesus, likewise the favorite of his father and surrounded by a band of twelve "brothers," is also betrayed by them, is killed and buried in a pit, and rises to sit at the right hand of his heavenly father, with whom he is identical according to the trinitarian doctrine. The pit is both a tomb and a maternal womb for rebirth before triumph. The principle of reciprocity demands that he who would rise high must first sink equally low.

But both the Joseph story and the Jesus story have happy endings, whereas the story of Moses does not, or has only a partially happy ending. The reason, I think, is that Moses, like Oedipus, actually killed his father, whereas Joseph and Jesus did not. Joseph rose to the top through a combination of prudence, foresight, and restraint. An "anti-Oedipus," he rebuffed the advances of his master Potiphar's wife when he was a bondsman, respected his true father, Jacob, and was diplomatic in his dealings with the pharaoh. As a result, he and the Israelite clan, though prosperous and politically favored, remained unfree, still finally dependent on the higher power of the pharaohs. This was amply demonstrated when a less friendly pharaoh ascended the throne and turned against the descendants of Jacob/ Israel.

Moses, by contrast, was destined to carry through the rebellion of the junior males against the senior male, achieving genuine liberation not only from Pharaoh but from the system of the primal horde altogether. But by virtue of the extremity of his deed, and by the law of reciprocity his own revolution inaugurated, he also required, by the logic of the myth, an equally serious retribution. No mere seven years in a pit would compensate for the murder of the primal father. It was the unfinished nature of the mythic scenario in the story of Moses that led to a vision of closure, first announced in the myth of the messiah foretold by the Israelite prophets. A historically successful attempt at messianic closure was realized in the Christian myth, the point of which, as I shall show, is to provide a mythic happy ending—the "good news" of the Gospel—to the apparently "unfinished" story of Moses, with its bittersweet, unresolved tension.

6

Death on the Nile

I

While Moses is tending the flocks of his father-in-law, Jethro, on the slopes of Mount Horeb in Midian, God addresses him from a burning bush and reveals his plans for the liberation of the Israelites from Egyptian bondage. When God informs Moses that he, Moses, is to lead the Exodus and guide the Israelites to the promised land of Canaan, Moses responds, "Who am I, that I should go to Pharaoh and free the Israelites from Egypt?" (Exod. 3:11). God might well have reminded Moses that he is prince of Egypt, that's who, but apparently this detail is not thought worthy of mention. Such moments as this, together with such occasions as the time Moses asks God to remind him who God is, support the view of scholars, including many upon whom Freud relied, that Moses was essentially a Midianite prophet who worshiped a fierce and warlike volcano god named YHWH and that to the tradition based on this historical reality, the biblical authors or redactors have appended a fictitious prehistory in Egypt.

Since I am not exploring how, if at all, the biblical text reflects historical reality but looking rather at how the text now coheres and operates as a sacred narrative and foundational myth for the Jews, as well as for Western civilization, my concern in these passages, and in the story of Moses's encounter with God on Mount Horeb, is with Moses's altered relationship with the various figures who represent the senior male in his story.[1]

In Midian, Moses has achieved a modified senior status: he is a married householder with sons of his own. But several factors mitigate his full attainment of senior status and keep him still partially a junior male. He has his wife (and therefore his children) and his flocks only because of the benevolence of a man senior to him, Jethro. Moses is thus still beholden to an older and more powerful man and in that sense junior and a "bondsman." He is also, as we recall, a fugitive from Egypt, where his life is being sought by another who stands in a senior relation to him, Pharaoh, and this for the crime of having killed a senior male in the form of the Egyptian taskmaster. This deed, far from bringing Moses senior status, has put him even more at the mercy of the senior male—one of whose decompositions is now dead, it is true, but who cannot be killed off so easily. The spirit of paternal punishment and vengeance is embodied in a mightier and more powerful senior male figure, the persecuting Pharaoh. Moses's developmental task of moving from junior to senior status, as well as his historic task of liberating a subject people and doing away with the regime of the primal horde, have therefore not yet been accomplished. Having fled Egypt for Midian, Moses will have to return to Egypt to play out the rest of his destined scenario, much as Oedipus, having been transported from his native Thebes to Corinth to escape his fate, nonetheless has to go back to Thebes and fulfill the prophecy that governs his career.

Because Moses has rebelled and killed the overseer, he is under threat of death (not for the first time) from Pharaoh, in accordance with the law of the talion. But having acquired a new and magnified version of the persecuting senior male, he also obtains the benevolent, rescuing counterpart, the good half of the decomposition, in the form of God, who suddenly tells him to go back and confront Pharaoh. (I shall return later to a consideration of the fact that the pharaoh Moses confronts is not the same one who sought to kill him.)

God, in ordering Moses to confront (and ultimately kill) Pharaoh, enacts the part of the protective, empowering father who says, "You must kill your (bad) father!" Only after it is too late will Moses discover that this God also gives the command "You must *not* kill your father!" thus leaving Moses—and the Jews, and the Judeo-Christian world—in the moral impasse from which we have yet to extricate ourselves.

II

In the logic of succession stories, the split representation of the senior male makes possible the expression of the apparent paradox that in order to overcome the bad, adversarial senior male, the succeeding junior male draws on strength made available to him by his identification with the good, loving senior male. Freud recognized this paradox in the case of the normal development of the Oedipus complex. The boy wishes to be like his father and identifies with him not least because his father has achieved the boy's goal of making his mother his sexual object: "Identification is known to psycho-analysis as the earliest expression of an emotional tie with another person. It plays a part in the early history of the Oedipus complex. A little boy will exhibit a special interest in his father; he would like to grow like him and be like him, and take his place everywhere. We may say simply that he takes his father as his ideal" (1921, 105).

It is with the aid of this ideal father of identification, a model that derives its power from the fact that it retains the child's sense of his own disavowed omnipotence and grandiosity, that the boy, by becoming like the father, can compete successfully with the father. The relationship is thus profoundly ambivalent: the boy unites or identifies with the father so as to gain strength to get rid of the father, to "take his place everywhere." "Identification, in fact, is ambivalent from the very first; it can turn into an expression of tenderness as easily as a wish for someone's removal" (1921, 105). It is this ambivalence that is expressed in myths by decomposition, primarily by the splitting of the senior male into a good, protective, empowering father who represents union and harmony between the generations of males and a bad, persecuting father who is a sexual rival and whom the junior male wants to get out of the way.[2]

The required empowerment from the good father is often seen as an ingestion or incorporation of his phallus or of a symbol of his phallic power. As an "incorporation," the ingestion is clearly based on an oral prototype, as Freud recognizes: "It [identification] behaves like a derivative of the first, *oral* phase of the organization of the libido, in which the object that we long for and prize is assimilated by eating and that way is annihilated as such. The cannibal, as we know, has remained at this standpoint; he has a devouring affection for his enemies and only devours people of whom he is fond" (1921, 105). The act of eating thus resolves the paradox of wanting to be something while wanting to get rid of it because to eat and make something part of oneself is also to get rid of it as an object in the external world. Eating father, or his phallus, would thus be a way of accomplishing two imperatives of oedipal succession: to be like father and to get rid of him.

Of course, most objects, once eaten, are thereby really eliminated. The same is not true, however, of the first experiential object. The apparent miracle of the milk-giving breast is that one can "eat" it, incorporate it, drain it dry, and yet it is there, full again, the next time one is hungry. This ability to replenish itself, or survive a loving/devouring cannibalistic attack, is also transposable to the (mature) phallus, which is likewise able to recover from apparent depletion. These prototypes probably lend support to the belief that people can be killed (and eaten) but survive and live again. Therefore, if one is killed as a victim of a persecuting and/or cannibalistic father, one can hope to be regenerated and live again. The negative side is that, even though one kills the senior male, he can still rise from the dead and return to seek vengeance. This process is illustrated in the story of the killing of the overseer, which brings upon Moses a yet-more-dire filicidal persecution by Pharaoh. When Moses in turn kills Pharaoh, God himself will emerge as the immortal agent of paternal vengeance who cannot be eliminated.

Jacob Arlow, in a classic article on the application of the insights of ego psychology to the study of mythology (1961), uses the theme of ingesting the father's phallus to explore how the same idea is figured in various tales according to different levels of ego development. In this demonstration he includes a discussion of Moses. Arlow points out that the wish to incorporate the father's phallus or phallic power is expressed in three apparently different traditional tales: "Jack and the Beanstalk," the myth of Prometheus, and the story of Moses receiving the Ten Commandments on Mount Sinai.

According to Arlow's analysis, Jack, who climbs the phallic beanstalk, kills the giant, and escapes with the stolen treasure to live happily ever after with his mother, is the hero of the most primitive form of the story. His tale represents pure wishful fantasy. As such, the story of Jack corresponds to the situation of the sons in the primal horde, who imagine their deed without the influence of the internalized punitive superego that will emerge after they have acted. The Prometheus story occupies the next level of development, when the fantasy is dominated not by the image of gratifying a wish directly but by the anxiety of a castrating punishment for the wish: for having stolen fire from Zeus, Prometheus suffers eternal punishment by having his liver pecked out daily by an eagle. The power of the organ to regenerate, like a phallus, is now not a boon but a nightmare. In this story we have a correspondence to the remorse and guilt that follow from having acted on the wishes represented by Jack's fantasy.

In the Moses story, the ego has developed sufficiently to accept submission to and identification with some superego demands without experiencing this submission as castrating defeat: Moses receives from God a boon that establishes a relatively mature morality. The rules Moses brings down from the mountain represent a compromise, in which the vengeful paternal God is placated, but a system is instituted of inhibitions, rules, and prohibitions that simultaneously defend the ego and serve the requirements of a viable form of social life.

All three of these stages are found in quick succession in the story of Jethro's rod. First, there is instant and effortless oedipal success: Moses seizes the rod, succeeds in detaching it from its owner, and thus wins the hand of the woman. Then comes the prolonged suffering in retaliation: Jethro throws Moses in a pit and subjects him to repeated oral torture (instead of being "eaten" by the rod, or pecked at by a phallic bird, he is starved). And finally, we have reconciliation with the father: nurtured by the care-giving woman, Moses survives his ordeal and is accepted by Jethro, in a relation of exchange—marriage—that epitomizes the rule of reciprocity (and hence guilt) that will be at the core of the social order he will later establish.

All this is to be played out again in the story of Jesus: as a child he has sole possession of his mother, successfully eliminating his apparent father, Joseph, from the scene. Then comes the suffering on the wooden cross or "rod." Finally, he rises in triumph from the pit to sit at the right hand of the (divine) father as enforcer of a renewed version of the Mosaic laws.

III

Where, we must now ask, are the women in these stories? Even if the only role they are destined to play in these heavily masculine fantasies of conflict and succession is that of the object of the rivalry between men, why does there seem to be no major female figure depicted even as a prize, let alone as an active character in the story? There can be little doubt that, historically, the Torah narrative was composed and interpreted by—and served the interests of—men.[3] It generally adopts a male perspective, and by and large addresses concerns, conflicts, wishes, and anxieties likely to be experienced by men. It is, as recent scholarship has shown, possible to discover traces in the text of a less obviously male-oriented social and cultural world that have been overlain with a tendentiously masculinist ideology. Nonetheless, as it stands, the Torah bears the marks of a work written by, for, and about men, in which the feminine dimension of life is pushed into the background and in which women are rarely seen as protagonists.

In the story of Moses we can point to four female characters of some importance, but we cannot truthfully say that any one of them or even all four taken together constitute a major figure in the story. They are Moses's birth mother, Jochabed; his sister, Miriam; the pharaoh's daughter, who becomes his second mother; and his wife, Zipporah. Edmund Leach, in his ambitious and important structural reading of the Moses story (1983), focuses on the figure of Miriam. Leach makes a persuasive case for seeing in her elements of the sort of eternal mother/wife/sister/daughter figure represented in a more undisguised fashion by Isis in the Egyptian mythic tradition. (He also argues that the Virgin Mary is another, sublimated and disguised representation of the same mythic character role.) Be that as it may, the Torah as it stands makes only scant use of this potentially rich field of symbolic meaning, and all that remains of it in the text are traces that require extrabiblical materials to fill them out.

My own line of reasoning about where the mother is to be found in the Torah follows from the observation that Moses's adopted mother and his wife are both the daughters of senior men in non-Israelite lands. The pharaoh's daughter, as the daughter of a pharaoh, clearly represents the land of Egypt. Zipporah is the daughter of a Midianite priest and thus represents the land of Midian. (The tradition has apparently tried to forge a connection between the two nations, by such maneuvers as depicting Jethro as an Egyptian diviner or courtier who flees to Midian in horror at the bad advice given by the diviner Balaam; while the latter also somehow ends up in Midian, where he is killed in the raid described in Exodus 31.)

If his adoptive mother represents Egypt and his wife represents Midian, what nation do Moses's birth mother and sister represent? The answer, of course, is Israel, which is indeed a nation in the sense of being a social group united by common descent. But unlike the nation of Egypt or that of Midian, "Israel" has no native land. The Israelites are a subject and foreign nation living within the territory of the land of Egypt.

What, then, is the native land of Israel? It is the land that God, in his previous interventions into proto-Israelite history, has promised to the patriarchs Abraham, Isaac, and Jacob/Israel: the land of Canaan, through which each of them traveled as an alien herdsman. Moses's lifelong mission, as we know, is to lead the people of Israel to their destined native land, one they have never yet occupied but that is nonetheless rightfully theirs by virtue of the divine covenant with Abraham.

It is my assertion that the land of Canaan figures in the Torah narrative as the closest representation this highly masculinized text can offer of the female, specifically the mother, who is the object of contention among the senior and junior generations of males. In Western culture we frequently picture a land as represented or symbolized by a female figure. The concepts of the "motherland," or the "mother country"; the iconography of a nation in the form of a female figure, like Britannia or Columbia; and the conceptualization of the land or the earth as Mother Nature or Mother Earth: all are familiar even without the invocation of unconscious symbolism. In the ethnographic context of the Jewish tradition, however, these generic possibilities for maternal imagery are given specific shape.[4]

In the case of this particular land, the land of Canaan, we are told that it is a "good and spacious land, a land flowing with milk and honey, the home of the Canaanites, the Hittites, the Amorites, the Perizzites, the Hivites, and the Jebusites" (Exod. 3:8). (The same imagery is repeated in Exodus 3:17.) If the land is symbolic of the oedipal mother, then all these hostile tribes are to be understood as decomposed versions of the oedipal rival, who must be cleared from the land so it can be taken (back) by its one rightful owner. But what of the land itself?

Literally, it would appear, a land of milk and honey must refer to a locale suitable for the raising of cattle and goats and for the growing of dates, as well as a home to wild bees (since the honey in question, *davash*, can be either honey from bees or date nectar). Regardless of whether Canaan meets that particular description, one can clearly recognize in the image of a land giving forth flowing fountains or streams of "sweet milk" an evocative symbol of the maternal body as it is experienced in infancy.

But the mother-land connection can be made in a more specific and concrete ethnographic way. To follow it out, we may begin with this midrash, which deals with an episode from the time when Pharaoh issued his edict against the male children of the Israelites: "The women . . . would go out into the field when their time of delivery arrived, and give birth to their children and leave them there. The Lord, who had sworn unto their ancestors to multiply them, sent one of His angels to wash the babes, stretch their limbs, and swathe them. *Then he would give them two smooth pebbles, from one of which they sucked milk and from the other honey*" (Ginzberg, 1911, 2:257, my emphasis).

Here, then, in the folk tradition, is imagery of milk and honey flowing from stones in the field or on the earth. These stones are in turn depicted as filling the role of maternal breasts, which confirms the conceptual link between "milk and honey" and breast milk, as well as the link with the earth or land, since the stones are the "breasts" of the fields. These fields, in turn, act as nursing mothers to the infants after they have been abandoned there by their human mothers, at the behest of their infanticidal persecuting senior male.[5]

The connection between the earth and the mother is further spelled out later in the same story: God "ordered the earth to receive the babes, that they be sheltered therein until the time of their growing up, when it would open its mouth and vomit forth the children, and they would sprout up like the herb of the field and the grass of the forest" (2:258).

In this remarkable bit of folklore, the earth literally becomes the mother of the Hebrew children, who emerge like plants out of her "body" to be born. (There are strong echoes here of the scene of Moses being fed by Zipporah while he is hiding in an underground pit to escape the infanticidal wrath of the persecuting senior male, Jethro.) The basis for this imagery is the biblical text to which the midrash serves as a commentary, Deuteronomy 32:13: "[He] fed him on the fruit of the fields; He nourished him with honey from the rock." The word translated "fields," sdy, could actually be read as either "fields" or "breasts." The second line emphasizes the imagery of suckling from the breast, since the root here translated as "nourish," ynq, means "to suckle" or "nurse."[6]

We can pursue this symbolism further. There is a commentary on Numbers 21:15 according to which there are two mountains in the valley of Arnon near the border between the land of Moab and the land of Canaan. From the top of each mountain one can speak and be heard on the other. The Israelites, passing through the land of Moab on their way to the land of Canaan, traverse the narrow valley between the two mountains, where they find all the people of Canaan arrayed to halt their advance. Some of the enemy soldiers are poised in caves in the mountain overlooking the valley, waiting to strike. Opposite the caves, as the midrash tells us, "in the mountain facing this one, there were numerous rocky projections resembling breasts [shadayim]; as is borne out by the text, 'and the eshed of the valleys' " (Numbers Rabbah, 773–774). Numbers 21:15 mentions "the slopes of the ravines [or 'valleys'] that lead to the site of Ar." Since the word for "breast" (shad) is similar to the word for "slope" (eshed), the commentary, by a punning etymology, interprets the rocks on the mountain at Arnon as being shaped like breasts.

The adversaries of the Israelites agree that some of them will block the valley, while those in the caves will fall upon the trapped Hebrews. But when the Israelites reach the spot of the planned ambush, God beckons to the mountains, "and the breasts of the mountain referred to entered into the caves, and all the occupants were killed" (774).

The "rocks shaped like breasts," in other words, penetrate into the caves where the enemies of the Israelites are hiding, crushing them to death. This image reminds us of a primal-scene fantasy, in which a victim is crushed by the violent penetration of a destructive organ into the cavity in which he is (in fantasy) hiding. But the penetrating organ here is a "breast," not a phallus. This indicates a preoedipal, oral dimension to the symbolism, which I shall consider shortly. For the moment I shall concentrate on the more obviously oedipal aspects of the tale.

There are, as we recall, two mountains in the story, one in Moab, the other in Canaan, the land promised to the Israelites. During the battle, the two behaved rather differently: "The mountain in the land of Moab in which the caves were did not move, while the mountain from the Land of Israel in which were the rocky projections resembling breasts moved and joined the mountain opposite. Why did it move? Because it belonged to the Land of Israel. It may be compared to the case of a handmaid who, on seeing her master's son coming to her, advanced quickly to meet him and welcomed him" (774). A footnote further clarifies the structure of the parable for us: "The handmaid is the mountain, the master is God, and the son is Israel" (774n2).

This striking product of the folk imagination offers confirmation of the equation between rocks or stones, on the one hand, and breasts on the other. Mountains also easily lend themselves to such symbolic usages (witness our own Grand Tetons). In the present story the stones on the mountain are like breasts, while the mountain itself is likened to a servant woman who is excited to see her young master. The mountain/woman in the scene is synechdochic for the land of Canaan. The master whom she serves is God, the senior male. The master's son, or junior male, is Israel, whose coming she is eagerly anticipating. Here is a beautiful portrayal of the situation in the triad of the primal-horde schema: the master's "woman" awaits a (re)union with the approaching junior male who intends to "liberate" her. We are on the verge of oedipal triumph. But of course, as we know, Moses is destined not to make it across the border, thanks to the prohibiting will of that pesky senior male.

The situation has a nice parallel in the story of Moses's own life: he spends his first three "prehistoric" months with his Hebrew mother, Jochabed (like the other Israelite infants hidden in the earth-mother for three months). Then he is taken away to a new mother, the pharaoh's daughter. But the wet nurse, or "handmaiden," to whom he is handed over is in reality his own Hebrew mother, so that what appears as exile is actually a homecoming. The land of Canaan, the place the Israelites have never actually occupied but which is their true home—and which was promised to them in previous generations—can be seen as the body of the oedipal mother, the woman who is currently owned by usurpers but who beckons from a mysterious and unattainable yonder. As Freud writes, "The uncanny place . . . is the entrance to the former home of all human beings, to the place where each one of us lived once upon a time and in the beginning. There is a joke saying that 'Love is homesickness'; and whenever a man dreams of a place or country and says to himself, while he is still dreaming: 'this place is familiar to me, I've been here before,' we may interpret the place as being his mother's genitals or her body" (Freud, 1919, 246).

IV

There is an important theoretical dimension to this maternal imagery. A psychoanalytically oriented reader can hardly look at these stories, in which breasts both help the Israelites (and quiver with joy at their approach) and act as persecuting agents of destruction that crush people to death in the dark interior of the female body symbolized by a mountainside, without thinking of the fantasies discussed in the works of Melanie Klein.[7] In the midrash just cited, for example, there are two mountains/women/breasts. The Moabite, non-Israelite breast/mountain is a hostile weapon of death, while the one in Canaan/Israel is an eroticized, loving woman/breast. Here we have a really marvelous depiction of Kleinian splitting, in which the breast is imaginatively decomposed in fantasy into a good, loving breast and a hostile, persecuting breast. (I do not know to what degree the fact that breasts come in pairs plays a role in determining all this symbolism.)

An important implication of this Kleinian split is that the primary mother-child dyad is already, in fantasy, a triad, consisting of the child, the good breast (or mother), and the bad breast (or mother). It is possible to see this triad as the forerunner of later fantasy transformations, in particular that of the oedipal triad. According to this view, the good mother and the feared, punishing father of the oedipal triad could in fact be seen to derive from a split in the maternal imago, with the bad, persecuting mother being transformed into an image of the oedipal father. This would be especially easily seen if we assume that the bad mother were depicted as a phallic woman. In that case, the breast would serve as the original prototype of what later in fantasy becomes the symbol of the paternal phallus.

Thus, for example, we have seen that Moses's original mother, Jochabed, is both good and bad, in that she complies with the pharaoh's infanticidal order yet rescues Moses from death. We might then see the later development that contrasts a persecuting, senior-male Pharaoh with his benign, rescuing daughter as a split representation of the ambivalently experienced original mother. By this logic, then, the feared persecuting, oedipal father would be a derivative of the more primary persecuting breast of the Kleinian "paranoid position." This would in turn account for some of the oedipal father's more uncanny and horrifying features.

With these considerations in mind, too, we can see the story of Moses in Jethro's pit as a regressive fear of being dominated/feminized/castrated/raped by the senior male, calling upon primitive oral fears of being attacked by the persecuting maternal breast of the paranoid position. The source of the belief that there is a bad, persecuting breast is the infant's experience of its own destructive impulse, aroused by ungratified hunger: a frustrated demand to be fed. These impulses and the bad, internal states of feeling that accompany them are then assigned, by the primitive defensive maneuver of projection, to the absent breast itself. We can now see that Jethro's starving of Moses is like a transformation of the bad, persecuting breast, while Zipporah's feeding of him represents the good, providing, nurturant breast. Underlying the wish to eliminate the persecuting father and be united with the mother/woman would be the deeper oral fantasy of destroying and eliminating the bad, frustrating breast and being united only with the good, gratifying breast.

The fact that the biblical narrative is so resolutely male-centered, to the point where important females can be represented only by an abstract disguise like the land of Canaan, could be interpreted from a Kleinian point of view as a case of neurotic oedipal defense against a psychotic preoedipal core. By such a reading, the underlying fear of the bad or persecuting side of the maternal imago from the preoedipal dyad is so potentially anxiety-producing that it is disavowed and contained by the procedure of resolutely excluding or suppressing reminders of female power and replacing these by, or translating them into, male imagery. It is certainly striking that there is almost no explicit "bad mother" imagery in the Torah story. (A point that might be pursued elsewhere is that the Bible story recurrently features a

foreign king, usually bad, like Pharaoh, but occasionally good. These figures
are probably projections of the bad and good mother imagoes, respectively.
As such, they are not, as they might appear, incidental to the myth but are
rather intrinsic aspects of it. The biblical insistence on the Israelites as a
self-contained people separate from all others misleads us into regarding
the foreign kings as intruders or extraneous figures. No doubt this serves
defensive purposes.)[8]

According to a Kleinian interpretation, much if not all the imagery of
senior male power in the biblical narrative (as well as elsewhere) would
conceal a disguised, apparently excluded but really transformed, primary
model rooted in maternal symbolism drawn from the experience of the
preoedipal dyad. By the same token, many observers have pointed out that
if in Freud's model of the primal crime there is a primordial cannibalistic
fantasy embedded in the human psyche, surely it derives more plausibly
from the relationship to the mother than to the father, whom Freud, like
the biblical writers themselves, exalts, excluding the female, maternal dimension in his own myth.

Perhaps the most striking evidence in support of the Kleinian view
from within the Torah narrative itself would be the passage in which Moses
speaks of himself at a time when he has already achieved the status of leader
and lawgiver to his people and may thus be understood in relation to the
Israelites as a senior male. The scene is appropriate enough for our theme:
The Israelites wandering in the wilderness are complaining about the food,
their diet having been restricted to manna. " 'If only we had meat to eat!
We remember the fish that we used to eat free in Egypt, the cucumbers,
the melons, the leeks, the onions, and the garlic. Now our gullets are shriv-
eled. There is nothing at all, nothing but this manna to look to!' " (Num.
11:4–6). Moses, hearing their weeping, turns in anger and distress to the
Lord, asking: " 'Did I conceive all this people, did I bear them, that You
should say to me, *"Carry them to your bosom as a nurse carries an infant,"* to
the land that You have promised on oath to their fathers? Where am I to
get meat to give to all this people, when they whine before me and say
"Give me meat to eat!" ' " (11:12–13, my emphasis).[9] Moses is here reacting
to the charge of being a "bad mother" to the group, and he is himself feeling
persecuted. Indeed, a little later in the passage he asks God to kill him
rather than subject him to the torture of leading the Hebrews. His impa-
tience with his charges' demand to be fed contrasts interestingly with his
own experience of having a surfeit of indulgent and nurturing mothering.

(If, as the midrashic tradition holds, the longing for Egypt was a longing for "incestuous unions," as I discussed in Chapter 4, then these scenes
could be analyzed as representing a longing for the mother in whom the
nurturant and erotic functions are as yet undifferentiated. Cast out from
incestuous Egypt by virtue of the guilt incurred through rebellious patricide,
Moses pursues the unattainable chimera of the "promised land flowing with
milk and honey," which will always remain out of reach.)

I find the idea that the masculinized stories of the Bible have preoedipal precursors that break through now and again persuasive. It helps explain
why the narrative tradition as well as the social organization to which it
refers have been exclusively male in orientation, and it provides for a source
of unconscious fantasies, wishes, and fears upon which the symbolism of
the narrative can draw to render itself convincing to individuals under its
sway. The only proviso I wish to insist upon—and it is central—is that the
preoedipal period is, except in extreme cases, followed by an oedipal phase.
The fantasy resolutions of the oedipal period, no matter how influenced
they may be by what came before, become the foundations of nuclear individual and cultural fantasies. Whatever role "Kleinian" fantasies play in
the creation and reception of the text, there can be no doubt that insofar
as they do appear, they almost always do so translated into an explicitly
oedipal guise.[10]

V

In the light of these considerations, we can now examine why Moses, despite his years of loyal and largely obedient service to God, is denied the
achievement of his mission to take the Israelites into the promised land,
dying on the eastern shore of the Jordan River within sight of his goal. The
biblical account is in Numbers 20.

Once again the Israelites have quarreled with Moses and Aaron as
"bad mothers," this time because there is no water. God instructs Moses
and Aaron to take Jethro's rod, which Moses still has, and, before the assembled multitude, to order the rock to yield water. Moses, who seems
quite out of patience with his charges, says to them: " 'Listen, you rebels,
shall we get water for you out of this rock?' And Moses raised his hand and
struck the rock twice with his rod. Out came copious water, and the community and their beasts drank" (vv. 10–11).

It is apparently for this infraction—that Moses strikes the rock with his rod instead of verbally ordering it to produce water as God had commanded—that Moses is punished: "But the Lord said to Moses and Aaron, 'Because you did not trust me enough to affirm My sanctity in the sight of the Israelite people, therefore you shall not lead the congregation into the land that I have given them' " (v. 12).

Commentators have puzzled over this episode, which is called "the waters of Meribah," or "the waters of strife," because the offense seems so slight and the punishment so cruel. Many interpretations of the incident are possible and even plausible; mine is based on my symbolic analysis. We may easily suppose, I think, that the rock that gives forth water to a thirsty and demanding people can be understood as a breast. Since the rock refuses to give the water contained within it, it is the equivalent of the bad, withholding breast. Moses's rod, with which he strikes the rock, is both a sign of phallic empowerment bestowed by a senior male (Jethro and, before him, God) and also a symbol associated with oral aggression and starvation. When Moses strikes the rock with his rod, he is giving expression to erotic, sadistic, and destructive impulses, of a combined oral and phallic nature, that he ought to have controlled.

Lacan's language can serve us here (largely because it is itself drawn from biblical language). The paternal law, enforced by the Name-of-the-Father—God himself—requires that the boy forego the "imaginary" preverbal relationship with the mother and enter the linguistic, symbolic dominion of the father and his law. This law is at root the prohibition on incest, which the agreement to engage in rule-governed symbolic speech represents. Language is itself one of the forms of reciprocity, the exchange of information encoded in circulating symbolic forms, that characterizes "society" or civilization as such.[11] At the waters of Meribah, Moses disobeys the paternal injunction to speak, to use language, and reverts to a preoedipal demand for the breast and its withheld bounty. It is thus for a symbolic incestuous infraction of the oedipal law of the father that Moses is punished.[12]

Of course, God does not have to give a reason for denying Moses the promised land. He is a senior male, after all, *by virtue of* his prevention of junior males from achieving his own senior status, which, in the model of the primal horde, means denying them access to the females. Since, as we have seen, the land of Canaan is the mother/woman sought by the junior males but owned by the senior male, Moses by definition as prototypical rebellious junior male cannot enter but is kept out by the restricting will of the senior male.

In the waters of Meribah incident, Moses violates the senior male's control over access to the female, giving expression to wishes that are at once oral, phallic, and sadistic (anal) toward the mother's body. In response, God forbids Moses to cross the waters of Jordan but grants him a final trip to the mountain top, where he can look upon but not touch or enter the forbidden object of his desires.

Moses's "oedipal victory" in his rebellion against the primal father is mitigated, as is required in Freud's scenario: the brothers in that myth agree to deny themselves the object for which they rebelled, sexual access to the female(s) of the horde. In the story from Artapanus, we recall, Moses kills the assassin representing his persecuting father at the same moment he mourns the loss of his mother. Still more explicitly, in the story of the kingship in Ethiopia, Moses deliberately refrains from sleeping with the queen out of fear of the stern God of his fathers, who represents the up-holder of the law of the dead predecessor.

VI

From this excursion into the realm of the occluded maternal symbolism of the Torah story, let me return now to examine further the situation of the primal horde as it is represented by Israel in Egypt and to establish the context within which the rebellion of the junior males, led by Moses, takes place. Not all the sons, it turns out, are equally oppressed in Freud's mythic picture of the original social life of humanity: "For natural reasons, youngest sons occupied an exceptional position. They were protected by their mother's love, and were able to take advantage of their father's increasing age and succeed him on his death. We seem to detect echoes in legends and fairy tales both of the expulsion of elder sons and of the favouring of younger sons" (1939, 81).

This favored youngest son, in Freud's view, would have been the first among the group of brothers to imagine that things could be different. In the "exigency of his longing," he invents for himself the hero myth. He becomes an epic poet, a mythographer who portrays for his brothers a scenario in which a hero slays the father, perhaps in the guise of a mythical monster or dragon. In the "hero" of his myth—who is at bottom a grandiose version of himself, remembered from his childhood as the favorite of the mother—the youngest brother/poet constructs an ego ideal, a model of what he and his audience of young men hope to become: "The transition to the hero was probably afforded by the youngest son, the mother's favorite, whom she had protected from paternal jealousy and who, in the era of the primal horde, had been the father's successor. In the lying poetic fancies of prehistoric times the woman, who had been the prize of battle and the temptation to murder, was probably turned into the active seducer and instigator to the crime" (1921, 136). Freud perhaps has in mind Helen of Troy in this final sentence, since it was she who set in motion the events that are described in the Homeric epics. In the Bible story, Eve is depicted as the active seducer of Adam, instigating his fall. The story of Joseph and Potiphar's wife also comes to mind. But whatever Freud may have intended, it is nonetheless worth noting that his description of the ringleader of the rebellion against the primal father forms a remarkable fit with the character of Moses. Moses is, as it happens, a younger brother, the favorite of his mother, and a great epic poet and the composer of a hero myth.

That Moses led a band of brothers is no secret. The family of the patriarch Israel who settled in Egypt comprised simply a band of twelve brothers and a sister. Furthermore, in societies with strong traditions of lineages and patrilineal descent, like that of the Israelites, not only what we would call brothers (male offspring of a one couple or parent) but also lineage mates related agnatically (descendants through males from a single male ancestor, even one several generations back) would be considered brothers and would be called by the same term. Thus, for example, in the scene of the killing of the Egyptian overseer, the Israelite who is being beaten and whom Moses saves is described as his "brother," 'ḥ implying only that he is a kinsman, a member of the Israelite lineage, not necessarily the child of the same parents.

On a more immediate and concrete level, Moses is presented throughout the narrative specifically as a brother, indeed, as a youngest brother in a sibling set of three, paralleling the fairy-tale structure to which Freud refers. Even as God announces his liberating mission to Moses on Mount Horeb, he includes Aaron in the role of spokesman, and from that time forth, until Aaron's death in the land of Zin, described in Numbers 20, Moses is always accompanied by his brother. His oldest sibling is Miriam, who also accompanies him throughout much of the wandering.

Now, admittedly, these three do not literally make up a band of brothers, since one of them is a sister. But the text works hard to keep constantly before one's awareness that Moses is a brother, and a youngest brother, who nonetheless is the highest in rank, the one whose word is law and who speaks directly with the voice of the father.[13]

As for whether Moses is the favorite of his mother, I have already indicated that the doubling of good, rescuing mothers, as well as the repetition of the theme of rescue from abandonment or filicide and reunion with a care-giving mother, signify symbolically the extra maternal care, love, and protection that fell to Moses's lot.[14] Freud also notes that the woman/mother protects her favored youngest son from paternal jealousy. This theme, as we have seen, appears repeatedly in the myth and folklore surrounding Moses.

Finally, we have seen that for Freud, the favored youngest brother who is to become ringleader of the uprising is an epic poet who invents the hero myth. Here too Moses fits the description, although this may not be immediately obvious, thanks to our iconographic image of Moses as a humorless and wrathful smasher of tablets. But not only is Moses the protagonist-hero of the Torah narrative but he is also, as the tradition has ardently insisted for two millennia, the author of the narrative itself. Scriptural foundation for this claim may be found in such passages as these from Deuteronomy: "So Moses wrote down this law and gave it to the princes, the sons of Levi, who carried the ark of the covenant of the Lord, and to all the elders of Israel" (31:9). Or: "Moses finished writing in a book the words of this law from beginning to end" (31:26). Whether the Torah narrative is strictly speaking an epic poem, it is certainly a titanic mythic hero narrative, and Moses is certainly to be understood as its author as well as its hero.

We do not usually picture Moses on the model of blind Homer, spinning out flawlessly metered verse to the accompaniment of his lyre, a mortal medium for the promptings of the divine muse. But Moses too, that slow-of-speech defier of pharaonic edicts, is just such a bard, as can be seen in Deuteronomy 31. God appears there in the Tent of Meeting, in a pillar of cloud, and gives Moses a rather grim prophecy about the future of the Hebrew people after Moses is gone. Then he says to Moses: "Therefore, write down this poem and teach it to the people of Israel; put it in their mouths" (v. 19). From this passage, we can see that we are to picture Moses's prophecy of God's words as being sometimes given in verse, which is taught as a poem to the people, and it is *also* written down as law in the book that will, when completed, be the Torah itself.

I also cite the passage in Exodus 15 which introduces the "Song at the Sea": "Then Moses and the Israelites sang this song to the Lord" (v. 1). On at least some occasions, then, Moses is actually an inspired singer, and his prophesies are songs, or poems.

So we may conclude that not only is the situation of the Israelites in Egypt under Pharaoh directly analogous to Freud's image of the primal horde but also that the hero Freud described as possessing the necessary qualifications to serve as liberator and ringleader of the rebellion matches perfectly a description of Moses himself. He is the youngest of a band of brothers, his mother's favorite and the one she protected from the father's jealous wrath, and the inspired composer of a great mythic epic describing the deed he himself performs: the murder of the father, the establishment of a more just social and moral order, and the liberation of the captive junior males and the females.

What now remains to be answered is a question that I have so far avoided by leaving it vague, namely, who exactly is the pharaoh whom Moses overthrows?

VII

In psychoanalytic terms, the pharaoh, as a great emperor deified by his subjects as a living embodiment of a god, serves aptly as a symbolic representative of the paternal imago, and there are evident oedipal dimensions to Moses's defiance of and rebellion against the pharaoh.[15]

What I wish to demonstrate more specifically here is that the pharaoh whom Moses confronts and finally kills in a spectacular scene of destruction, and whose identity the text masterfully conceals and reveals simultaneously, is Moses's father. To do so, I shall simply add specificity to what is already suggested by the text. For this obviously political story about the liberation of an oppressed people also conveys a more covert message, which gives it a familial dimension well designed to speak directly to the reader's own unconscious fantasies, wishes, and anxieties.

Let me clarify, once again, that I am speaking only of evidence internal to the myth. I do not ask the historical question "Under which pharaoh did the Exodus from Egypt occur?" I wish to demonstrate only the relationship between Moses and Pharaoh that the story itself constructs for us, even while keeping its operation away from fully explicit awareness.

We learn at the beginning of Exodus that a new pharaoh has succeeded to the throne, one who does not know Joseph. Even if the new pharaoh is, in fact, the old pharaoh with a meaner disposition, as the midrash says, there is no reason to assume from what is written anything other than that it is the daughter of this new pharaoh who rescues Moses from the bulrushes after the pharaoh orders the slaughter of the Hebrew boys. Since Moses becomes the son of the daughter of the pharaoh, this makes him the grandson of the pharaoh who ordered his execution.

There is no textual basis for assuming that the pharaoh who seeks Moses's life upon hearing that Moses has killed the Egyptian overseer is anyone but the pharaoh who ordered the infanticide.

In ensuing passages we learn of Moses's flight to Midian, his marriage to Zipporah, and the birth of his first son, Gershom. Then, in Exodus 2:23, we encounter the following, introduced without apparent connection either to what precedes or what follows it: "A long time after that, the king of Egypt died." Once again, we must assume that the pharaoh whose death is reported here is the same pharaoh who ordered Moses thrown in the river and who sought his life over the affair of the overseer, Moses's maternal (Egyptian) grandfather.[16]

A little later in Exodus we read: "Now the Lord had said to Moses in Midian: 'Go back to Egypt, for all the men who sought to kill you are dead' " (4:19). It is not clear who "all the men" are, but surely one of them is the pharaoh who tried twice to kill him. Perhaps the other ill-wishers include Balaam and the advisers who have gone along with Pharaoh's treacherous scheming. One might argue that it is possible that "all the men who wanted to kill you" refers not to one but to many pharaohs, who have succeeded one another during this long period, each inheriting his predecessor's animus against Moses. But there is no textual support for this theory, and indeed the statement in Exodus 2:23 seems strongly to support the view that only one pharaoh has died, and he has been succeeded by another.

In Exodus 3:10 God addresses these words to Moses: " 'Come, therefore, I will send you *to Pharaoh,* and you shall free my people, the Israelites, from Egypt' " (my emphasis). These lines clearly indicate that *somebody* is pharaoh at this time, so we know that not only has the king of Egypt died but that he has been succeeded. The pharaoh who has died was Moses's grandfather. Who, then, is the successor pharaoh, whom Moses is to confront at God's behest?

The obvious and indeed the only justifiable deduction we can make is that the new pharaoh is the son of the old pharaoh. While another sce-

nario may be imaginable—a coup or invasion leading to a change of dy-
nasty, for example—there is no warrant for it in the text. This son of the
former pharaoh must therefore also be the brother of Moses's mother, the
daughter of the now-deceased old pharaoh. A mother's brother in any patrilineal society is of course important, as a long tradition in social anthropology has amply demonstrated, and well suited to play a senior male role.[17]

But once we have come to this point, our knowledge about the marital
habits of pharaohs becomes immensely relevant. Of course, it may be that
Moses's mother was only one of many sisters of the new pharaoh, and he
actually married another of them, but we have no textual basis for assuming
that the deceased pharaoh had more than one daughter. The deduction that
requires the least deviation from or addition to what is actually in the text,
then, is that the man who inherited the throne from his father and became
the new pharaoh in this story is the brother and, by that same token, the
husband of Moses's mother: in other words, Moses's (Egyptian) father.

While other possibilities can be imagined, there is no basis in the text
for preferring any of them to this one. We may therefore reasonably conclude that the text tells us the following: Not only is the situation of the
Israelites in Egypt at the time of the Exodus *like* the oedipal triad of the
primal horde, it *is* the oedipal triad of the primal horde. There is a senior
male married to a woman who is both his sexual partner and his sister. He
jealously persecutes the son and excludes him from sex with this woman,
who has shown herself willing to disobey or "betray" the senior male out
of love for the junior male.

This demonstration that the pharaoh is Moses's father serves as a good
example of how the text is able to communicate vital information to the
audience while at the same time disguising the fact that it is doing so.
Certain facts are presented that, together with knowledge the reader can be
presumed to have, lead to an inevitable conclusion. But that conclusion is
never stated, and the pieces of information leading to it are scattered
throughout the text. Readers make the connections and the right assumptions unconsciously while (possibly) remaining unaware that they have
done so.

Moses's situation when he confronts Pharaoh is precisely that of the
junior male in the paradigmatic triad of Freud's primal horde. He is a would-
be usurper of and successor to the position of the senior male, a role whose
present occupant is incestuously married to the lone woman in the story.
She is simultaneously Moses's mother, Pharaoh's sister, Pharaoh's wife, and

Pharaoh's daughter. In other words, Moses, like Horus, seems about to send his father/Osiris to rule in the underworld while he marries Isis, the wife/sister/daughter/mother. Instead, however, he foregoes the prize of the queen and the kingdom and goes in search of his own other, "real" mother, symbolized by the promised land he is fated never to enter.

VIII

The climax of this segment of the story comes at the moment of rebellion itself, when Moses, together with Aaron and supported by God's might, confronts, challenges, visits plagues upon, and finally kills his father, Pharaoh. This sounds somehow inappropriate. Moses's actions are not usually phrased in that stark way, in contrast, for example, to the way we more comfortably say, "Oedipus killed his father Laius, at the place where three roads meet." (The conjunction of the theme of plague with that of patricide, by the way, is common to the two stories.) If we examine the sentence "Moses killed Pharaoh," we can raise two kinds of doubts. One doubt concerns the subject of the sentence: can we really say that *Moses* kills Pharaoh? The second involves the verb and its object: was Pharaoh really *killed?* Do we know that he died as a result of actions on the part of Moses?

There is no doubt that Judaic tradition insists that all the deeds making possible the Exodus of the Hebrews from slavery in Egypt were the work of God alone, that only he has the power to work such miracles, and that no human, Moses or anyone else, deserves credit for the great deliverance: that credit belongs to God only.

At the same time, this same tradition, and its Christian inheritors, insists no less firmly that each human has free will by virtue of God's intention. One can freely choose either obedience to or defiance of God's commands. These latter do not act like commands to a computer, which automatically enacts whatever program is commanded. They are rather orders given to autonomous conscious beings who can freely decide whether to execute them. Even Moses, who is (almost) always obedient, loses his chance to enter the promised land for his act of disobedience at the waters of Meribah.

In the actual description of the scene of the destruction of the Egyptian host at the Red Sea, *both* Moses and God appear as agents. Moses parts the waters by a gesture of his hand, then God hurls or sweeps the Egyptians back into the sea: "Then the Lord said to Moses, 'Hold out your arm over the sea, that the waters may come back upon the Egyptians and upon their chariots and upon their horsemen.' *Moses held his arm over the sea,* and at daybreak the sea returned to its normal state, and the Egyptians fled at its approach. But *the Lord hurled the Egyptians* into the sea" (Exod. 14:26–27, my emphasis).[18]

The relevant question for my purposes, however, is not the theological one of whether, in the face of God's attributes of omnipotence and omniscience, humans really have the power to act independently; and if so, how this independence is to be imagined. The question of whether God *really* worked a miracle at the Red Sea is likewise irrelevant, lying outside the text. The question is, Did Moses *act* at the Red Sea? It certainly seems to me that humans, and among them Moses, are given the possibility of freely willed action by God; if that were not so, God could just as well have left Moses to graze his father-in-law's sheep in the deserts of Midian and destroyed the Egyptians himself. That Moses could not have destroyed the Egyptian army *except* by calling on divine power seems obvious, but then the issue becomes a question only of the means used by Moses to destroy his enemy, not of the fact that he actively did so.

God is not outside the story, but a character in it. As such, he is clearly a decomposition of the figure of the senior male. In the split that also produces the bad, persecuting, jealous senior male, Pharaoh, God is the good, protecting, loving senior male, without whose incorporated might it is impossible for the junior male(s) to overthrow the bad senior male. Within the myth, then, Moses accomplishes the destruction of the Egyptians at the Red Sea. That he can do so only at the behest of, and with the superhuman assistance of, God is consistent with how events must occur according to the logic of the primal-horde scenario itself.

(I might suggest, going further, that the insistence in Judaic tradition that only God acted during the Exodus serves a defensive purpose insofar as it proclaims on Moses's behalf, "Don't blame me. *I* didn't commit this catastrophic deed against Father—you did it yourself!")

We may now turn to the question of whether, when Moses with God's miraculous help destroys the pursuing Egyptian army, he also kills the pharaoh. The answer to this question is almost certainly yes, but it is interesting that, as with the question of Moses's actual relationship to Pharaoh, the matter is never explicitly spelled out in the text.

After Pharaoh agrees, in the wake of the death of the Egyptian first-born, to let the Israelites go, he once again has a change of heart (though as the text makes clear, this occurs through God's will). He readies an army of six hundred of the best chariots, along with the rest of the chariots of Egypt, and they pursue the fleeing Hebrews: "The Egyptians gave chase to them, and all the chariot horses of Pharaoh, his horsemen, and his warriors overtook them encamped by the sea" (Exod. 14:9). Was Pharaoh himself among the pursuing Egyptians? We may cite Exodus 14:8 in reply: "The Lord stiffened the heart of Pharaoh, king of Egypt, and *he gave chase* to the Israelites" (my emphasis). Similarly, Exodus 14:10 expresses itself thus: "As *Pharaoh drew near,* the Israelites caught sight of the Egyptians advancing upon them" (my emphasis).

Passages like these, which refer to Pharaoh's pursuing the Israelites to the fatal shores of the Red Sea, strongly imply that Pharaoh himself was among the Egyptian host that met death in the waves, but they are not conclusive. After all, when we say, in speaking of a military campaign, that, for example, "Sherman breached the Confederate defenses at Peachtree Creek," we do not picture General Sherman himself doing the breaching, rather, we see his troops acting on his behalf while he surveys the battle scene from a safe remove. Likewise, we can easily imagine Pharaoh watching in horror from a nearby hillside while his entire army vanishes in the flood.

Exodus 14:6, however, seems to argue strongly for the view that Pharaoh is actually at the head of the troops that pursue the fleeing Israelites, and so would be among the first to drown: "*He* [Pharaoh] ordered his chariot and took his men *with him*" (my emphasis). This passage seems to mean that Pharaoh personally got in his chariot and chased the Israelites, with his troops following, or going with, him.

In Exodus 14:17–18 the words of the Lord to Moses seem further to specify that when the final cataclysm comes, Pharaoh is among the victims: " 'And I will assert My authority *against Pharaoh* and all his warriors, his chariots and his men. Let the Egyptians know that I am Lord, when I assert My authority *against Pharaoh,* his chariots, and his horsemen' " (my emphasis).

From this point on, the text refers no more to the pharaoh, speaking only of "the Egyptians," or of "Pharaoh's army." The climax of the scene is expressed as follows: "But the Lord hurled *the Egyptians* into the sea. The waters turned back and covered the chariots and the horsemen—*Pharaoh's entire army* that had followed after them into the sea; not one of them remained" (14:27–28, my emphasis). The phrasing maintains a studied vagueness, refraining from saying specifically that Pharaoh is killed. But since we know that he himself got into his chariot to chase the Hebrews, the fact that "the waters turned back and covered the chariots" so that "not one of them remained" seems quite decisively to indicate that Pharaoh perished along with his army. The vagueness of the text on this point may be designed to convey the information that Pharaoh is killed while preventing too clear an awareness of this unvarnished reality.

The phrase "not one of them remained" may be literally rendered as "did-not-survive among-them up-to-one" (lo-nishar bahem ad-echad). Rabbinic commentators have seized on the tiny ambiguity in this expression to suggest that one person did survive, Pharaoh. Even if valid, this interpretation does not undo the argument that Pharaoh is killed by Moses. For if Pharaoh's life is spared, it is only with the intent of reserving for him a worse fate. Thus, according to one rabbinic tradition, Pharaoh did indeed enter the sea and drown but his soul was preserved alive to stand forever at the gates of Gehenna. There he is doomed to berate all the subsequent tyrants who persecuted the Jews, saying, "Why did you not learn from my example?" Others argue that while Pharaoh did die, he was the last to do so, so that in addition to dying he was condemned to witness the destruction of his army.[19]

Insofar as it is at all possible to maintain that Pharaoh alone among the Egyptian forces did not die in the waters of the Red Sea, it is only because death would be too good for him. For revenge to be truly sweet, the persecutor must not only die but, perhaps even more important, must remain conscious so as to suffer at the knowledge of his own discomfiture. In the same way, one regrets that Hitler, for example, could only die the death of an ordinary man and not suffer some far greater punishment, more proportional to his deserts. Even if one reads the biblical account in such a way as to preserve Pharaoh's life, one still has to imagine him bereft of his empire, with his entire army destroyed, his country in ruins thanks to the disasters visited on him during the ten plagues, his people decimated by the slaughter of the first-born, and himself left with the knowledge that the despised Hebrews and their God have reduced him and all he treasured and ruled to less than nothing.

In conclusion, then, what happened at the Red Sea was this: A tyrannical, incestuous senior male, who recognizes no distinctions between wives and kinswomen and who (at least through his double, the former pharaoh) persecutes junior males with real or threatened infanticide, is put to death (or an utter defeat more painful even than death itself) by the junior males.

Their ringleader is one of a band of brothers among whom he stands as leader by virtue of being the youngest, an epic poet, the composer of the hero myth, and the favorite of his mother. His purpose is to liberate the oppressed band of brothers as well as the women trapped by the tyrant's jealousy and to gain possession of the woman/mother/land that is rightfully his. Or, in other words, Freud's primal crime.

IX

My analysis sheds light on an obscure dimension of Freud's mythic scenario. The implication of Freud's myth is that the brothers were only able to rebel against the primal-horde system when they were first able to unite against their common enemy: "United, they had the courage to do and succeeded in doing what would have been impossible for them individually" (1913b, 141). Freud goes on to propose what may have led to the development of the united front: "Some cultural advance, perhaps, command over some new weapon, had given them a sense of superior strength." Later in the same essay (*Totem and Taboo*) Freud gives yet another opinion on what accounted for the brothers' success when he alludes to "the organization which had made them strong—and which may have been based on homosexual feelings and acts, originating perhaps during the period of expulsion from the horde" (144).

In his study "Group Psychology" (1921) Freud pursues some of these ideas. The difference between the primal father and the brothers, he argues, is that the former is absolutely narcissistic and devoted to the gratification of every wish. The brothers, by contrast, forced by the father into (hetero)sexual abstinence, are able to develop aim-inhibited erotic ties with each other, leading to real social relationships based on object-love rather than on narcissism: "It may perhaps also be assumed that the sons, when they were driven out and separated from their father, advanced from identification with one another to homosexual object-love, and in this way won freedom to kill their father" (1921, 124n).

What Freud intends to convey here, I believe, is the idea that unlike the senior male, who is never thwarted in his drives and so remains unshaken from his narcissistic and self-oriented stance, the frustrated brothers turn their erotic impulses through sublimation into the long-lasting, aim-inhibited feelings of friendship, comradeship, and concern for as well as identification with others that form the underpinning of social life. Whether the brothers enacted the specifically "sexual" dimension of their "homosexual" attachments to each other is unimportant. What matters is that through their love for one another—brotherly love—forced upon them by the father's privations, the sons in Freud's myth are able to transcend the rivalry, envy, and hatred that would otherwise pit them against one another. The "cultural advance," the "new weapon," then, that enabled the sons to come together to defeat their father in a new way was, by Freud's account, the capacity for brotherly love, a love of the group, its members, and its totality that is able to override narcissistic ambition (though paradoxically, it itself ultimately derives from disavowed narcissism).[20]

Where did this brotherly love come from? We can gain insight into this matter by turning to the biblical story. Here, the new weapon that gives Moses the strength to lead his brother Israelites in defiance and overthrow of the primal father/Pharaoh is the power of an omnipotent and protective God, who has appeared out of nowhere and who gives the junior males strength beyond that of the martial prowess of the senior male/Pharaoh.

Proverbially, "God is love," and we can now see what this means in the primal-horde context: "God" is the name for the strength in unity that arises from the brotherly love in the group of exiled junior males. In this way we are led to Emile Durkheim's assertion that God is a collective representation of the strength of society itself, which is greater than that of any individual member. The brothers are united through bonds of aim-inhibited object-love. Their ensuing sense that the group itself is a source of power, love, and life-enhancing value is symbolized in the figure of a protective and benevolent God pictured as presiding over it and empowering it with his all-encompassing spirit.

The model for this God is the narcissistic self-representation marked by grandiose omnipotence that each group member has been forced to curtail or abandon in order to join the group. Inhibited in their own individual wishes for total love and power, the brothers mutually identify with a hypostasized and idealized senior male who is as loving and benevolent as the primal father is jealous and persecutory. This image of the idealized protector can be maintained only under certain conditions, however, and we already know what these are. Since the privations of the bad senior male enforce the formation of the solidarity of brothers based on aim-inhibited love, the purely good senior male/God can flourish only when there is also a bad, prohibiting counterpart to form the balanced decomposition of the ambivalence. The good father is imagined precisely by contrast with the persecuting father, as Freud writes: "We have seen that . . . this contrivance is the illusion that the leader loves all of the individuals equally and justly. But this is simply an idealistic remodelling of the state of affairs in the primal horde, where all the sons knew that they were equally *persecuted* by the primal father, and *feared* him equally" (1921, 124–125).

The illusion of the benevolent and omnipotent God of the group can itself survive, then, only because the hostile, competitive feelings and narcissistic self-serving ambitions of the individuals toward one another, as well as their hatred and fear of the father, are projected out of the group and displaced onto the figure of the external persecuting enemy. This is precisely the "paranoid process" that W. W. Meissner (1978) finds at the core of the formation of religious "cults."[21]

In the primal horde, there is no God, or rather, the father *is* a god. Because he has never been forced to abandon his own grandiosity and narcissism, he can remain his own ego ideal and need not project that function into some idealized other. Thus, as we know, in the case of Egyptian society, functioning as the primal horde, the pharaoh is the god Horus, who has married his sister/mother—and rules the earth while his father is relegated to the land of the dead.

The aim of the rebellion of the band of brothers, then, is not to replace one narcissist with another but to replace the reign of narcissism with that of object-love, the love of brothers for one another and their collective love for their own unity, symbolized by an omnipotent God who loves them all, before whom they stand as equals, and who is himself the condition making possible cooperative social life.

The question that remains, however, is what happens to the band of brothers after they have actually rid themselves of their persecutor. As we have just seen, the existence of a bad persecuting side of the split made possible the sustaining of the unity of the brothers and the perceived benevolence of the idealized good father. But what happens to the negative dimension of junior/senior male ambivalence when the hated antagonist is removed from the picture and can no longer be the focus of projected hostility? What happened to the Hebrews "after the death of the primal father"?[22]

7

After the Death of the
Primal Father

I

Foremost among the events that occurred after the defeat of the primal father/Pharaoh at the Red Sea is an occurrence that, on the surface at least, seems to precede the Exodus itself. This is the first Passover, which takes place in Exodus 12–13, after the pharaoh has let the people of Israel go but before the final showdown at the Red Sea. But I believe that it can be regarded as an aspect of the aftermath of the primal rebellion.

We have seen how insistent Freud is that the killing of the primal father includes the eating of the victim. I have suggested that his conviction reflects his method of working backward from the ceremony of the Christian Eucharist, which contains graphic imagery of oral incorporation in the act of communion. It is, as I have noted, striking with what nonchalance Freud takes it for granted that he can speak with certainty about what must have happened on that momentous occasion in prehistory: "Cannibal savages as they were, *it goes without saying* that they [the brothers] devoured their victim as well as killing him. The violent primal father had doubtless been the feared and envied model of each one of the company of brothers: and in the act of devouring him they accomplished their identification with him, and each one acquired a portion of his strength" (1913, 142, my emphasis).

Freud reiterates the theme in *Moses and Monotheism:* The brothers "united to kill their father and, *as was the custom in those days,* devoured him raw. There is no need to balk at this cannibalism; it continued far into later times. . . . We can . . . understand the cannibalistic act as an attempt to ensure identification with him by incorporating a piece of him" (1939, 81–82, my emphasis). For Freud, the act of identifying with another through cannibalism is profoundly ambivalent: one becomes the object one identifies with while at the same time destroying it.

We must not forget, of course, that Freud was working within the context of the anthropological opinions of his day. In that climate, the idea that the so-called totem meal was the earliest form of religious ritual was widespread. It was in part by linking the concepts of the Christian Eucharist and the totem meal of "primitive peoples" with psychoanalytic findings about cannibalistic impulses in human development that Freud came to reconstruct his myth of the primal crime in the first place. I want to dwell on this detail a bit to demonstrate that here too there is an unexpected and rather remarkable correspondence between the specifics of Freud's apparently fantastic construction and the actual text of the Torah narrative. We do indeed discover right there in the text a description of, as well as a prescription for, a full-fledged totemic meal directly linked with the events I have identified as the primal rebellion of Freud's myth.

The key text in Freud's reconstruction is the work of the British theologian and forerunner of social anthropology, William Robertson Smith.[1] In *The Religion of the Semites* (1894) Smith traced the idea of sacrifice, central to contemporary Christian theology, to practices of ancient Arabia. Freud thought highly enough of Smith's insights to use his book extensively in constructing his own theory, quoting from it at length. After showing that for Smith the sacrifice was originally a meal in which the victim represented the shared substance of groups of kinsfolk, Freud cites Smith's description of a "sacrificial ritual current among the Bedouin of the Sinai Desert at the end of the fourth century A.D." (1913, 138), as recorded (at least apocryphally) by Saint Nilus.

According to the saint's account, repeated by Smith, the sacrificial victim, a camel,

> "is bound upon a rude altar of stones piled together and when the leader of the band has thrice led the worshippers round the altar in a solemn procession accompanied with chants, he inflicts the first wound . . . and in all haste drinks of the blood that gushes forth. Forthwith the whole company fall on the victim with their swords, hacking off pieces of the quivering flesh and devouring them raw with such wild haste, that in the short interval between the rise of the day star which marked the hour for the service to begin, and the disappearance of its rays before the rising sun, the entire camel, body and bones, skin, blood and entrails, is wholly devoured." (Smith, 1894, 338, cited in Freud, 1913, 138)

Are there parallels to this particular feature of Freud's story of the primal horde in the biblical narrative?

A positive answer is to be found in Exodus, chapters 12 and 13, immediately before the deliverance from the pursuing Egyptians at the Red Sea. The Lord has just announced that he is about to bring upon Egypt the final plague, the death of the first-born, notwithstanding which, he will also toughen Pharaoh's heart so that he will not let the Israelites go but will chase after them. God's stated purpose for this otherwise rather senseless farce is so his "marvels may be multiplied in the Land of Egypt" (Exod. 11:9): that is, so he can demonstrate his superior might for all to see, especially those who hold themselves insuperable.

In Exodus 12, the narrative of the plagues is abruptly interrupted, and the Lord speaks thus to Moses and Aaron: "Speak to the whole community of Israel and say that on the tenth of this month each of them shall take a lamb to a family, a lamb to a household. But if the household is too small for a lamb, then let him share one with the neighbor closest to his household in the number of persons; you shall apportion the lamb according to what each person should eat" (vv. 3–4). He specifies that the sacrificial animal may be either a lamb or a goat kid, and it must be a yearling male without blemish. It is to be kept until the fourteenth day of the month, and then all the households of Israel are to slaughter their individual lambs at twilight. They are to take some of the blood and put it on the doorposts and lintels of their houses, after which they must eat the lamb.

God continues: "They shall eat the flesh that same night; they shall eat it roasted over the fire, with unleavened bread and with bitter herbs. Do not eat any of it raw, or cooked in any way with water, but roasted—head, legs, and entrails—over the fire. You shall not leave any of it over until morning; if any of it is left until morning you shall burn it" (vv. 8–10). These instructions for the keeping of the Passover service—for this is what it is—continue at considerable length, through the whole of Exodus 12 and up until Exodus 13:16, interwoven with the narrative of the tenth plague, the death of the Egyptian first-born, and the sparing of the Hebrew first-born by means of the lamb's-blood sign on the doorposts that warns the Destroyer.

Among the other Passover instructions are these: The meal must be eaten in haste, with loins girded and with sandals on the feet; only unleavened bread can be eaten during the seven days of the Passover season; and, several times reiterated, the feast is to be performed annually as a commemoration of the Exodus from Egypt (which has not actually happened at this point in the story). In addition, the law of the Passover offering requires that no foreigner may eat it, though it may be eaten by circumcised slaves; that it shall be eaten in the house; that there shall be no bones broken; and that the whole assembly of Israel must offer it. An additional commandment requires the Israelites to consecrate to God every first-born, whether man or beast.

It is evident that in these passages, and hence in the ceremony they prescribe, the Exodus is symbolized and memorialized.[2] Interestingly, the episode chosen to represent in future memory the parting from Egypt is the tenth plague, the death of the Egyptian first-born, for which the Passover sacrifice is understood to be a substitute and an apotropaic warding-off. Nor can there be any dispute that the sacrifice of the Passover animal inserts into the Exodus scenario the elements of cannibalism that Freud insisted ought to be there. As we know from Smith, for the pastoral peoples among whom it was practiced, the act of animal sacrifice represented the sharing of family or kinship substance, for the domestic animal was understood as an individual, a member of the household, and in some ways even as a kinsperson. Any reading of the ethnography of a pastoral people, from the Lapps to the Nuer, will show Smith's reading to be plausible.[3]

There is thus a clear thematic link between the symbolism of the devouring of a sacrificial victim in a ritualized way and the event I here analyze as a depiction of the primal crime of killing the senior male of the primal horde. I am nevertheless forced to admit that while the Arabian camel sacrifice depicted by Saint Nilus could symbolize the killing and eating of a primal-father figure by a community of junior males (especially since the camel is a large animal with respect to humans), the Passover ritual is different in significant ways. Perhaps the most crucial of these is that the victim is by no means a "paternal" animal, but, on the contrary, is quite clearly specified as a "junior male": a year-old, intact male lamb or kid. (The junior status is entailed in the victim's age, not its uncastrated condition.)

Let me approach these problems by briefly comparing the Passover injunctions in Exodus with Saint Nilus's camel sacrifice invoked by Freud. The similarities between the two sacrificial feasts are these: the animal is devoured collectively by the members of the sacrificing group, with no exceptions; it is eaten whole; and it is consumed within definite time limits in the confines of single night (though the exact time limits differ).

The main differences are that in the Passover, the feast is limited to the household rather than partaken of by a larger group; the Bedouins circumambulate the animal and drink its blood; and the Bedouins eat the animal raw, while the Israelites are distinctly enjoined from doing so, being instructed to roast it directly over the fire.

The difference between the size and definition of the group sharing the eating of the animal can be directly correlated to the character of the sacrificial animal in question: obviously, many more people can be fed off a camel than a lamb, which is big enough only for a single household. The collective, suprafamily nature of the Israelite ritual is ensured by the fact that *all* households are performing the same rite simultaneously.

From a psychological perspective, as Freud makes clear, the point of insisting on the communal eating is to bind a community, first by shared substance and second by shared guilt: everyone is implicated in the killing and devouring, and there is no one who can stand apart to accuse, condemn, or judge the others.

The second difficulty, that the Bedouins are supposed to circumambulate the animal and drink its blood, may be answered in two parts. Circumambulation seems to represent a setting apart of a sacred space within which the ritual act will be performed. Acts with similar functions occur in the Hebrew rite, like scouring the house for leavening and casting it out. In both cases, the space as well as the time of the ritual are clearly demarcated from ordinary space and time.

As for drinking the blood (and I realize that this is not an explanation), the Israelite Deity exhibits a particular horror concerning blood and the spilling of blood. Indeed, one of his first commandments in the Bible text, long before the Sinaitic revelation, is one given to Noah (and so is considered to apply to all people, not just the Israelites): "But you must not eat meat that has its lifeblood still in it. And for your lifeblood I will surely demand an accounting" (Gen. 9:4–5).

The blood represents the life of an animal or human, and as such is hedged about with sacred precautions. In the Bedouin rite, the drinking of the blood can be understood as the acquisition by the collectivity of the life force of the sacrificial victim—the literal oral incorporation of its strength, as Freud proposed.

It is hard to imagine the Israelite God asking for the drinking of blood even under conditions of the ritual reversal of ordinary regulations. But the blood is used for a "life-enhancing" purpose: smeared on the lintels and doorposts, it preserves the lives of the household members from the Destroyer who slays the first-born in every unmarked home.

One must bear in mind, too, that in the days of the Temple, the collective sacrifice produced vast quantities of blood, some of which was sprinkled on the audience. Going further, one might speculatively interpret the injunction to drain meat of blood as a preventive reaction-formation against a wishful devouring or draining fantasy like the one spelled out in Saint Nilus's description.

Finally, as to the matter of the eating of the animal raw, as the Bedouins do, the Passover victim must also be eaten in a strictly prescribed way, which excludes other, more ordinary ways of cooking meat, such as cutting it up to grill it, stewing it, boiling it or smoking it. Lévi-Strauss's analysis of the "culinary triad" comes to our aid here.[4] For him, the category of raw food stands in relation to cooked food as "untransformed nature" to "transformed nature." Transformation itself can be subdivided according to whether it is brought about by a natural or a human process. In the former case, raw food is transformed into rotten food; in the latter, raw food is converted into cooked food, which thus represents culture, as opposed to nature.

Freud's myth, as well as the biblical one, concerns the passage from the precivilized state of nature to a state of culture or civilization. Lévi-Strauss's analysis focuses on cooking as a symbol of the transformation of nature into culture, by the subjection of something raw and hence inedible to those in a state of civilization into something edible by means of a technological—cultural—operation. Eating a sacrificial animal raw, then, is a temporary reversion in ritual time to the last moment of precivilized history, the moment of devouring the body of the father. The Israelite Passover does not involve eating the victim raw but rather achieves a compromise whereby the precivilized is represented from within the boundaries of the already civilized cosmos. This is one reason I categorize the Passover as coming after the primal rebellion.

Lévi-Strauss's triadic structure—raw, rotten, cooked—is reproduced as a structure within the category of cooked foods themselves. There are three main kinds of preparation of meat: roasting, boiling, and smoking. Roasting is a process "in which the meat is brought into direct contact with the agent of conversion (fire) without the mediation of any cultural apparatus or of air or of water; the process is only partial—roast meat is only partly cooked" (Leach, 1970, 27). Boiling, by contrast, reduces raw food to a state similar to rotten but does so through the medium of water contained in a receptacle, that is, an item of culture. Smoking, the most complete form of cooking, occurs without a cultural artifact, through the medium of air. In this triad, then, roasting occupies the same structural position in relation to boiling and smoking as raw meat does to rotten and cooked. Roasting, being only "partial cooking" accomplished without a cultural medium, most closely approximates in structural terms the state of being raw among the various forms of cooking.

We can assert, then, that while it is true the Israelites do not eat their Passover meat raw, they eat it *more* raw, that is, less culturally processed, than if it were boiled or cut up and stewed or skewered like shish kebab. Roasting whole is the least transformed state of meat and is thus the closest thing to being raw without actually being raw.

Furthermore, cutting up meat to cook it disguises the fact that what is being eaten is an animal. Cooking the whole animal serves to emphasize the fact that a fellow creature is being cannibalized. There is no culturally interposed masking, as would be achieved, for example, by skewering chunks of meat in a kebab.[5] The Bible specifies that one is to eat the "head, legs, and entrails" (Exod. 12:9) of the victim. These parts forcibly remind the eater that he or she is eating what was a living being, not some affectively distanced "food."

But we still have not addressed the question of the nature of the sacrificial animal: not so much the species—which simply reflects different pastoral practices involving different animals in different times and places—but rather its suitability to represent the sacrificed and eaten primal father. Freud had no qualms about asserting that the father is regularly symbolized by an animal, but the Passover lamb is, as I have said, without question described in terms appropriate to a junior male, not a senior one.

This is, of course, logical in the context, since the Passover lamb is killed in place of the first-born child of the household. But how does it come to reflect the primal crime, which is the killing of a senior male? Why should the commemoration of the Exodus in the Passover ritual enact the killing and eating of a sacrificial substitute for a son rather than the father of the household?

We have seen that the events leading up to the Exodus are set in motion by an order to carry out the mass filicide of the Israelite children by the Egyptian high command. In accord with the talionic principle the Egyptians will suffer just retribution and the Israelites will be redeemed by God's intervention. The retribution actually occurs in two parts, which apply to the two generations of males. In the tenth plague, the sons of the Egyptians are killed, just as they had killed the sons of the Israelites. And at the Red Sea, the senior males themselves are killed in revenge for the crime of having persecuted the Israelites as a junior, enslaved people, as well as for having killed their sons.

The Passover ritual, which is thematically related to the tenth plague rather than to the parting of the Red Sea, enacts the first part of the retribution, the more perfectly talionic part. It affirms: "Your senior male killed our sons; now our senior male (God), who is bigger and stronger than your senior male, will kill your sons."

At the same time, the sacrifice of the Passover lamb enacts the killing of a senior male by junior males: Freud writes, concerning the origins of the punitive superego, "A considerable amount of aggressiveness must be developed in the child against the authority who prevents him from having his first, but nonetheless his most important, satisfactions. . . . But he is obliged to renounce the satisfaction of this revengeful aggressiveness" (1930, 129).

This renunciation is made possible by means of identification: the child (the son or junior male, for our purposes) takes the unattackable authority into himself, turning it into his superego, which thereby comes to possess all the aggressiveness of the father that the son would have liked to have exercised against him in revenge. But the son's own ego, in order to obtain this vicarious satisfaction, has to content itself with "the unhappy role of the authority—the father—who has been thus degraded. Here, as so often, the [real] situation is reversed: 'If I were the father and you were the child, I should treat you badly' " (1930, 129). Thus, in the Passover rite, by killing and eating an animal substitute for a junior male, Moses and the Israelites are saying, "If you (Pharaoh) were the junior one and I the senior one, I would treat you like this, just as you treated me."

Following Freud's analogy with obsessional neurosis, we may here recall that for Freud, an obsessional ritual or ceremony is a symptom that is always a compromise formation between the original wishful impulse and the defensive measures taken to counteract it. During the process of the return of the repressed, the apotropaic rituals of atonement originally designed to undo the offending forbidden deed come to be invested more and more with the significance of the wishful fantasy that led to the deed. If we view the Passover sacrifice as the collective equivalent of such a compromise formation, we can observe that the ritual contains the fantasy of punishment for the crime of aggression toward the pharaoh as a substitute for the deed itself. For having killed a senior male, the Israelites, through the sacrifice of a junior male/son/animal, must pay the retributive price for the guilt they have incurred by turning the tables on their oppressor. But at the same time the ceremony is a commemoration and reenactment of the rebellion. If the religious ritual did share the dynamics of an obsessional symptom, this is, then, what we might expect it to look like.

The association of the redemption of the first-born, animals and children alike, with the Passover sacrifice (Exod. 13:11–15) helps us understand the nature of the compromise in the Israelite symbolism.[6] First-born sons in the narratives of Genesis come off second best, from Cain through Ishmael, Esau, Reuben, and even Aaron. I contend that by his structural role, the first-born son is well suited to absorb the negative dimension of the senior-junior ambivalence between males. Like the father's younger brother, who also can play this role (Claudius or Seth, say), the older brother is junior to the father but senior to his younger brother(s). He can thus serve as a lightning rod for the hostility of the senior male toward the potentially usurping junior, at the same time that he becomes the focus for the aggression of the junior male against an interfering, obstructing senior. Both the bad, persecuting senior and the bad, defiant junior, the first-born can be sacrificed as the talionic price for his own murder as the senior male.

The Passover sacrifice, then, is a commemorative ritual enacting the killing of the primal father, but only as it would be defensively distorted or transformed *after* the institution of the superego, or "civilization." This at first seems inappropriately anachronistic, since the real instauration of the Israelite cultural superego does not occur until later in the narrative, at Mount Sinai. The commandments concerning Passover in Exodus 12 and 13 are thus premonitory, a foretaste of things to come. Their positioning, however, is more appropriate than it seems, since while the Passover commandments occur *before* the primal crime, in the narrative chronology they describe something that is, in effect, part of the *aftermath* or *consequence* of the crime. For they establish a *later* commemorative festival that will look back upon and reenact the deed now being done in the narrative present. This is made evident by the fact that, in giving the Passover instructions,

God speaks to Moses as if the Exodus had already occurred: "You shall observe the [Feast of] Unleavened Bread, for on this very day I brought your ranks out of the land of Egypt: you shall observe this day throughout the ages as an institution for all time" (Exod. 12:17). The use of a perfect form of the verb here (hotzeti) indicates that God, in enjoining the Passover service, speaks as if he has already brought the house of Israel out of Egypt.[7]

Because the description of the sacrificial meal of the Israelites on the eve of the Exodus is a reading back into mythic history of a later commemorative ritual (dating from after Sinai), and therefore after the construction of the superego, the primal meal can be recalled only as it would appear in the presence of the superego, that is, in the disguised and guilty way I have described. Had we been able, *per impossibile,* to see it as it appeared before our consciousness was transformed by the events that followed, we might have seen what Freud expected to find: the brothers feasting on the (uncooked) body of the father. Interestingly, in the Christian transformation of the Passover into the Eucharist, a step in this direction is taken: in eating the body and blood of the divine son, the communicant simultaneously, by the mystery of the Trinity, also eats the father (raw), since father and son are identical. This development would be consistent with Freud's view of the progress of an obsessional neurosis, in which the repressed fantasy/memory emerges more clearly under the guise of the representation of the punishment for the wish invoked as a defensive undoing. The Christian rite in effect confirms our suspicion that hidden beneath the image of a sacrificed son is the fantasy of the murdered and cannibalized primal father.

II

We may now turn to an examination of the events that occur directly after the overthrow of the Egyptians at the Red Sea. Chapter 14 of Exodus ends with the dramatic imagery of the drowning of the Egyptian army, which contrasts with the miraculous safe-passage of the six hundred thousand Israelites. Chapter 15 is devoted entirely to the so-called *Shirat ha-Yam,* the Song at the Sea.

Led by Moses, the Israelites, on seeing the wondrous power of God and being thus stirred to fervent faith, sing a poem of praise to the Lord. A triumphant rejoicing and a hymn to God's greatness, the song also expresses contempt for enemies past and present and derides the Egyptians for their boasting in light of their complete discomfiture. The people occupying the lands the Israelites must seize to take possession of Canaan are also fore-warned to tremble before the invincible might of the Israelites under the protection of God.

After Moses and the Israelite men have sung their song, Miriam takes up a timbrel and leads the women, also playing timbrels, in a chant that, though it occupies only two lines, is deemed especially important and is considered one of the most ancient fragments preserved in the entire biblical corpus: "Sing to the Lord, for He has triumphed gloriously; Horse and driver He has hurled into the sea" (Exod. 15:21).

For one moment, in the wake of the miraculous events of the day, the Israelites feel complete elation, the perfect fusion of wish and reality, the accomplishment of victory and vindication. The persecuting tyrant is dead, his subjects freed from restrictions and threats of danger. Everyone shares the triumph, including unborn infants. A midrash tells us that "even the sucklings dropped their mother's breasts to join in the singing; yea, even the embryos in the womb joined the melody" (Ginzberg, 1911, 3, 34). Complicity in, as well as both credit and guilt for, the primal crime is, as we saw, spread throughout the community. There was no one who did not join in the song of victory, no one who did not benefit from the liberation, and no bystander with innocent hands who could call his fellows to account.

The euphoria that reigns for all-too-brief a period after the liberation from Egypt will, according to tradition, be experienced again only in the "world to come," the messianic era: "As Moses and the race that wandered from Egypt with him sang a song to the Lord by the Red Sea, so shall they sing again in the world to come. . . . In other respects, too, it shall be in the world to come as it was at the time of the song by the sea" (Ginzberg, 1911, 3, 35). It is said that when the Israelites sang the Song at the Sea, God himself put on a festive robe embroidered with promises for a happy future. When Israel sinned—which, as we know, they didn't take long to get around to doing—God rent the festive robe, and according to legend, he will mend it and put it on again at the time of the world to come, the era to be ushered in by the messiah, when the perfect happiness at the sea will be the everyday state of affairs.

When the Torah portion containing the Song at the Sea is read in the synagogue, it is traditional for the worshipers to rise to their feet. This singular honor it shares with only one other passage: the Ten Commandments. As we shall see, this pairing is a fitting one.

III

According to Freud's account of the primal crime, once the hatred of the primal despot had spent itself in murder, and the initial wave of exultation had passed, "the affection which all this time had been pushed under was bound to make itself felt. It did so in the form of remorse" (1913b, 143). Coming back to their senses, the Israelites, realizing they are stuck in the middle of a desert with no water or food, almost at once begin to grumble against Moses and Aaron and, by implication, against God. They feel remorse for what they have done; they long for the security, and the fleshpots, of Egypt. (Perhaps these pots of meat, or stews, form the contrasting "profane" fare with which the "sacred" roasted whole animal of Passover is to be contrasted.)

On this first appearance of the rebellious, grumbling, doubting, and stiff-necked attitude of the Israelites, God does not lose his temper, perhaps realizing that the demand for water and food is, after all, legitimate. He first provides water, by enabling Moses to sweeten the waters of Marah ("bitter") with a piece of wood. Then he supplies food in the form of manna and quails, hedged about with strict instructions as to their use. Later grumbling will not be so kindly dealt with. Throughout the wandering in the desert, the Lord is repeatedly provoked by his people, who appear too often to be a pack of disobedient ingrates, driving him almost to abandon or even annihilate them.

It is perhaps relevant that the first instance of grumbling in the story is oral: the people are hungry and thirsty, and God feeds them. The people have left a land that, though it kept them in inferior status, at least kept them well fed. The Exodus, like separation-individuation, brings with it both the push to freedom and a fear of autonomy and a longing for the lost dependency on the providing mother. In this light, the elation at the sea could be partly understood as a hypomanic defense against the depression over the oral loss that is sustained by rebelling and declaring independence.

In feeding the Israelites, in a situation in which there really are no other options (since the desert cannot sustain life), God creates in them a new and equally profound dependency. He also announces the terms of his care: at the waters of Marah, God "made for them a fixed rule [*hok umishpat,* "statute and ordinance"], and there He put them to the test. He said, 'If you will heed the Lord your God diligently, doing what is upright in His sight, giving ear to His commandments and keeping all his Laws, then will I not bring upon you any of the diseases that I brought upon the Egyptians, for I the Lord am your healer' " (Exod. 15:25–26). This announcement sets the general terms of the future relationship between God and Israel: God will *withhold* his powers of destruction, provided the Israelites obey his "fixed rule." He is their "healer" in that he voluntarily holds in check his powers as a destroyer. At this point, obedience is required only in the abstract: the actual commandments to be obeyed concern the regulations for collecting and storing manna. The single more enduring and important commandment is the observation of the Sabbath, on which no manna can be collected. Even this rule, however, awaits its fuller exposition at Mount Sinai.

We learn from these passages that following the unmitigated joy and triumph of the Song at the Sea, a profound ambivalence enters the relationship between the Israelites and God, a new development in what had previously been a wholly positive alliance against the pharaoh. This is evident, on the side of the Israelites, in their complaints about having to leave Egyptian bondage/security. On God's side, it takes the form of his showing his dual nature as both preserver *and* destroyer, who will let the preserving side of the ambivalence hold the destroying side in check as long as his absolute position as master goes unchallenged.

The reason for the emergence of this new dimension of ambivalence is that the conditions that previously made possible a split between characters exemplifying good and bad dimensions of the junior male–senior male relationship no longer prevail. Until the demise of the Egyptians at the Red Sea, the Israelites' mythic paternal senior-male imago was split between antithetical good and bad representatives: God could be all good precisely because Pharaoh was all bad. I have shown in the previous chapter how the idealized human-God relationship of the oppressed band of brothers was made possible because all the negative side of the ambivalence between junior males and senior males could be expelled from within the group and projected onto the image of the evil (non-Israelite) persecutor.

But when the pharaoh no longer exists to offset God, and to absorb and embody the hostile dimensions of the senior-junior relationship, Moses and the Israelites find themselves in an unprecedented moral dilemma. The God who protects, loves, and provides for them is also now the one who may become jealous, wrathful, prohibiting, and infanticidal (as he demonstrated in the tenth plague). The sacrifice of Passover, which served originally as an apotropaic rite, makes it plain that God's "protection" consists in his being prevented, or preventing himself, from destroying.

From a Kleinian perspective, what has happened is that the Israelites have moved from the paranoid to the depressive position. In the paranoid position, a persecutor can be identified and opposed vigorously with violent countermeasures because of a fantasied split that separates the negative from the positive aspects of the breast. The depressive position is reached when the split is overcome conceptually, and one realizes that the evil withholding or persecuting mother is not a separate person but the same mother who nurtures, protects, and loves.

In attacking and killing the evil mother, then, one has also unwittingly killed the good, providing one. This attitude is represented by the Israelites rejoicing that they have triumphed over the wicked Pharaoh only to realize that they must now do without the fleshpots of Egypt—the symbols of the providing breasts of the mother hidden in the overt image of the father the Israelites have slain.

The depressive position, then, is that state of mind in which the child mourns the loss of the beloved object, is overwhelmed by the removal of the source of life upon which it has been dependent, and experiences guilt for having been the cause of the loss through its own destructive attack on what was (mistakenly, it is now realized) seen as a malevolent persecutor. According to the Kleinian view, only after fully experiencing the grief attendant on fearing that one's own wrath has killed what one wanted and needed most can one truly love others in an unselfish, altruistic way. One strives to do good out of guilt, by way of reparation for the damage one has caused in the paranoid position. The concept of reparation—*tikkun*—seems to reveal the roots in and affinity of Klein's thought with the Jewish tradition out of which it emerged.

Klein's view, in turn, is a development of Freud's insight about the origin of civilization, namely, that social life is possible only after one begins to feel guilty about having slain the parent. But this sword cuts both ways. Overcoming the split representation forces one to recognize that the beloved parent was also a persecutor. An additional source of guilt is thus the rage at the parent that one must defensively turn upon oneself in order to protect the good parent from the attack she or he deserves for having been a source of distress and pain. Healing the split does not necessarily heal the patient, as the case of Moses well exemplifies.

IV

Having killed Pharaoh, Moses, acting as protagonist/representative of the Israelites whom he now leads and on whose behalf he has acted, finds himself in an impossible position. For it now becomes evident, and will soon be made explicit, that the God who gave the command "You must kill your father (Pharaoh)" is also the God who gives the command "You must not kill your father." It will do no good to respond to the latter by blustering, "But you said . . ." Both commands are absolute and admit of no disobedience; but in obeying one, we necessarily disobey the other; God's promise that he will hold his aspect as destroyer in check so long as his will is obeyed cannot possibly be sustained.

In the insightful view of Roland Barthes, man, on perceiving the cruel dilemma in which his relation to the father (God) has him trapped, responds by taking upon himself the transgression of the father, accepting guilt himself. This is the "paradoxical moment when the child discovers that his father is wicked, yet wants to remain his child" (1983, 45). As Barthes continues: "The hero's guilt is a functional necessity: if man is pure, then God is impure, and the world falls apart. Hence man must *cling* to his transgression as his most precious belonging: and what surer means of being guilty than making oneself responsible for what is outside oneself, previous to oneself? God, Blood, the Father, the Law—in short anteriority becomes incriminating in essence. . . . The world is tribunal: if the accused is innocent, the judge is guilty; hence the accused takes upon himself the judge's transgression" (46, my emphasis). Without the split-off bad father, the hostile side of the ambivalence between generations becomes an intolerable scandal from which the unified, good-enough God/parent must be protected. This hostility is therefore redirected against oneself, the only object left for it to attack, which results in a greatly augmented sense of guilt.

The second part of chapter 17 and chapter 18 of Exodus provide a beautiful illustration of the ambivalence that, as I have argued, becomes painfully explicit upon the slaying of the primal father/Pharaoh. The passage divides thematically in half, contrasting two very different non-Israelite foreigners of senior rank encountered in the desert: Amalek, the eponymous ancestor of the Amalekites, and Jethro, Moses's father-in-law.

Amalek (who is not actually a person but a personified tribe, the "house of the ancestor Amalek") "came and fought with Israel at Rephidim" (Exod. 17:8). After Joshua defeats Amalek, thanks to God's intervention,

God orders that Amalek's memory be blotted from under heaven (vv. 9–14). From then on, far from being obliterated from memory, Amalek serves as the prototype of all enemies of Israel. Thus, "Amalek" has appeared and reappeared throughout Jewish history in many guises: as Haman, Antiochus, Titus, Hadrian, Torquemada, Chmielnitzki, and Hitler, to name some of the most egregious.[8]

Jethro, by contrast, though a Midianite, is depicted as faithful, wise, and benevolent. He recognizes the sovereign authority of God in the wake of what has happened in Egypt; he brings Moses's family to rejoin him after his mission at Pharaoh's court; and he gives sound advice about the setting up of an effective governing organization for the Israelite community as they continue their trek through the wilderness.

Amalek and Jethro force Moses and the Israelites to face the question of how to organize themselves into a continuing society in light of the presence among them—and between them and others—of *both* hate and love. The answer to this question will be delivered, spectacularly and, as far as the Jews are concerned, definitively and for all time, at Mount Sinai.

8

Facing Mount Sinai

To recapitulate briefly, the biblical narrative, paralleling Freud's scenario of the primal horde, has so far reached this point: Moses, as leader of a band of oppressed brothers, has led a successful rebellion, done away with the rule of his father, the jealous, persecuting patriarch, and, instead of placing himself in the role of the old senior male, now aims to establish a new form of social organization, governed by just and legitimate laws. In the wilderness, after experiencing the joyful moment of victory and wish fulfillment, Moses and his band have had to face the deep ambivalences in human life that render his task of establishing a just society difficult.

Now, at Mount Sinai, the God who has led them out of Egypt reveals at last the terms of the covenant Moses has already, in effect, accepted by allowing himself and his people to be guided by God's hand in the commission of the primal patricide at the Red Sea. God makes it known that in return for having liberated Israel from Egyptian bondage, and for his continued protection and benevolence, the Israelites must commit themselves to unswerving obedience to a set of laws that he enunciates through Moses. These rules include prescriptions—especially instructions for religious practice and observation like the rules for the performance of rituals and for the construction of religious buildings, garments, and paraphernalia—and prohibitions and regulations designed to prevent certain actions. God thus becomes as demanding a taskmaster as Pharaoh ever was, indeed more so. But now the "tasks" are supposed to result in a society that will not only serve the primary purpose of realizing God's unchallengeable intentions but also lead to a harmonious, self-governing, and prosperous life for the Israelites themselves.

A passage from *Totem and Taboo* captures with uncanny precision the spirit of the psychological shift from the moment of the death of the pharaoh to the revelation of God at Mount Sinai:

> They [the band of brothers] hated their father, who presented
> such a formidable obstacle to their craving for power and their

sexual desires; but they loved and admired him too. After they got rid of him . . . a sense of guilt made its appearance, which in this instance coincided with the remorse felt by the whole group. *The dead father became stronger than the living one had been.* . . . What had up to then been prevented by his actual existence was thenceforward prohibited by the sons themselves, in accordance with the psychological procedure so familiar to us in psycho-analysis under the name of "deferred obedience" (1913b, 143, my emphasis).

The alternative to having one of the victorious brothers set himself up as a new pharaoh—as Moses himself might have done, had he simply stayed in Egypt, succeeded to his father's throne, and married Miriam—is for all the brothers to renounce this ambition, as well as prohibit anything that might serve as a motivation for competition, rivalry, and jealousy among themselves. The insistence on the binding of each by a universal, equalizing law is, paradoxically, fueled by the jealousy and envy each feels for the other, according to the powerful principle "If one cannot be the favourite oneself, at all events nobody else shall be the favourite" (Freud 1921, 120). Either there will be one self-evidently supreme senior male or no senior male. Therefore, no one may have those things that established the senior male as senior male: the women of the horde and supreme political authority.

As Freud expresses it: "The new organization would have collapsed in a struggle of all against all, for none of them was of such overmastering strength as to be able to take on his father's part with success. Thus the brothers had no alternative, if they were to live together, but . . . to institute the law against incest, by which they all alike renounced the women whom they desired and who had been their chief motive for dispatching their father" (1913b, 144). Later in the same section of his essay he puts the matter this way:

There was one factor in the state of affairs produced by the elimination of the father which was bound in the course of time to produce an enormous longing for him. Each single one of the brothers who had banded together for the purpose of killing their father was inspired by a wish to become like him and had given expression to it by incorporating parts of their father's surrogate in the totem meal. But, in consequence of the pressure exercized by the fraternal clan as a whole, that wish could never be fulfilled. . . . Thus after a long lapse of time their bitterness against their father, which had driven them to their deed, grew less, and their longing for him increased; and it became possible for an ideal to emerge which embodied the unlimited power of the primal father against whom they had once fought as well as their readiness to submit to him. (148)

The result of this longing for the slain father is his return in the form of an idealized and deified patriarch whose power is immeasurably greater than was that of the father who was slain: "The scene of the father's vanquishment, of his greatest defeat, has become the stuff for the representation of his supreme triumph" (150).

We may weave these observations together, in the context of our understanding of the Exodus as the scene of the primal rebellion and victory of the brothers, in the following way. After having killed the primal father (Pharaoh), the brothers (Israelites), having spent their fury, in the name and with the support of the idealized, benevolent decomposition of the senior male (God) they had been able to maintain because of the aim-inhibited state of group psychology into which the bad father's tyranny had forced them, become overwhelmed with remorse and guilt.

Why? First, the brothers have lost the father's love and protection, for although he persecuted them, as long as they were docile he also provided sustenance, security, and protection from rival patriarchs. In addition, since, as we have seen, in the biblical narrative the males tend to take over and represent figures who were originally female, the pharaoh's feminine aspect—the land of Egypt itself—has also been lost, in the form of the preoedipal mother who gives care and nourishment directly from her own body. (In this aspect of the scenario, the Israelites are motivated less by the fear of castration than by the fear of the loss of parental love.)

Second, the ambivalent attitude of the sons had included a wish to identify with and emulate an admired and beloved senior model. Having vented their hatred, they were left with their now unfulfillable love and affection for a lost object, which their own hateful impulses had destroyed.

Furthermore, once they were rid of the bad father, their own rivalries and jealousies could no longer be projected onto their persecutor and began to interfere with the harmonious group identification that had prevailed as long as the brothers remained in a state of oppression. The idealized God who had come to represent their mutual love and unity of purpose now had to absorb the negative, persecuting aspect of the senior male previously embodied by the wicked Pharaoh, as well as the internecine hostility, previously suppressed or projected outward, of the brothers.

Thus, the brothers found that the aim-inhibited bonds of homosexual object-love, which had welded them into an effective social unit before the primal crime, threatened to deteriorate into a war of all against all as their envy of and hostility to each other returned.

Facing a renewed struggle for primacy among themselves, mourning the loss of their loved and admired protector, and longing for the feeling of being approved of by the ego ideal they had set up as God in their rebellious unity, the brothers arrive at the only viable solution short of reverting to the primal horde. Drawing upon both their longing for the dead father and their fear of punishment for having killed him, they agree to impose restrictions upon themselves that make it impossible to become a true senior male. These privations can be effectively enforced precisely because the combination of a repressed earlier love of the father, as well as the guilty dread of what would happen after he found out that they had killed him (if I may so phrase it), combined with the fear of the possibility of internecine war and the envy and jealousy felt by each for the others, motivates each one to accept a compromise of his own ambitions, provided everyone else does too.

The stage is thus set for the Israelites voluntarily to embrace the covenant presented to them as a fait accompli by their deliverer at Sinai. Freud, though he did not (at least explicitly) realize the significance of what he was saying, nonetheless managed to envision this moment with striking clarity:

> The first effect of meeting the being who had so long been missed and longed for was overwhelming *and was like the traditional description of the law-giving from Mt. Sinai.* Admiration, awe and thankfulness for having found grace in his eyes—the religion of Moses knew none but these positive feelings toward the father-god. The conviction of his irresistibility, the submission to his will, could not have been more unquestioning in the helpless and intimidated son of the father of the horde. . . . A rapture of devotion to God was thus the first reaction to the return of the great father. (1939, 133–134, my emphasis)

This passage accurately describes Moses when we cast him not, as Freud did, as the *victim* of the primal rebellion but rather as the leader of it. Moses has every reason to turn from willful rebel against the authority of Pharaoh to punctiliously obedient servant of the new deity whose will he announces as prophet. We have seen that God expresses his benevolence in the form of a restraint of his penchant for destruction and that he has further announced that he will protect Israel from his wrath provided they obey his rules. But these rules, as Freud has analyzed them, are at root rules against doing exactly what Moses has just done: rebelling against the father's authority and killing him for his power and his women. Since Moses is already guilty—albeit at the behest of this same deity—it is in his interest to be very careful around the new, immortal, omnipotent, and omniscient senior male who has now appeared to replace the deposed one. In effect, Moses, for having rebelled against his father, now stands under eternal threat of punishment by the new father-avenger. Hence, his willingness to demonstrate his deferred obedience and to insist upon obedience from his Israelite brothers.

The God who is fully revealed at Sinai now combines both sides of the ambivalent feelings between the generations of males. He is an embodiment of the idealized, loving, protecting divinity who ruled the rebellious brother group *and* the wrathful, jealous, demanding, prohibiting tyrant of the primal horde itself. Which aspect of him will predominate it is up to the Israelites to determine, by their choice of whether to overmatch their desire to rebel, backslide, or indulge their senses with their obedience, brotherly love, and fear of their Lord.

II

The covenant at Sinai is the social contract that the culture hero Moses establishes to transform the realm of the primal horde into the state of civilized society, governed by an absolute and universal law in which each person is assured a measure of respect and justice equal to that of the others.[1] It is enforced by the twin motivations of love for the father and for one's fellows, and guilty fear of the hostility one has renounced and projectively assigned to God.

What, then, are the actual laws and statutes that God, through his prophet Moses, establishes for the Israelites in the revelation that begins, and may symbolically be seen to have its apotheosis, at Sinai? According to

Freud, the original patricide was followed by the self-imposition by the brothers of two commandments, which he identifies as the two fundamental rules of the religion of totemism (which, following the anthropological thought of his time, he believed was the founding human religion): "They revoked their deed by forbidding the killing of the totem, the substitute for their father; and they renounced its fruits by resigning their claim to the women who had now been set free. They thus created out of their filial sense of guilt the two fundamental taboos of totemism, which for that very reason inevitably corresponded to the two repressed wishes of the Oedipus complex" (1913b, 143).

Contemporary anthropology no longer concerns itself with issues derived from a model of universal evolution of society or religion from "primitive" to "civilized." We need not share Freud's interest in showing how his myth accounts for what was once taken to be the Ur-religion but that today is not recognized as a meaningful entity.[2] But leaving aside the question of what relation the primal crime might have to a supposed totemism, we are still entitled to ask whether Freud's expectations that the taboos of the Oedipus complex will form the core of the social contract are met in the biblical narrative. The Torah contains a total of 613 commandments, which constitute the complete guide to a Jewish life in accordance with God's law. These commandments make up the greater part of the Torah text after the episode of the arrival at Sinai. In Exodus, of the remaining twenty chapters, chapter 21 and parts of chapter 33, which relate the incident of the Golden Calf, alone concern something other than instructions regarding ritual practices. The book of Leviticus is wholly devoted to the enunciation of laws and ordinances, and the final book in the set, Deuteronomy, almost completely so as well, often restating regulations that have already been given elsewhere.[3] Only the book of Numbers devotes most of its space to narration rather than instruction, recounting the forty years of wandering through the wilderness on the way to the promised land of Canaan; though even in Numbers, there are significant segments devoted to law.

Just as the moment at Sinai symbolizes the completeness of revelation through Moses, so the Ten Commandments received there have come to be seen, by synechdoche, as representing the whole of God's Law. One could certainly read these ten as *including* the two Freud proposed as deriving from the Oedipus complex. One could, for example, take the fifth commandment—"Honor your father and your mother, that you may long endure on the land which the Lord your God is giving you" (Exod.

20:12)—as encompassing some such thought as "Don't kill the one and have sex with the other" as one of the many ways to fail to honor one's parents. Likewise, the sixth and seventh commandments—"You shall not murder. You shall not commit adultery" (Exod. 20:13)—would necessarily include the oedipal injunctions within their far wider scope. But this is stretching things to the point of absurdity.

To follow up in a more fruitful way, using a Freudian approach to making sense of the Law and commandments, I think we must begin by looking at the corpus of revealed statutes and ordinances in the light of Freud's dynamic understanding of why there are laws at all. Here we must turn to the analogy Freud posited between the history of Judeo-Christian religion and the dynamics of the "obsessive-compulsive character."

I must reiterate that we cannot accept any suggestion that a culture, or civilization, or society can have either a neurosis or a personality: these are the attributes of individuals. But what I propose is that we read the Torah text as an instruction manual for how to have a socially acceptable and culturally valued personality; and in the process by which people form themselves as individuals with certain character structures, and do so in the context of a particular social and cultural milieu, the Torah text provides a model and a guide for the formation of the obsessional and/or normal "conscientious" personality. In this sense the text is what Melford Spiro (1987c) has referred to as a "culturally constructed defense mechanism": that is, a concrete and institutionalized cultural artifact individuals can use in the structuring of their own psychodynamic organization, which channels the individual's personal psychodynamics into a mature and stable personality organization consonant with the continued, relatively harmonious, operation of the social-cultural system of which the individual is a member.

III

At this point in my exposition I draw upon the validity I believe remains in Freud's application of the clinical understanding of obsessional neurosis to the Judeo-Christian tradition. While a society cannot have an obsessional neurosis, a text, such as the Torah, certainly can exhibit in its form and content traits distinctive to the obsessional style of personality. An individual predisposed to that mode of character organization would then find the text congenial and would be able and inclined to organize his or her psy-

chodynamic defenses and adaptations in the socially approved way illustrated by the text. Before I continue, however, I must clarify what I mean
by the obsessional or conscientious personality.

All humans may be characterized as having a distinctive and relatively
stable psychodynamic organization consisting of compromises between impulses and defenses against them. Whereas in a "normal" person this compromise allows the person to function in a way that is both congruent with
the cultural and social milieu and consonant with his or her own ideals,
ambitions, and expectations, "neurosis" consists in a compromise that seriously inhibits or impairs the person's adaptive capacity, as evaluated both
by social norms and by the person him- or herself. The defenses deployed
in any particular neurotic syndrome are not in themselves pathological
symptoms. Rather, the inappropriate or excessive deployment for defensive
purposes of normal adaptive operations of all kinds (and not just certain
specific "mechanisms") results in what is socially deemed pathological.[4]

What is called obsessional is a particular and distinct mode of organization or characterological personality style that is typified by a certain set
of defenses used to manage a particular constellation of impulses. The origin
of this distinctive style is probably to be found in a combination of tem-
peramental endowment and the accidents of family dynamics and early life
history. This particular style is not in itself necessarily neurotic or pathological (nor is it be regarded as in itself more or less pathological or normal
than any other mode of psychodynamic organization). Freud himself assumed that the various defenses, fantasies, and fears typical of the obsessional character were produced by natural selection and would thus have
a primarily adaptive purpose.[5] Recent research supports this view; thus, for
example, one can suppose that the obsessional's fear of contagion or dirt
serves the adaptive function of reducing the likelihood of infection. In moderation, this is a culture- and ego-syntonic trait. It becomes neurotic or
pathological when it occupies a place in the psychic organization far beyond
what it merits or what is either realistically useful or congruent with the
wishes of the individual, who finds this compulsive cleanliness involuntary
and unwanted.[6]

We may thus differentiate between the obsessional dynamics consistent with normal life and those that are so exaggerated as to be counter-
productive for the afflicted individual. I wish, therefore, to make a
distinction here among three different but related syndromes, each based
on the same characteristic complex of defenses but ranging along a contin-

uum from the pathological to the normal—indeed, the desirable and admirable.

Current psychiatric practice, as represented by the *Diagnostic and Statistical Manual of Mental Disorders* (DSM-IV), recognizes two different pathological syndromes both characterized as "obsessional." The more serious Axis I disorder is called Obsessive-Compulsive Disorder.[7] It features full-blown obsessions and/or compulsions, that is, thoughts and behaviors that are involuntary and unwanted; persistent; irrational or unrealistic; and ineffective in removing anxiety or accomplishing their ostensible purpose. Typical obsessions cited by DSM-IV include thoughts about contamination, repeated doubts, aggressive or horrific impulses, and unwanted sexual imagery. Typical compulsions include repetitive and unrealistic or nonfunctional handwashing, ordering, or checking, as well as praying, counting, or repeating verbal formulas involuntarily and at wasteful length. Obsessive-Compulsive Disorder shows signs of being stimulated by serotonin agonists, and it responds in some cases to antidepressant drugs, thus suggesting an organic foundation in neurotransmitter imbalance. The disorder is equally common among males and females.

The generally less serious syndrome, not associated with organic disturbance and constituting a character type rather than a disorder with a set of "symptoms," is treatable with psychotherapy or analysis rather than drugs. It occurs twice as often in men as in women. This is the Axis II category called Obsessive-Compulsive Personality Disorder.[8] The striking ceremonials, rituals, and verbal formulas of the Obsessive-Compulsive Disorder are absent. Rather than being seen as a disease, this pathology is understood as being a stable character structure, organized in a way that, in the judgment of the patient, is not optimally successful in meeting the demands of life and realizing his or her wishes and intentions. The diagnostic criteria for this personality disorder include: excessive preoccupation with details, lists, rules, order, and schedules; a perfectionism that interferes with the completion of tasks; excessive devotion to work and productivity; overly scrupulous morality or ethics; inability to discard things; need for control and inability to delegate tasks; miserly attitudes toward money; and general rigidity or stubbornness.[9]

In addition to these two pathological manifestations of the obsessional personality style, I wish to draw particular attention to a third, nonpathological form of obsessional character. Following Oldham and Morris (1990), I refer to this as the "conscientious personality." Most authorities are agreed that whereas Obsessive-Compulsive Disorder and Obsessive-Compulsive Personality Disorder are undesirable conditions that merit treatment, there is a kind of obsessional personality that is not only normal but is even exceptionally well-suited to life in our present sociocultural environment. Thus DSM-IV closes its discussion of the Obsessive-Compulsive Personality Disorder with this caution: "Obsessive-compulsive personality traits in moderation may be especially adaptive, particularly in situations that reward high performance. Only when these traits are inflexible, maladaptive, and persisting and cause significant subjective distress do they constitute Obsessive-Compulsive Personality Disorder" (1994, 672).

Freud himself was the first of a long series of psychoanalytic writers to emphasize the positive value of the obsessive, or conscientious, character to our civilization: "[People of the obsessional type] exhibit, as it were, an internal instead of an external dependence. They develop a high degree of self-reliance; and, from the social standpoint, they are the true, preeminently conservative vehicles of civilization" (1931, 218).

More recently, Burness Moore and Bernard Fine remark in their dictionary of psychoanalytic terms, under the heading "Obsession-Compulsion": "At one end of the continuum are well-organized, productive, hard-working, conscientious people. They think logically and are able to carry out their ideas effectively" (1990, 132). David Shapiro, in his influential study of different neurotic cognitive styles, writes of the obsessive-compulsive personality: "The most conspicuous fact about the activity of the obsessive-compulsive is its sheer quantity, and along with this, its intensity and concentration. These people may be enormously productive in socially recognized ways, or they may not be; however that may be, they are, typically, intensively and more or less continuously active in some kind of work" (1965, 31). Roger MacKinnon and Robert Michels, in their authoritative textbook on the clinical interview, characterize the obsessive-compulsive patient thus: "His punctuality, conscientiousness, tidiness, orderliness, and reliability are derived from his fear of authority. These can be highly adaptive traits of great social value" (1971, 89–90). Humberto Nagera writes in his psychoanalytic monograph on the obsessional neuroses: "The obsessional character is one of many possible outcomes in normal personality development and, where it remains within limits, a useful and desirable form of personality organization" (1993, 139). D. A. Freedman notes that in choosing a surgeon (and the same goes for most professionals upon whom one might call) one would likely actively seek out someone "obsessional," that is, meticulous, scrupulous about following procedures, and a perfectionist. He writes: "One does not seek to eradicate [with psychotherapy] social proprieties, sense of duty and a host of other aspects of functioning which are taken for granted in civilized society" (1989, 8).

Joseph Sandler and A. Hazari distinguish between the obsessive-compulsive neuroses proper and a second form of personality that operates with the same dynamics but that is ego-syntonic and adaptive rather than pathological. The traits characterizing their second type appear to be "well-integrated into the personality, a source of pride and self-esteem rather than of anxiety and tension. . . . They represent traits of character . . . which conform to their possessor's ideal standards for himself—standards which are rather more demanding than those of the average person." One may think, for example, of the difference between a person who is always tidy, well-groomed, and smartly dressed and another who wastes endless hours washing his or her hands until the skin is raw. In both cases, their actions are "reaction formations against unconscious and unwanted . . . smearing and dirtying impulses" (1960, 120), but one is "normal," adaptive, and admirable, and one is not.

Of particular interest in the context of this book is the work of Joseph Michaels and Robert Porter, who, writing shortly after World War II, studied frequencies of psychopathology in the military. They point out that the army and navy, "with their discipline, regimentation, reports, rules, regulations and their emphasis on orderliness, cleanliness and economy, may be considered as vast compulsive organizations" (1949, 128). The authors suggest that the military favors the obsessional who uses the institution to augment and strengthen his own defenses. They cite studies showing that obsessionals make exceptionally good bomber pilots and combat fliers, able to defend themselves against anxiety by their meticulous, rigid, ritualistic devices. They conclude that some level of compulsiveness is essential to strength of character, remarking that "a certain degree of compulsiveness is considered worthwhile to all citizens of current civilized society as well as to members of military forces. . . . Early training which instills some compulsive character traits in children by virtue of respect for authority remains necessary in our present-day culture" (1949, 132).

Responding to the clear need for a delineation of the normal variant of the obsessional style, John Oldham and Lois Morris propose the term *conscientious personality* and offer a list of positive traits typical of this type. These traits represent healthy expressions of those attributes that, exaggerated, form the diagnostic criteria for the DSM-IV category of Obsessive-Compulsive Personality Disorder. Oldham and Morris's personality profile of the conscientious personality includes an interest in hard work, strong moral values, a belief in a right way to do things, perfectionism, love of detail, orderliness, pragmatism, prudence, and a tendency to collect things.[10]

In a 1994 article the economist and historian Donald McCloskey tries to describe what kind of "virtues" might be proper to the much-maligned "bourgeois" and comes up with a list that seems to me a version of the set of positive character traits I have just been describing: "A modern society needs poetry and history and movies about bourgeois virtue: integrity, honesty, trustworthiness, enterprise, humor, respect, modesty, consideration, responsibility, prudence, thrift, affection, self-possession" (1994, 180). I shall refrain from citing the twelve attributes of the good Boy Scout; I simply wish to point out that a thoughtful and sympathetic description of an ideal type that is obviously central to our civilization, the bourgeois, is not far from a description of the "good obsessional," or conscientious, personality.

It should now be clear that when I characterize the personality style consistent with modern civilization, which I find represented in the Torah text, I do not necessarily imply a diagnosis of pathology. Rather, I am describing a certain more-or-less identifiable syndrome of typical impulses and defenses, which can be manifest in a particular case in either healthy and adaptive or neurotic forms, or both. I intend neither to condemn nor to applaud, only to understand how it comes about that our civilization exhibits, through the actions of the individuals who compose it, its characteristic style.

IV

With these considerations in mind, we may turn our attention to the question of what the dynamics of the conscientious or obsessional personality organization are.[11] At the root of this distinctive variety of character organization is the phenomenon of emotional ambivalence—the simultaneous existence of equally powerful feelings of love and hatred directed toward the same person. While everyone experiences this phenomenon, it is especially marked in those destined to become conscientious personality types. The loving aspect of the relationship is ego-syntonic and hence easily acknowledged and consciously felt, but the hostile dimension poses a continuous threat, a fear that one may in an unguarded moment do harm to the person one loves. Therefore, hostile impulses must be kept out of consciousness and restrained from leading to actions.

The psychological operation most typical of the conscientious character involves deploying what is called reaction-formation. This is the defensive maneuver whereby the positive side of the object relation is strengthened by adding to it the affect belonging to the hostile dimension. Transformed into its opposite, the negative ideation accompanying the destructive impulse is denied access to consciousness, while its propulsive or motivational force is added to heighten the positive impulses. What is conscious, then, is not just love but an enhanced, positively militant or "aggressive" charitable or protective attitude that is overtly benevolent but is in reality partly fueled by the disguised aggression proper to the unconscious hostile wishes.

In spite of a commitment to do only the good and oppose the bad, however, conscientious people live with a fear that the destructive impulses may at any moment elude their own efforts to deny and control them. They also harbor a profound guilt, which may be more-or-less consciously felt, based on the unconscious knowledge that they indeed have the impulses they condemn consciously; furthermore, they are convinced they have acted on these impulses in the past.[12] There is sustained in unconscious memory from childhood a fantasy or set of fantasies in which aspects of reality are interwoven with wishes and fears deriving from hostile, sadistic impulses, together with dread of their consequences, to form an apparently "real" recollection of an event of a sexual, violent, and narcissistic nature. In most cases, the activities and impulses were real enough—indeed, so overpowering as to threaten the ego and thus result in their exclusion from consciousness. But the remembered acts are often exaggerations or fantasies, corresponding to what the child, in its rage, *would* have done had it possessed sufficient strength and skill to put its impulses and wishes into practice, or what, looking back, it retrospectively imagines it has done.[13]

While at first Freud believed that the original disavowed impulses were primarily sexual, he and his followers came to be impressed by the equally essential role of aggressive, destructive, and hostile impulses at work in the obsessional personality. Freud clarified the issue by proposing (in 1913a) that the impulses generating obsessional defenses and adaptations stem from the "pregenital" period of development. At this point in maturation, the child's ego is sufficiently developed for it to establish and maintain true object relations with others, who are recognized as independent of self. One loves others *as* others rather than simply as extensions of the narcissistic love of the self. But the precocity of ego development, common to humans as a species, and especially typical of those destined for the conscientious or obsessive style of personality organization, leads to the result that the ability to form object-ties coincides not with the attainment of genital organization in the sphere of sexual maturation but rather with the pregenital position. This form of sexual organization, not yet directly linked with an aim of genital union with the other, is built instead primarily on the anal-sadistic components of human sexuality. As a consequence, the first wishes directed at the object of one's love are not tender or genitally pleasurable but sadistic, that is, typified by wishes to perform acts that combine feelings of sexual pleasure with the infliction of harm, violence, or destruction on the love object, or with the subjecting of the loved one to mastery and domination. Other typical fantasies involve performing excretory functions with the loved one or combining these functions with the more typically "sexual" ones.[14]

Therefore, from the point of view of the mature ego, the remembered wishes one has harbored toward the person one loves are bound to seem dangerous, repulsive, and in general reprehensible, and are hence subjected to conscious disapproval and defended against. The usual pattern is for the person (I shall use a male example, since men are more typically associated with this form of personality; in addition, it is more relevant for my overall purposes) to experience castration dread at the height of the oedipal period of childhood and, when that dread is for one reason or another unacceptably anxiety-producing, to opt instead for a favoring of pregenital impulses. These may be experienced in active form, as sadistic wishes and disorderly conduct. More usually, it involves a defensive turning against the self and the disavowal of overtly sadistic impulses. These impulses are then projectively assigned to the love object, toward whom the person adopts an attitude of submission, masochism, and a wish to be the "passive" partner in a sexual or dominant-submissive relationship.[15]

Because with his ego the conscientious personality is horrified at his unconscious recognition of his own wishes and impulses, he devotes himself to the construction of a psychological defense system designed to prevent the possibility that his own unacceptably destructive wishes could eventuate in action. In his unconscious fantasy, he is already a guilty murderer and tyrant, who must forever subject himself to stringent controls and surveillance to ensure that he is never again free to give unbridled expression to his angry and sadomasochistic impulses.

In addition to reaction-formation, the principal defensive strategies of the conscientious or obsessional person are splitting, isolation, and doing and undoing. We have already examined splitting and seen numerous examples of it. It originates in the child's ambivalent relations to the breast and comes to the fore during the period of separation-individuation, especially the conflictual "rapprochement" phases, in which the opposed wishes to separate from and reunite with the mother result in decomposed images of both the self and the object as either good or bad.[16] The bad mother is the one from whom one flees and seeks liberation; the good mother is the one with whom one seeks to reunite. In the biblical narrative, we saw this beautifully illustrated in the attitude of the Israelites to the land of Egypt after the Exodus. It was at the same time the tyrannical land of bondage and domination from which they escaped and the land of security and succulent fleshpots to which they longed to return.

"Isolation" refers to a set of operations whereby, instead of repressing a disturbing wish or fantasy from consciousness altogether, as is done with the mechanism of repression proper, the ego achieves the goal of defusing a dangerous impulse by separating, or isolating, the thought from the affect, and attaching the strongly felt affect, by means of the mechanism of displacement, to some trivial or unthreatening arena. The original dangerous idea is retained in consciousness but robbed of its affect: its real significance is neither understood nor recognized. Not only are ideas detached from affects, but ideas are also isolated from each other, so that the implications of their overall pattern are deliberately not seen or grasped. Therefore connections between ideas are denied or broken and thoughts occur in fragments or details. While originally these defenses are instituted to dismantle the offending sadistic or hostile impulse or fantasy, because of the proneness of the conscientious person to resort to displacement the technique of isolation comes to be applied to thoughts in general. One common result is "intellectualization": in this defensive pattern, the conscientious person can contemplate otherwise dangerous or anxiety-provoking thoughts by robbing them of emotion and viewing them as abstract, depersonalized, formalized concepts. The connections to oneself are denied, and the thoughts are experienced as objective bits of external reality in which one has only an observer's interest. The pathological result of these defenses can be that the overly conscientious person denies himself the capacity to feel any emotions whatsoever, for fear that the especially forbidden and dangerous one might emerge, overwhelm the defenses, and reach consciousness or, worse yet, motor enactment.

The defense of doing and undoing expresses the two aspects of an ambivalent relationship by means of responding first to one side of it, then "undoing" that action with another, expressing the other side of the ambivalence. Acts that seek to reverse, make up for, or counterbalance previous actions fall into this category and may often take the form of rituals that express contrition or atonement.

Having given up responsibility for his own emotions and impulses—even his own thoughts—the conscientious or obsessional person feels himself beholden to some external arbiter who holds him to a high standard of moral behavior. This arbiter is in fact his own superego, but phenomenologically it is experienced as an abstract demand originating outside himself. It is manifested in a concern with generalized rules, schedules, instructions, standards, and boundaries. These are the defenses one has erected against the dangerous impulses but that have been projected into a highly intellectualized and abstract realm of principles, which are held to apply to everyone and exist in an apodictic, self-legitimating way.

Toward this external, abstract authority, with its rules, restrictions, and right ways of doing things, the ego adopts the position of the submissive and dominated one in an abstracted version of the relation of dominance and submission that characterizes the pregenital sadomasochistic mode of sexual organization. This submissive attitude, which one is forced to adopt out of fear of the castration attendant upon advancing to the oedipal position and becoming a "master" oneself, brings with it a precarious sense of security, but it also arouses renewed rage at and resentment and envy of the dominating authority. As a consequence, the typical psychological attitude of the conscientious person oscillates between fear of the authority, obedience, and increased conscientiousness in the performance of the defensive operations designed to prevent the expression of sadism and rage, on the one hand, and rageful rebellion against and defiance of that same authority, who originally forced one into the submissive position, on the other.

The latter attitude, which simply serves to express the hostile side of the ambivalence against which the vigilance and conscientiousness have been instituted, constantly reinforces the feeling of guilt and the consequent need for punishment. It reinforces fear of the impulses, which in turn leads to renewed dedication to the precautions and preventative measures that have been undertaken in defense.

Since conscious acknowledgement of responsibility for any of these operations is denied by the psychological operations to which I have alluded, mental life is felt as an attempt to maintain a calm, clear, objective and "rational" point of view as a well-meaning and sensible observer of external reality. This attempt, however, is subject to intrusive, disruptive thoughts and impulses, which are themselves counteracted by defensive operations. These, since they are habitual and drained of their intelligible ideational significance, appear as meaningless rituals and ceremonials or "superstitious" apotropaic operations and formulas.

V

With this picture of the conscientious personality and its obsessive-compulsive variants in mind, we can see how the commandments that, from Sinai on, constitute the bulk of the Torah text exemplify for the audience of intended executors instructions or models for the construction of defensive and adaptive devices and strategies typical of the person with conscientious or obsessional dynamics. I contend that, having "connected" affectively with such a person by reflecting to him his own oedipal conflicts and fantasies in a culturally valorized myth embodying the paradigmatic scenario of the primal horde and the primal patricide, the instructions in the text guide the person in socially appropriate ways in the deployment and management of the impulses, anxieties, and defenses or adaptations of his own, still-forming psyche.

I do not treat religion like a personality disorder or neurosis, nor do I claim that it inculcates defenses in a person that are essentially on the pathological or defensive end of the spectrum rather than on the normal, socially adaptive end. While this may be one result of involvement in religion, it is just as possible that the socially sanctioned, external, ritualized actualization of some of the defenses discussed here liberates the person from the necessity of having to deal with them on his own. The more pathological Obsessive-Compulsive Personality Disorder would thus be understood as the result of an attempt on the part of an individual to construct by himself and from scratch a set of psychic organizations that would otherwise have been dealt with for him by immersion in a community guided by the religious practices enjoined in the cultural myth, such as the one contained in the Torah. So while I shall often describe the more exaggerated and defensive end of the continuum, I do not think that people who follow these practices are thereby neurotic—quite the contrary. The exaggerations, however, allow us to perceive the operative dynamics all the more clearly and distinctly.[17]

We can begin with the obvious observation that the rules *are* rules: they are written in a book external to the individual and are experienced as having an objective reality, value, and authority. As David Shapiro writes, the obsessional personality type functions, to use Shapiro's very appropriate words, as "his own overseer" (1965, 34) and is constantly telling himself: "I should . . ." He "does not feel that he issues these directives wholly on his own authority and by his own free choice" (39). Rather, he feels he is prompted by some "compelling objective necessity, some imperative or higher authority than his personal choice or wish, which he is obliged to serve." When he acts as his own demanding overseer, it is not on his own behalf, as he perceives it, but rather is experienced as being "in response to the requirements of some objective necessity, particularly some moral necessity. He feels in the capacity of agent or representative to himself of that objective necessity or imperative" (39).

In Egypt, the Israelites are under the domination of real overseers, who compel obedience by force. Moses, as leader of the rebellion, kills the real "overseer," first in the episode with the Egyptian taskmaster, and then at the Red Sea. But, consistent with the dynamics we have observed, he follows the deed by installing in place of these tyrannical overseers a far greater one, with omniscient and omnipotent powers, who, being immortal and spiritual, can never be overthrown. This new authority issues moral demands for which Moses acts precisely as "agent or representative" to himself as well as to the people he now leads.

The feeling of being under a constant obligation to obey externally imposed rules, many of which appear pointless or picayune, is not necessarily experienced as a new submission to external domination, as was the case under the real overseer. On the contrary, the laying down of guidelines may be felt as profoundly liberating because it provides a means of escaping from the burden of guilt that results from having already rebelled (at least in fantasy). This it does by stating terms for forestalling the punishment from the vengeful senior male that would otherwise be certain to strike sooner or later.

In addition, there is a heightening of self-esteem and a sense of moral achievement, if not superiority, in laboring under and working hard at fulfilling some such obligation. Having rebelled against the father as persecuting superego, one derives a sense of security, as well as narcissistic self-satisfaction, in receiving from the positive ego ideal a set of clear expectations about how to return to a state of approval and love. As a list of externally imposed rules, the biblical commandments provide for the individual a ready-made set of guidelines matching the needs of his own internal psychodynamics.

Let us now look at the commandments themselves. We recall that for Freud, the two fundamental commandments at the root of civilization are the oedipal injunctions not to kill the father in his guise as the totemic animal, except under ritual circumstances, and the prohibition on incest. If we examine the text with this in mind, we discover, first, that a large part is given over to instructions for the ritual killing of animals. It is one of the most interesting dimensions of the Torah as a set of instructions that, in addition to giving rules for the conduct of social life for the community, it also prescribes methods for ritual practices in a temple that has not existed for close to two thousand years. The study of the Torah is thus the study of the instruction manual for a great many ritual practices that are never performed (though they once were, and there is of course always the hope that a day of restoration of the Temple may come about in a future age).

The first seven chapters of Leviticus are all concerned with the central act of temple worship, the sacrifice. With the exception of the grain sacrifice described in chapter 2, these sacrifices entail the ritual killing of an animal, usually as expiation for sin or guilt resulting from some failure to adhere to the Law. Much of the text of these chapters contains instructions for the actual slaughter and dismemberment of the animal in question, as for example, these rules for the "sacrifice of well-being" (that is, a peace offering):

> He shall lay his hand upon the head of his offering and slaughter it at the entrance of the Tent of Meeting; and Aaron's sons, the priests, shall dash the blood against all sides of the altar. He shall then present . . . the fat that covers the entrails and all the fat that is about the entrails; the two kidneys and the fat that is on them, that is at the loins; and the protuberance on the liver, which he shall remove from the kidneys. Aaron's sons shall turn these into smoke on the altar. (3:2–5)

Among the animals that can be slaughtered in some version of ritual sacrifice are lambs, goats, bulls, and (for the poor) pigeons and doves. Chapter 17 of Leviticus makes it plain that no sacrifice is to be performed except by priests at the gate of the Tabernacle, or Tent of Meeting. This means that even animals killed purely for food must be offered as sacrifices and killed by the priests authorized to do so: "If any man of the house of Israel slaughters an ox or sheep or goat in the camp, or does so outside the camp, and does not bring it to the entrance of the Tent of Meeting to present it as an offering to the Lord, . . . bloodguilt shall be imputed to that man: he has shed blood; that man shall be cut off from among his people" (vv. 3–4). While it is true that this passage seems to be contradicted in Deuteronomy 12, it nevertheless indicates the movement on the part of the sacrificing priests to arrogate to themselves the sole right to kill anything, and to specify the place, time, and manner of such killing.

Given that the central act of worship is sacrificial killing and that only priests may perform it in specially demarcated sacred spaces, it follows too that the laws about the dedication of the Tabernacle and the ordination of priests in Leviticus 8–10 are also, in an extended way, a set of instructions concerning the ritual performance of sacrifice.

We may also argue that the dietary laws, comprising chapter 11 of Leviticus, concern the killing of animals, since they specify what animals may be killed and eaten. The laws of *kashrut* handed down in Leviticus 11 mainly concern *killed* food. The restrictions and regulations thus bear indirectly but no less genuinely on the killing of animals. Since, as we have seen, Leviticus 17 forbids slaughtering animals for food except by priests in the Tabernacle, the dietary laws may be understood as pertaining to or encompassed by the sacrificial or ritual killing of animals.

For Freud, the primary injunction was that the primal father, represented by an animal, was *not* to be killed, but we must recognize the fact that this prohibition will appear as a compromise between both an impulse and the fear of its consequences. We have seen that defenses typical of the conscientious personality result from the struggle to control an impulse to express aggression. In any practice that serves as a model for a defense, one expects to find a compromise formation, in which both the impulse and the defenses against it are represented equally. Therefore, it is not surprising to find that a matter that figures at the heart of the practices described in the Torah involves the regulation and containment of the killing of animals.

The defensive side of the equation is represented in a number of ways. The first and perhaps most self-evident is that no animals have actually been killed in Jewish religious practice since the destruction of the Temple; rather, the "sacrifice" consists of the reading of a book which *describes* how to kill an animal. Instead of the affectively laden act of killing, there is an act marked by isolation and intellectualization, in which the careful study of a text about killing satisfies the demand for the expression of the aggressive impulse, while at the same time the affect is dissociated from the ritual act itself.

In the second place, the killing is not impulsive; on the contrary, it is set about with all manner of rules and restrictions. The focus of attention is on the observance of correct procedure, rather than on the violence that has thus been rendered less affectively charged and is thus in a sense "bound" by the ritual regulations encasing it. This would have been true even in the days of the Temple, when sacrifices were performed, since ritual sacrifice is still contained within a strict regime of regulation. When sacrifice ceased to be the focus of religious observance, this change introduced a second degree of isolation or distancing of the Torah texts concerning ritual killing from the actual destructive deed. Furthermore, the killing was all done in a setting that, being sacred, is set apart from everyday life. In the realm of the sacred, ritual specialists are delegated to enact on behalf of ordinary citizens acts of slaughter that are otherwise forbidden.

As Freud says, totemic religion, or that aspect of it in which patricide is symbolized by the killing of an animal representative of the father, is informed with the ambivalence typical of the personality configuration we are examining: "Totemic religion not only combined expressions of remorse and attempts at atonement, it also served as a remembrance of the triumph over the father. Satisfaction over that triumph led to the institution of the memorial festival of the totem meal, in which the restrictions of deferred obedience no longer held. Thus it became a duty to repeat the crime of parricide again and again in the sacrifice of the totem animal" (1913b, 145).

The sacrifice of the animal is viewed as an expiation for some sin, fault, or impurity: an atonement which "undoes" the guilt for the original crime. The animal, or its blood and the odor of its burning, is offered to God, who, as the apotheosis of the senior male, is mollified by the remorse shown for having killed him. But, as Freud writes, "The importance which is everywhere . . . ascribed to sacrifice lies in the fact that it offers satisfaction to the father for the outrage inflicted on him in the same act in which the deed is commemorated" (150). With this incisive stroke, Freud accounts for the highly dynamic aspect of religious practices, that is, for how they reproduce themselves over time with undiminished energy. The ritual practice assures that the acts undertaken to reduce guilt simultaneously serve the purpose of re-creating it and thus generate the need for a subsequent ritual, and so on. The killing of the animal, or even the reading about it, is both the atonement for and (at least in fantasy) the enactment of the deed itself, precisely in the manner of the ambivalent acts of doing and undoing typical of the conscientious personality type.

As regards the dietary laws, the analysis of Mary Douglas, according to which the forbidden animals are those that violate the categories of edible animals defined by certain typical exemplars—fish for the sea; goats, cows and sheep for land; and fowl for the air—has been criticized by some psychoanalytic thinkers as being too intellectual and as not giving enough credit to the underlying passions.[18] What this critique overlooks is that, in Douglas's analysis, as well as in the cogitations of the rabbis, the violence—and the aggressive impulses implicated in it—are transformed precisely by the typical obsessional operation of intellectualization. Turning a discussion of bloody slaughter into a list of forbidden and permitted animals, fit for endless debate over ritual minutiae, is a perfect example of an obsessional defense at work. The affect itself is displaced from the topic to which it is proper, namely the killing, and fuels instead the passion and rigor with which the rules and regulations are studied, debated, and enforced.

One might object, however, that while this may apply to the killing of animals, there is no reason to assert on the basis of the biblical text (rather than on the basis of Freudian theory) that the killing of animals in the Torah really does refer to the killing of the senior male in any human form. Yet as we have seen, all killing was drawn into the category of priestly sacrifice, and priestly sacrifice was assigned to a particular lineage, namely, those directly descended from Aaron, Moses's brother.

There is a myth that serves as a charter for the establishment of Aaron's line as the sole legitimate lineage of sacrificial priests, a fact that was actualized in history during the reign of King Solomon, who appointed the Aaronid priest Zadok and his descendants as proprietors of the Temple in Jerusalem. This myth occurs in chapter 25 of the book of Numbers. The Israelites, camped in Moab before crossing the Jordan and entering the promised land, fall into apostasy, seduced by Moabite women into the worship of their god, Baal Peor. In punishment, a plague sweeps through the

Israelite camp, in which 24,000 people perish. Moses appears powerless to stop the plague, but rescue is provided by Phinehas. Phinehas is the grandson of Aaron (who has died), the son of Aaron's son and heir as chief priest, Eleazar. Phinehas observes an Israelite man of the tribe of Simeon named Zimri and a Midianite woman named Cozbi go into a tent to have sexual intercourse. Phinehas follows them into the tent and runs his spear through the copulating couple. The plague is checked. Then the Lord says to Phinehas, " 'Phinehas, son of Eleazar son of Aaron the priest, has turned back My wrath from the Israelites by displaying among them his passion for Me, so that I did not wipe out the Israelite people in My passion. Say, therefore, "I grant him my pact of friendship. It shall be for him and his descendants after him a pact of priesthood for all time, because he took impassioned action for his God, thus making expiation for the Israelites" ' " (vv. 11–13).

We thus have warrant in the biblical text for asserting that the act of expiatory sacrifice performed by the hereditary Aaronid priests—who are established as hereditary priests by this act—is the sacrificial killing of a pair of humans in the "primal scene." We may therefore argue that the sacred nature of the Aaronid line, and their right to kill in a ritualized way, has to do precisely with an original "oedipal" murder, which the Aaronid priests are doomed or privileged to perform endlessly in simultaneous expiation and reenactment.

In addition, as I have demonstrated elsewhere (1994a), we should recall that the theologian Ernst Sellin, whose book helped motivate Freud to write *Moses and Monotheism,* interprets precisely this passage as a thinly disguised description of the killing of Moses. Arguing that Moses alone had a Midianite wife among the Israelites, and that only the sacrifice of a man of Moses's stature could have stemmed a plague of such vast proportions, Sellin proposes that "Zimri and Cozbi" are pseudonyms for Moses and Zipporah and that the deed for which Phinehas is so extravagantly praised and rewarded by God is nothing other than the sacrifice of Moses himself. If there were anything to this argument, it would ground the Aaronids' title to the communal service of expiatory sacrifice in a deeply "patricidal" act, since Moses is not only the leader and lawgiver of the Israelites but also the great-uncle of Phinehas.

Since there are also grounds in the commentaries and midrashim for suspecting that there was a tradition that Moses himself had sacrificed Aaron, Phinehas's act would make sense as just retribution, if Sellin's construction has any merit.[19]

But even without this particular argument, we are entitled to conclude that one of the great themes of the laws enunciated at Sinai is the killing of the sacrificial animal and that this deed can be understood as simultaneously expressing and atoning for a deed of homicidal violence, against the memory of which the typical conscientious defenses of reaction-formation, doing and undoing, isolation, and intellectualization have been deployed.

VI

As for the other dimension of the twofold oedipal prohibition—on killing (and eating) the sacrificial animal (except under ritual circumstances) and on incest—let us look at the first verses of the first biblical chapter addressing sexual offenses, Leviticus 18. The Lord speaks thus to Moses:

> None of you shall come near anyone of his own flesh to uncover nakedness: I am the Lord. Your father's nakedness, that is, the nakedness of your mother, you shall not uncover; she is your mother—you shall not uncover her nakedness. Do not uncover the nakedness of your father's wife; it is the nakedness of your father. The nakedness of your sister—your father's daughter or your mother's, whether born into the household or outside—do not uncover their nakedness. (vv. 6–9)

In the next verses (10–18), using similar language, the code prohibits the following relatives as potential sexual partners: the son's daughter, the daughter's daughter, the father's wife's daughter born into one's household, the father's sister, the mother's sister, the father's brother and his wife, the son's wife, and the brother's wife. Further, one may not have sex with both a mother and her daughter or with two sisters, as long as both are alive.

The text proceeds to prohibit sex during a woman's menstrual period, adultery with a neighbor's wife, child sacrifice, male homosexuality, and bestiality (vv. 19–23). Leviticus 20 essentially repeats this list, slightly rearranged, with punishments specified.

It should be mentioned that the "you" addressed by the Lord, speaking through Moses, in these verses is self-evidently a male. It is an unstated assumption that men are the sexual actors and controllers of sexual relations. Looking at the quotation from Leviticus 18:6–9 one can observe that these are exactly the rules which the newly victorious brothers in Freud's myth might be expected to give themselves, assigning to these instructions the authority of the now deified and omnipotent father. The women of the horde, the father's consorts, who in the day of the unregulated sexual life of the horde would have been the mothers, aunts, and sisters of the junior males, are now prohibited; primarily, so it is possible to gather, out of (deferred) respect for the father: "Your father's nakedness, *that is,* the nakedness of your mother you shall not uncover" (my emphasis).

We can conclude, then, that in this respect, too, the biblical commandments exemplify Freud's insight that after liberating themselves from the primal horde and its jealous tyrant, "the brothers had no alternative . . . but to institute the law against incest, by which they all renounced the women whom they desired and who had been the chief motive for despatching their father" (1913b, 144).

VII

It is not possible within the scope of this book to address all the laws and regulations in the Torah revealed at Sinai and thereafter. I have demonstrated that the text exhibits the characteristics one would expect from it according to the Freudian dynamics and mythology, but of course there is a great deal else in it too. The Torah is the written constitution of a nation and addresses itself directly or implicitly to the proper conduct of almost every facet of social life. I do believe, however, that the juxtaposition of ordinary rules for secular social life with ritual commandments deriving their meaning and power from the fantasies and psychodynamics I have been describing serves the purpose of imbuing the former with the affect and authority generated and shaped by the latter. In this way the observance of the most ordinary law of daily life possesses the same sense of sanctity, authority, compulsion, and anxiety about infraction that pertains to the awe-inspiring wishes, conflicts, and fears of the oedipal scenario in which they are embedded.

We may say, in other words, that the affect surrounding the central oedipal fantasy, despite the defensive efforts taken to isolate it, "seeps out" by displacement and pervades the rules and regulations designed to ward it off and contain it. The tendency to displacement of the erotic and aggressive impulses involved in the central fantasy is experienced by the conscientious or obsessive personality as a threat of contagion and impels the deployment of further efforts to isolate and make distinctions between things, so as to keep apart ideas that, by associative chains, might become pathways of further displacement. In the psychology of the obsessional or conscientious personality, one observes these features in a tendency to focus on details at the expense of seeing connections or larger wholes; a concern with categorization and clear boundaries and borders; an anxiety about disorder; and, on a more exaggerated level, obsessional and compulsive ideas about touching or cleanliness, in which wishes to express hostility and to soil are counteracted, through reaction-formation, by a great emphasis on avoiding contact with things or people, or an emphasis on avoiding dirt, defilement, or "contagious" things.

When we turn to the biblical text, we are struck by a number of related themes that illustrate the operation of adaptive and defensive maneuvers and postures typical of the conscientious personality. A surprisingly extensive segment of the book of Leviticus is given over to instructions regarding purity, defilement, the combating of pollution, and, especially, the treatment of contagious diseases. Beginning with chapter 11, verse 24, four-and-a-half chapters are devoted almost entirely to these subjects—more space than is granted, for example, to the creation of the world and the fall of the first humans.

The first part of Leviticus 11 deals with food taboos. As we have seen, it is an exercise in categorization and distinctions and an expression of horror at the mixture or violation of categories. The second half of this chapter concerns animals that have died, whose carcasses may not be touched for fear of defilement or impurity. The underlying psychodynamics of a fear of contagion and the entering of an impure state by touching a dead animal would seem to be this: to touch something dead, in unconscious fantasy, may be understood as an attenuated version of laying violent hands upon someone. Anything that recalls the act of killing, or any person or animal that, by its helplessness and vulnerability, tempts one to release violence against it, creates dangerous feelings precisely because the conscientious person struggles tirelessly to subdue and contain the impulse to violence.

Under the social contract of Judeo-Christian civilization, each person has agreed to suppress his aggressive impulses on the condition that everyone else does so too; as Freud explains the matter: "Anyone who has violated a taboo becomes taboo himself because he possesses the dangerous quality of tempting others to follow his example: why should *he* be allowed to do what is forbidden to others? Thus he is truly contagious in that every example encourages imitation, and for that reason he himself must be shunned" (1913b, 32).[20]

The same sort of explanation applies to subsequent passages. Leviticus 12 is concerned with defilement incurred by childbirth. Freud writes that special dangerous and uncanny powers are attributed to "*exceptional* states, such as the physical states of menstruation, puberty, or birth" (1913b, 22); and he explains that "dead men [or their animal representatives], new-born babies and women menstruating or in labour stimulate desires by their special helplessness. . . . For that reason all of these persons and all of these states are taboo, since temptation must be resisted" (33).

That the temptation that is aroused in each case of an unclean or defiling thing, person, or circumstance is, at base, a violent, sadistic, soiling impulse is demonstrated by the ritual measures taken to purify a person who has been defiled. A woman who has given birth, for example, ends her unclean time after delivery when a priest offers on her behalf a sacrifice at the entrance to the Tabernacle: a year-old lamb for a burnt offering and pigeon or dove for a sin offering. The blood of the sacrificial victim "expiates" the mother and cleanses her of her own flow of blood at delivery, similar to that of menstruation. The killing that the person in a vulnerable state seems to invite, in being disavowed by the sense of taboo danger, is expressed in a manner sufficiently distanced from the offending person and hedged about with ritual precautions, in the bloody measures taken to "undo" the original temptation.

Leviticus 13 deals at great length with the procedures for treating people with skin afflictions. After a priest ascertains that the disease, sore or eruption or scaly rash, is an impurity and not the result of some "clean" circumstance, he "shall isolate the person for seven days" (v. 21). If it is determined that the diseased man is leprous, "his clothes shall be rent, his hair shall be left bare, and he shall cover over his upper lip; and he shall call out 'Unclean! Unclean!' . . . Being unclean, he shall dwell apart; his dwelling shall be outside the camp" (vv. 45–46).

Without doubt, the impulse to isolate a contagious person is sound from the point of view of public health. But contagion itself has a deeper, unconscious psychological meaning that these passages also express. As in the case of childbirth, the treatment for a contagious condition is an animal sacrifice, after which the priest daubs sacrificial blood on the right ear, right thumb, and right big toe of the affected person. Unclean houses, too, are cleansed by a ritual sacrifice.

Finally, a special chapter, Leviticus 15, is devoted to the uncleanness that results from unusual discharges of the sexual organs, as well as menstruation. Here it seems clearer that sexual as well as aggressive impulses are being addressed. But of course in the oedipal scenario expressed in the myth of the primal horde, the two are co-implicated and can never be separated: the motivation for the bloody deed is sexual jealousy, and the result of sexual desire is deadly competition with a rival or rivals.

VIII

In *Totem and Taboo,* Freud argues that the socially imposed taboos sanctioned by various religious beliefs display dynamics similar to the prohibitions and precautions ritualized in apparently meaningless ceremonials by obsessional neurotics (and, as I would add, in attenuated and more ego-syntonic forms, in persons with a normal conscientious personality). He summarizes the results of his comparison of the two phenomena thus: "Taboo is primaeval prohibition forcibly imposed (by some authority) from outside, and directed against the most powerful longings to which human beings are subject. The desire to violate it persists in their unconscious; those who obey the taboo have an ambivalent attitude to what the taboo prohibits" (1913b, 35).

The Israelites, despite the direct warnings from God about what is in store for them if they fail to abide by his commandments, as well as promises of the good fortune they will enjoy if they obey, are depicted throughout their sojourn in the wilderness as subject to doubt, grumbling, quarreling, rebellion, and backsliding. This unpleasantness makes up the bulk of the narrative in the book of Numbers. Emblematic of all these rebellions, however, is the story of the Golden Calf in Exodus 32.

The apostasy of the Golden Calf is a good example of a representation by splitting of the ambivalence underlying the self-imposition of taboos and prohibitions. Even as Moses is atop the mountain receiving the Law amid awe-inspiring theatrical effects, his brother and double is at the foot of the mountain leading the Israelites in the enactment of some of the crimes being prohibited above: the Israelites are dancing boisterously before an image made of gold and naming it the god who led them out of Egypt.

Moses is so angry when he sees what has happened that he grinds the Golden Calf to dust, pours it in the water, and makes the Israelites drink it. This procedure is similar to the method for testing and punishing an adulterous wife, described in Numbers 5:11–31. The analogy of Israel in its stiff-necked doubting, disobeying, and rebellion with an unfaithful wife or with sexual misbehavior pervades the Hebrew Bible. The apostasy at Baal Peor, described in Numbers 25, which may be read as a doubling or continuation of the Golden Calf story, specifically equates the worship of Moabite gods with the "harlotry" with the Moabite women.

God thus acts toward the Israelites in the manner of the jealous sire of the horde, insisting on complete loyalty as both master and symbolic husband. He is so angry about the Golden Calf that Moses with difficulty prevents him from annihilating the Israelites, by pointing out, first, that their destruction would give satisfaction to the Egyptians (or what is left of them), and second, their death would break God's promise to Abraham to multiply his descendants like the stars in the sky. Moses also offers himself as a sacrifice on behalf of the Israelites (Exod. 32:32). Without accepting Moses's offer, God in his rage sends an angel to lead the Israelites forward, rather than leading them himself, as has been his custom, out of fear of what he might do to the Israelites were they still in his sight: "The Lord said to Moses, 'Say to the Israelite people, "you are a stiff-necked people. If I were to go in your midst for one moment, I would destroy you. Now, then, leave off your finery, and I will consider what to do to you." ' " (33:5). In this passage, God himself is depicted as having obsessional psychodynamics: he is frightened of the destructive effects of his own anger, and, placing a defensive inhibition on himself, he withdraws to ruminate.

When the Israelites express the rebellious, defiant aspect of the ambivalent relationship to the senior male, they are confronted with the sire of the primal horde: jealous, tyrannical, and prone to outbursts in which he threatens destruction for disloyalty. When they are cooperative and obedient—when they fear God—they are guided by a benevolent Providence toward a longed-for land of milk and honey.

IX

There is a great deal more one could point to by way of exemplification of the cognitive and psychodynamic style of the conscientious or obsessional personality in the text of the Torah: the fascination with lists, the repetitive and often circuitous prose, the intermixture of matters of supreme importance with trivia and nonsequiturs, and the focus on such details as measurements or time, often to the detriment of the larger picture. Nahum

Sarna, for example, remarks that "notwithstanding the wealth of particulars recorded in the Torah, the Tabernacle cannot with confidence be reconstructed solely on the basis of the biblical data" (1987, 191). Recall David Shapiro's characterization of the typical cognitive style of the conscientious personality, in which he refers to such a person's "preoccupation with technical detail, and his missing the flavor and impact of things" (1965, 49–50). The same considerations apply to the "numbers" from which the fourth book of the Torah takes its (English) name. Gunther Plaut's commentary echoes that of Sarna: "Despite the detailed descriptions given, we are not entirely sure how the tribes were grouped" (1983, 2:3). What we find, in other words, is a situation in which precision and detail are employed apparently in the service of exact description. But at the same time care is taken to make sure that necessary pieces of information are missing so that no conclusion can be reached.

"Numbers," that is, counting in general, is also characteristic of the obsessional personality. As Freud explains about this and other dry, technical, and formulaic cognitive procedures, counting is a favorite pastime of the obsessive or conscientious person. Counting is originally employed defensively, being as "unemotional" a thought as can be imagined, and it is made the center of consciousness to keep out the unwanted obsessional thoughts that would arouse anxiety because of their derivation from impulses perceived as dangerous.[21] Having done this duty, counting and other such operations become "ritualized," in the sense that they take over the affect and compulsory quality of the ideas they were designed to ward off. Because they now have the significance of the original dangerous thoughts, they can no more be made to "add up" than could the original dangerous thoughts be allowed to emerge in fully coherent form.[22]

X

I think I have sufficiently indicated in what ways the Torah text as a document reveals the workings of typically obsessional strategies for dynamic conflict resolution. In conclusion, let me return briefly to its narrative line.

Moses, having led a rebellion of the subject people against their tyrant, has become the leader of the Israelites, who are on their own in the wilderness. He governs, however, not on the basis of his own narcissistic interest, like the original primal father, but on behalf of a supreme deity, who, using Moses as prophet and obedient servant, makes known a set of universal laws and commandments establishing the foundations for an ongoing social and moral life. The new leader is thus not a senior male in the sense of the term as it derives from the paradigm of the primal horde, which has now been overthrown. Moses is, rather, akin to a senior male to his followers but the junior male to the now deified senior male, whose ambivalent attributes of wrathful jealousy and protective love have been elevated to cosmic principles.

While most of Deuteronomy contains laws, commandments, prohibitions, and exhortations, the final chapters conclude the story of the life of the great culture hero of the myth. In chapter 31, Moses announces to the people that he is 120 years old and about to die. He reminds them that the Lord has told him that he will not himself be permitted to cross the Jordan, and he anoints his aide, Joshua, as his successor, to lead the invasion of Canaan. Moses commands the priests to put his teaching (*torah*) into writing and to make sure it is read regularly to successive generations, who will not themselves have had the experiences described in the book. Chapters 32 and 33 are known, respectively, as the Song of Moses and the Blessing of Moses; in them Moses addresses the Israelites as their supreme prophet for the last time.

In the Song of Moses, Moses thunders against the Israelites for their stiff-necked opposition to God.

> The Rock!—His deeds are perfect
> Yea, all His ways are just;
> A Faithful God, never false,
> True and upright is He.
> Children unworthy of Him,
> That crooked and twisted generation—
> Their baseness has played Him false.
> Do you thus requite the Lord,
> O dull and witless people?
> Is not He the Father who created you,
> Fashioned you and made you endure! (Deut. 32:4–6)

Moses depicts God throughout the song in a warlike mode, as vengeful and destructive; his foes are those who oppose Israel, but they can include the Israelites themselves should they forget him. (One may also read in this passage a veiled description of the primal crime.)

If the Song of Moses emphasizes the wrathful and punitive side of the

Deity, the Blessing of Moses stresses his promise to the children of Israel to stand by them. Here, Moses foretells the fate of each of the twelve tribes. The text seems incomplete, but it does stress the continuity of the people of Israel despite the "hiding" of God's protection that they will shortly incur because of their sinful ways.

Finally, in Deuteronomy 34, we learn how Moses ascends Mount Nebo and Mount Pisgah, where God shows him the whole land of Canaan, saying, "I have let you see it with your own eyes, but you shall not cross there" (v. 4). Moses dies in the land of Moab, and Joshua assumes command of the Israelites.

In telling Moses of his impending death, God reminds him: "You shall die on the mountain you are about to ascend, and shall be gathered to your kin . . . ; for you broke faith with Me among the Israelite people, at the waters of Meribath-kadesh in the wilderness of Zin, by failing to uphold My sanctity among the Israelite people. You may view the land from a distance, but you shall not enter it—the land that I am giving to the Israelite people" (Deut. 32:50–52).

If, as I have argued, the promised land across the Jordan represents the woman/mother, in order to be (re)united with whom Moses and the brothers have rebelled, then clearly God is now playing the role of the idealized and deified primal father to whom Moses owes deferred obedience: he allows Moses to look at, but not touch or enter, the object of his desire and of all his striving.

Commentators have long been bothered, as I have mentioned, by the apparent insignificance of the infraction for which Moses is made to suffer his cruel frustration. Some have suggested that there is a missing passage describing a greater offense at Meribah for which Moses suffers; others, that perhaps Moses is being punished for killing the Egyptian overseer. Moses himself seems to accept God's fury as a burden he assumes on behalf of the refractory Israelite people; he sees himself as a martyr or a sacrifice who absorbs God's wrath to permit the Israelites to cross the Jordan despite their disloyal grumblings, murmurings, and rebellions (see Deuteronomy 3:26 and 4:21).

Earlier, I proposed that the episode at Meribah symbolized an inappropriate outburst of sadistic rage at the withholding breast on the part of Moses. I would like to expand on that idea. The crime of Moses at the waters of Meribah is a substitute, by associative displacement, for the heroic deed/crime Moses committed at the Red Sea when he overthrew Egypt and killed his father, the persecuting senior male/Pharaoh. At Meribah, remember, God instructs Moses (and Aaron) to *order* the rock to yield water; instead, "Moses took the rod from before the Lord, as He had commanded him . . . and he said to [the congregation,] 'Listen, you rebels, shall we get water for you out of this rock?' And Moses raised his hand and struck the rock twice with his rod. Out came copious water" (Num. 20:9–11).

There is an undeniable parallel between this and the episode at the Red Sea. The Israelites, encamped by the sea, are frightened at the sight of the advancing pharaoh. But Moses tells them to trust in God. "Then the Lord said to Moses, 'Why do you cry out to me? Tell the Israelites to go forward. And you lift up your rod and hold out your arm over the sea and split it, so that the Israelites may march into the sea on dry ground' " (Exod. 14:15–16). In both instances, the senior party impatiently accuses the junior party of being rebellious or unfaithful; in both the rod is used, and a miracle occurs involving water. At Meribah, Moses strikes twice, and water appears where there was dry rock; at the Red Sea, Moses raises his rod, and the water splits in two to produce dry ground.

To carry the thought further, the idea of "two" in connection with water could refer to breasts, which are the underlying unconscious fantasy referent in both instances, especially at Meribah, as we have seen. Because Moses has angrily struck and prematurely demanded the nurturing maternal breasts, he will not be allowed to enter the land flowing with milk and honey by his vengeful father's prohibition.

There is, too, a thematic associative chain, well recognized in the commentaries and folklore, that stresses the theme of water in Moses's career: he is thrown in the river to die, he is rescued from the water, he overcomes the Egyptians by water, he dies by the water of Meribah, and he is prevented from doing what Joshua does—that is, crossing the waters of the Jordan into the promised land. And at that crossing, once again, the waters stop flowing and the Israelites cross on dry ground (Josh. 3).[23]

I have argued that in the biblical narrative, preoedipal fantasies are regularly transmuted into oedipal ones, with the father playing the role of the bad mother while the woman retains the characteristics of the good mother, but changed from an object of oral desire to one of phallic desire. We have already seen that a midrash ascribes the Egyptians' plunging into the sea to an illusory pursuit motivated by unbridled lust. I think it is plausible to speculate that the image of Moses raising his rod and striking the rock, or dividing the sea, can be understood to refer to intercourse with a woman, probably with a specifically maternal connotation. The cleaving of the Red Sea would thus be a symbolic oedipal triumph not only because father is killed but also because of the imaginary phallic mastery of the mother.

It seems possible to conclude that when he is a junior male, Moses's idealized father/God says to him, "You will not be senior male and attain the woman of your desires unless you kill your father." But at Meribah and the Red Sea, God, now that Moses is on the verge of becoming a senior male himself, seems to say, "No one who kills his father (and violates his mother) will be allowed to have possession of the woman of his desires." The very insolubility of this conflict between the generations of males after the downfall of the primal horde has provided the dynamism propelling our cultural tradition with never-decreasing force across the generations.

That this paradox is at the heart of the Jewish (and therefore the Western) tradition is recognized in the performance of worship, where two Torah portions are singled out for special respect. Normally the congregation sits while the Torah is being read in the synagogue, but on two occasions, as I have mentioned, the people stand: at the reading of the Song at the Sea and at the reading of the Ten Commandments.

This tradition tells Jews: "Because of your triumphant deed at the Red Sea, you must now forever be blessed/burdened with these laws, restrictions, and commandments; these commandments will be imposed upon you with ineluctable force and authority precisely because of your triumphant but guilty deed at the sea." Or: "Because you killed your father, your father will forever after demand obedience to his requirements; you must obey your father because, after all, you are guilty of having killed him."

9

The Living Myth

I

Freud's attempts at historical reconstruction in *Totem and Taboo* and *Moses and Monotheism* were not exercises in antiquarian curiosity but efforts to explain contemporary religious phenomena. How has it been possible for contemporary Judeo-Christian religious practice, and the civilization that has been in large measure organized around it for close to two millennia, to obtain its force, its persuasiveness, its compulsion, and its felt conviction? For Freud, the mere teaching or conscious inculcation of a doctrine could not produce the degree of unquestioning commitment and loyalty that religious ideas—on the face of it, many of them patently implausible—seem to command.

If Freud believed that ordinary instruction or traditional transmission could not account for the persistence and force of religious practice, that conviction rests on his faith in the power of reason, judgment, and the conscious critical faculties to arrive at rational, moderate, balanced, and realistic positions. Therefore, "A tradition that was based only on communication would not lead to the compulsive character that attaches to religious phenomena. It would be listened to, judged, and perhaps dismissed, like any other piece of information from outside; it would never gain the privilege of being liberated from the constraint of logical thought" (1939, 101).

By the time he wrote this passage in *Moses and Monotheism*, Freud had come to believe that the memory of a traumatic event in earlier history could be preserved in the unconscious collective mind and transmitted across generations without necessarily being actualized in individual experience. In this way, he explained the compulsory force of religious ideas on the model of neurotic symptoms, which likewise exhibit tremendous persistence and a compulsory quality impervious to conscious reasoning, judging, or willing. Since neurotic symptoms are given this power by an unconscious traumatic memory or fantasy that is preserved, also unconsciously, in the psyche of the individual, an analogous process on the collective, historical level would account for the persistent and tenacious qualities of religious beliefs and practices.[1]

But if we reject Freud's idea about the transmission of unconscious memories and the affects associated with them by phylogenetic inheritance, how can we account for the persistence of a tradition? My analysis here requires, after all, that the mythic paradigm of the primal horde not only be transmitted across generations but that it maintain its power to generate the unconscious guilt that leads to the re-creation of the motivational investment in the mythological system in successive generations of individuals.

I demonstrated in the previous chapter how the Torah text exemplifies an obsessional style of thought. I argued that this constellation of character traits is composed of defenses against unconscious guilt associated with an unconscious fantasy of having committed a violent and erotically motivated crime for which the merited retribution would be death or castration. This crime, I proposed, is the oedipal murder of Pharaoh by Moses. But if the guilt that drives the obsessional or conscientious personality organization of present-day actors is not a reaction to an inherited memory of a historical event, as Freud supposed, then how can that guilt be reproduced?

My answer to this question is that it arises from the intersection of two phenomena. One is the unconscious guilt that individuals feel, regardless of cultural setting, for fantasies of a broadly oedipal nature: fantasies involving some interplay of feelings of passionate attachment, jealousy, sexual excitement, murderous rage, and dread of punishment. The other is immersion in a sociocultural system organized around a shared and valorized myth that by its particular symbolism is able to arouse, address, and organize in a culture- and ego-syntonic way the individual's own powerful but inchoate fantasies, molding them into a personality suited to abide by the rules and conventions governing the social system.

I wish now to explore how unconscious guilt about an unconscious fantasy is communicated across generations—indeed, is re-created in new generations with undiminished intensity. Freud's considerations about the power of critical reasoning require us to suppose that both the fantasy and the greater part of the guilt remain unconscious. Otherwise, neither would have the compulsory force they exhibit. My task here is to show by what means a dominant cultural symbol—the Torah—is able to produce this effect, instilling a fantasy and a sense of guilt about it that is motivationally powerful yet unconscious.[2]

II

Twenty-five years before he wrote *Moses and Monotheism* Freud, without resorting to the Lamarckism, or "inheritance of acquired characteristics," so often mistakenly associated with his myth, proposed a solution in *Totem and Taboo* to the question of how an unconscious memory could be carried across generations, undiminished in power and unscathed by conscious reflection and criticism. In *Totem and Taboo*, contrary to prevailing opinion, Freud devotes to the idea of the phylogenetic inheritance of acquired characteristics only this single, qualified sentence: "A part of the problem [of cultural transmission] seems to be met by the inheritance of psychical dispositions which, however, need to be given some sort of impetus in the life of the individual before they can be roused into actual operation" (1913b, 158). This statement seems to me eminently reasonable, and it is certainly no cry for a commitment to the theory of the inheritance of acquired characteristics. At the most, Freud here suggests that inherited "dispositions" (*dispositionen* in German) contribute only *part* of a solution to the puzzle of the psychological continuity of successive generations.

But in the next few sentences, Freud offers a highly satisfactory solution to his own dilemma. This passage deserves to be quoted at length:

> Even the most ruthless suppression [of a traumatic memory] must leave room for distorted surrogate impulses and for reactions resulting from them. If so, however, we may safely assume that no generation is able to conceal any of its more important mental processes from its successor. For psycho-analysis has shown us that everyone possesses in his unconscious mental activity an apparatus which enables him to interpret other people's reactions, that is, to undo the distortions which other people have imposed on the expression of their feelings. An unconscious understanding such as this of all the *customs, ceremonies and dogmas left behind by the original relation to the father* may have made it possible for later generations to take over their heritage of emotion. (1913b, 159, my emphasis)

For Freud, then, the memory of the hypothesized killing of the primal father, and the anxieties and defenses associated with it, are instilled anew in each generation of individuals by means of religious myths, rituals, and practices. The customs, ceremonies, and dogmas that are a distorted re-representation of the original memory or fantasy, defensively transformed and translated into primary-process symbolic imagery, can be unconsciously deciphered by new generations of participants in their parents' practices and thus acquired by them as well without the intervention of any conscious critical judgment.

What this theory tells us is that the supposed "memory" can be thought of as being actually *produced in individuals* by participation in the ceremonies and customs that express the dogmas of the mythic system. Therefore, the question of whether the "memory" is actually the recollection in the present of some original event in the past is moot: it might be, but on the other hand, it might not. All that is required, for our purposes, in understanding how religious traditions are reproduced in undiluted force in succeeding generations of cultural actors, is that the new generation possess the unconscious "apparatus" (whatever it might be) that allows its members to decode the customs, ceremonials, and dogmas to which they are exposed and in which they participate during the formative years of their enculturation. It is important, then, that these decoded meanings correspond not to a historical event, the reality of which cannot be established independent of the "memory" of it created in the rituals themselves, but rather to a predisposition to find a "fit" between one's personal unconscious experience and fantasy and the public "memory," or fantasy/myth/story, being communicated.[3]

To put the case concretely: Freud's intellectual accomplishment involved his becoming conscious of the operations of the unconscious apparatus we all possess that can undo the symbolic encoding and defensive distortions the psyche imposes on its productions. It was precisely thus that, on the basis of the Christian myth, he "reconstructed" the underlying myth of the primal horde, undoing the distortions in the symbolism of the Passion myth and the ritual of the Mass. But if Freud could do that, it seems probable that everyone else can too, albeit perhaps unconsciously. The implication is that anyone could (and would) perceive the same pattern Freud did underlying the rituals and symbols of religion in their "disguised" form. Freud's generation of the myth of the primal horde from the Christian myth means, in other words, not that the primal horde existed but that the "memory" (fantasy) of it can be, and, indeed, is, created in the present by virtue of the unconscious undoing of distortions performed unconsciously by participants in present religious life.

My aim here is to show that when Freud reconstructed the primal crime he produced an accurate description of the myth that, as we know, is the fundamental master narrative in the Western Judeo-Christian tradition. This fact raises his proposal from an unlikely conjecture to a profound, coherent interpretive construction.

The predisposition to understand cultural myths, rituals, and symbols unconsciously must have a genetic component, including some innate capacity that corresponds to Freud's proposed apparatus for undoing defensive distortion. That humans have such a capacity seems to me certain, and no more theoretically problematic than that they also possess a genetically inherited Chomskian language-acquisition device that enables them to incorporate the language of their milieu.

More important in the context of this book, the "memory" produced by participating in the appropriate religious practices must seem convincing by virtue of its correspondence to fantasies, as well as to conflicts, impulses, anxieties, and defenses, generated by the interaction of an infant human with its nurturing environment. Such fantasies, impulses, anxieties, and defenses certainly include oedipal ones. The specific constellation of oedipal fantasies adopted by a particular individual will be the result of the interaction of his or her genetic endowment and his or her early life experiences with the core mythic ideas to which the child is exposed through his or her parents, by way of the customs, ceremonies, and dogmas in which the parents themselves are actively and meaningfully involved.

In this way of understanding Freud, we see that the performance of religious practices creates, *in the present,* that sense of reality beyond any rational conviction with which a myth is experienced. Whether the events it purports to commemorate actually took place, the unconscious fantasy is evoked in the present *by the participant,* for whom it really does correspond to his or her experienced and recorded unconscious memories, fantasies, impulses, anxieties, and defenses. The myth gives shape to the individual fantasy, while the psychological energy of individuals is transformed through ritual symbolism into the fuel that animates the cultural symbol system.[4]

III

Freud's thinking about this matter leads us, unexpectedly but certainly, to the insights of his contemporary, Emile Durkheim. From a sociological perspective, Durkheim reasons that a religious idea could not have the efficacy and strength, the sheer ability to lift people above themselves, that it manifestly has, were it simply an abstract idea: "It is not enough that we think of them [religious ideas and objects]; it is also indispensable that we place ourselves within their sphere of action, and that we set ourselves where we may best feel their influence; in a word, it is necessary that we act, and repeat the acts thus necessary every time we feel the need for renewing their effects" (1915, 464).

The "sphere of action" of religious ideas and objects, where we may best feel their influence, is in the "cult," that is, the communal setting in which the public and collective symbols of religion are the focus of repetitive, ritualized action: "The cult is not simply a system of signs by which the faith is outwardly translated; it is a collection of the means by which this is created and recreated periodically" (1915, 464).

Those ideas that become the focus of such a cult are the chartering myths and principles informing the organization of the society itself: "For a society is not made up merely of the mass of individuals who compose it, the ground which they occupy, the things which they use and the movements they perform, but above all it is the idea which it forms of itself" (1915, 470). But this founding idea is not like a philosophical idea, which can be contemplated privately. This idea must evoke commitment and faith, and this faith can come only from a source that truly is, as religions proclaim, greater than and outside of the self and beyond the self's meager capacities. But how can an individual surpass her- or himself by his or her own forces? "The only source of life at which we can morally reanimate ourselves is that formed by the society of our fellow beings; the only moral forces with which we can sustain and increase our own are those which we get from others" (473). In a word, religious ideas take on efficacy, reality, and moral force when they are enacted and performed in the life of a cult formed by many people participating simultaneously in a life centered around shared symbols, objects, and ideas.

(The word *cult* in contemporary English has a number of connotations that are inappropriate and distracting in the present context; and Durkheim's use of *church* is also incongruous in a discussion of Judaic religious practice. I shall therefore use the ungainly term *cultus,* which at least has enough unfamiliarity to allow it to mean what I want it to mean: that is, the organized social groups and processes in a community that center around performed religious rites and symbols.)

The insights of Freud and Durkheim on the source of the "aura of utter actuality" that infuses religious ideas and feelings is elaborated by Clifford Geertz, for whom it is precisely this sense of the really real "upon which the religious perspective rests and which the symbolic activities of religion as a cultural system are devoted to producing, intensifying, and so far as possible, rendering inviolable by the discordant revelations of secular experience" (1973, 112). How is this trick accomplished? Geertz's answer, like those of Gregory Bateson, Roy Rappaport, Victor Turner, and many others, is ritual: "For it is in ritual . . . that this conviction that religious conceptions are veridical and that religious directives are sound is somehow generated."[5] The operative word here is, of course, *somehow.* For Geertz, borrowing a page from Milton Singer (1958), it is in "cultural performances," concrete religious ceremonies and rituals, that the characters of myth come to life, are experienced not as representations but as presences: "The acceptance of authority that underlies the religious perspective that the ritual embodies thus flows from the enactment of the ritual itself" (118).

If we wish to understand how Torah, its myth, and its commandments come to attain supreme authority for religious actors, then, we must look at its life as the focus of a cultus in the Durkheimian sense. For it is only here that the theoretical connection between individual fantasy and public symbolism becomes actualized, and participants feel the force of the religious conceptions and directives as something greater and more "moral" than themselves.

IV

The Torah commands us to keep the Sabbath, and by means of the Sabbath, the Torah comes out of its self-contained state and enters life in society. The prohibition on all profane activity means that the Sabbath can be and is a day on which the religious community, or cultus, regularly convenes. And the central liturgical act of this assembled congregation is the reading aloud of the Torah. As the exilic tradition developed, the Torah was subdivided into fifty-four portions, or *sidrot,* some of which may be combined so as to fit the particular calendrical requirements of a particular year.

Each portion is then read in weekly installments; over the course of a year, on the Sabbaths other than holidays (as well as in additional readings during the week), the entire Torah will have been read from beginning to end.

(As with my approach to the text of the Bible, my interpretation of Judaic religious practice is not a historical one, and I do not address the question of the origins and development of the written works. I am concerned with those elements that came to characterize Judaism both as it developed in the Western world as a reasonably consistent, persisting cultural institution and as we find it now. Thus, for example, when I discuss the annual cycle of Torah reading, I am speaking of modern practice, derived from the Babylonian tradition, and not of the ancient Palestinian tradition, in which the cycle took three years.)

The Five Books of Moses constitute the text of the Torah: I can thus assert that this part of the biblical text alone forms the basis of the life of the cultus as its grounding myth. Thus, for example, while there are historical and literary reasons for including the book of Joshua with the first five books in what is known as the Hexateuch (Six books), this grouping has no meaning in terms of the lived, experienced, or performed communal cultus. Only the story of Moses, told and retold in the Torah readings, is performed from beginning to end every year; it alone has central status. The laws contained in the Torah form the foundation of social life, and the narrative in which they are embedded constitutes an enacted, living myth constantly and repetitively experienced publicly in the present moment.

In his fine study of Jewish memory entitled *Zakhor* (1982), Yosef Yerushalmi emphasizes how until the eighteenth century—and then only under the influence of European Enlightenment ideas—Jewish thought and commentary consistently ignored contemporary affairs or post-exilic history as topics worthy of scholarly attention. "Memory," so central in Jewish self-identity, is exclusively the memory of the founding events—ultimately, those two defining moments, the creation of the world and the Exodus from Egypt. While the rest of the Bible contains much that is history as such, what is most centrally kept alive and constantly relived through ritual performance is the foundational mythic narrative.

There is a second yearly ceremonial cycle that depends not on the regular weekly Sabbaths but on the calendar of special festivals, holidays, and rituals. These festivals constitute an additional arena for the re-creation of the foundational myth in the social life of the cultus. Each is distinguished by its own symbols, traditions, and affective tone. It is beyond the scope of this book for me to examine these in ethnographic detail, especially since local traditions of observance vary widely throughout the Jewish world. Here, I shall look at the role of some of the central, constant features of the major festivals in the construction and enactment of the master narrative as a living social and individual experience.

Of course, Jews explicitly remember through retelling the story of the Exodus at Passover. Although in the days of the Temple, Passover was one of the great communal pilgrimage festivals in which public sacrifices were performed by the priests, under the conditions of exile the celebration of Passover has been entrusted to individual families. The seder is traditionally led by the father in each household, and in the ritual itself the ambivalent father-son relationship is emphasized. The importance of this fact is that here the cultural myth is brought into direct contact with the family, with its inner dynamics, and with the individual fantasies of its members—especially the junior males—about one another. In the closed arena of the household at the suspended time created ritually at Passover, there is, in effect, no Torah and no society beyond the family. Each family temporarily reexperiences itself as the primal horde. The ritual techniques that set off the Passover season from the rest of the year could be understood to demarcate and protect this period as a reconnection with the mythic era. The extraordinary purity one is required to establish during this period would signify that in the days before the Law, humans were living in a state of innocence, without the guilt upon which present society is grounded. (The very concepts of guilt, sin, and impurity, as I have shown, come after the primal rebellion.)

Each adult male is enjoined to pass on to his sons the memory of the primal deeds, and all present are required to experience the events as if they themselves had been there. And in a very real sense they *are* there. For, as Ruth Gruber Fredman writes in her excellent anthropological account of Passover, "The sequence of the Haggadah, as it shifts its focus from past to present to future, mirrors the historical progression, but the symbolic identifications turn history into myth at each stage. The result is that those at the seder sit in an eternal present, a moment in history whose meaning has been predefined by the Exodus" (1981, 113).[6] At the same time, participants are "there" because the myth itself is a symbolic analogue of the oedipal dynamics of the family now gathered and focused upon itself, with the father cast as the leader who seeks to induct his sons into the society of brothers that was founded on the basis of the original rebellious deed being recounted.

The ritual explicitly enacts continuity between the male generations and has a positive tone; but this is possible because the negative sides of the inevitable ambivalence are present in symbolically disguised form. The story being enacted has, as its two major incidents, the killing of first-born sons (of the Egyptians) by a father (God) and the killing of a father (Pharaoh) by his son (Moses). By means of the myth being reenacted, the hostile dimensions of the father-son relationship are evoked and given a symbolic, culture-syntonic form that can then serve as the basis for the integration of each family and its members into the society of allied households that are joined by the prohibition on incest and the practice of marriage exchange.

In this ritual, which aims at instructing the junior generation and socializing them into a state of civilization, it is traditional to distinguish four kinds of sons. These are the wise son, who can be told everything and be initiated into the circle of the scholarly elite controlling the essential mythic knowledge; the obedient son, who is not necessarily interested in the scholarly details but who commits himself to executing the prescribed practices of the religion; the wicked son, who distances himself from the proceedings, denying that they have anything to do with him; and the young son, who is not yet able to understand.

I suggest that it is possible to merge the first two as representatives— at different levels of skill and sophistication—of intergenerational conti- nuity and obedience. Together with the father, we now have four male roles that correspond precisely to those I presented in Chapter 5 as essential for enacting the scenario of the succession of the junior male to senior status. There are the senior male who is to be displaced by the rising generation and the junior male, who is split into representatives of the rebellious son, the good son, and the "innocent heir." Thus the ceremony seems to contain an acknowledgment of the paradigmatic structure that I have proposed lies at its root.

As Fredman points out, the role of "innocent child" is crucial to the Passover service. Young children are ritually pure already, unlike adults, who need to purify themselves. "This state of purity connects the child with the idea of redemption. Both the Talmud and the Zohar imply that children are the 'messiahs of mankind.' . . . If knowledge and moral perfection can bring redemption, then the pure children engaged in the study of the Law are the community's hope for the future" (1981, 119). I would add that the induction of the pure children into the Law has the paradoxical effect of ending their state of purity, for in causing them to identify with the story of the primal rebellion, the father inducts them into the ranks of the guilty, comprising all those complicit in the violation of the old order and, therefore, fit citizens of the new, civilized world. Only after the messiah comes will everyone be finally redeemed, that is, liberated from the debt that simultaneously makes society possible and makes living in it an exile, a state of "discontent."

It is well known that Moses is conspicuous in the Passover service by his near-absence; the great deeds are ascribed to the Deity alone. There are numerous explanations for this; I offer this one, consistent with my view that at the seder table the sons take on the guilt that makes society possible by identifying their own unconscious oedipal guilt with that portrayed in the foundational myth. Although Moses is not mentioned, it is no secret that he is the protagonist of the story being retold and reenacted. And when children hear a story read to them by their parents, they are inclined to form a fantasy identification with its hero.[7] The fact that the role of Moses, fully rounded on other occasions, is left vacant on the Passover seder night constitutes, I propose, an invitation to the son(s) of the family to identify with Moses: each may imagine that he personally held out his hand, parted the sea, and drowned the pharaoh and all his men, thereby rescuing his own beloved family. That irresistible fantasy has, however, the additional consequence of producing the fear of the wrath of the Lord that underwrites the social contract. And this is connected, in the here and now of the seder festival, with the son's existing oedipal wishes and fears, and it is given culturally valorized form as the ceremony unfolds anew each year.

V

According to Freud's story of individual development, the oedipal boy, frightened by the prospect of castration by the father for his erotic and self-assertive hubris, enters a period of latency. During this stage, the boy identifies with his father, subordinates himself to his father's rules, and imposes on himself a critical internal monitor—the superego—that is designed to detect temptations to act on the dangerous oedipal impulses. To keep himself in check, under the promptings of the superego, the boy's ego enters a phase of development in which defensive measures successfully relegate sexual and aggressive impulses to unconscious status and sublimate them, to allow the boy to become socialized in the skills necessary for adult life.

If the myth of the primal horde, and its biblical representation in the Torah narrative, is analogous, as Freud claims, to the pattern of the individual development of an obsessional or conscientious character, then the climax of the oedipal phase corresponds with the killing of the primal father/Pharaoh. Following this line of argument, I tentatively propose that the seven weeks of "counting the sheaves," the period between Passover and Shavuot, the next major holiday in the Jewish year, constitute the ritual and mythic equivalent of latency. In terms of the myth of the horde, after the death of the primal father, the brothers renounce the women for whose sexual favors they have rebelled and impose on themselves a prohibition on the sexual and murderous impulses that led to their deed.

Two aspects of the period of counting between Passover and Shavuot indicate that it is a ritual enactment of a latency period. The first is that, as I have mentioned, the act of counting is itself one of the foremost obsessional defenses employed during latency to ward off anxiety-producing impulses. This is why children of latency age are taught the skills of mathematics (and of literacy as well, of course) at just this age.[8]

The other aspect is that the seven-week counting period is a time of ritual restrictions, the most relevant of which, for my purposes, is that traditionally no marriages are allowed during this time. I interpret this, in the context of the myth, as a sign of the renunciation the victorious brothers impose on themselves before the emergence of marriage exchange. During this period, one might say, mythically speaking, the brothers are waiting anxiously to see what punitive response the father will make to their audacity in having killed him. They are being careful to do nothing further that might provoke him—or that might lead to the outbreak of destructive rivalry among themselves over the spoils of victory.

Shavuot, in the days of the Temple, was a joyful midsummer festival marking the end of the period of ritual restriction that followed Passover. In exile, it has become identified as the anniversary of the giving of the Torah on Mount Sinai. One might have thought this would be understood as the imposition, rather than the lifting, of a set of restrictions. But we can here understand why the giving of the Law by God to the Israelites, through Moses, would be greeted with relief. The brothers, in the wake of their momentous deed, might have expected talionic retribution, that is, death.

Instead, God, as representative of the senior male, offers a set of conditions that, if met, will avert his wrath. A list of rules to live by that will keep God happy would be most welcome under those circumstances, given the alternatives that could be imagined (of which God keeps reminding them).

More specifically, the giving and acceptance of the Law as the guideline for a society based on reciprocity provides a way out of the impasse of the ban on "marriage" that has been in force during latency. If people renounce their original incestuous objects and agree to exchange spouses, displacing their erotic attraction onto new, substitute objects, then sexual reproductive life can go forward, provided each individual acts fairly with respect to the Law. Shavuot, as the giving of the Law, would thus correspond to the end of latency and the beginning of adult life. In terms of Freud's myth, it would mark the period of entrance into the social system inaugurated by the band of brothers, a system in which marriage and reproduction are the primary goals and activities around which life is organized.

By this logic, the other important annual holidays, the cycle composed of the High Holy Days (Rosh Hashanah and Yom Kippur), Sukot, Shemini Atzeret, and Simchat Torah, correspond to the next life-cycle event, death. Here the yearly cycle of weekly Torah readings comes together with the festival calendrical cycle, and the Days of Awe, with their somber and penitent mood, parallel the reading of the final chapters of the Torah, those dealing with the death of Moses. As both the mythic narrative and its hero approach their end, we feel a strong wish to be pardoned and to atone for our guilty deeds. Like Moses, we are fated to die in exile, without having entered the promised land, but we would like to go to the grave reconciled and at peace, rather than in a continuing state of guilt before the Deity who represents the undying primal father. At Sukot, just after Rosh Hashanah, we identify literally with Moses and his companions, by staying in booths, or temporary dwellings similar to those used by the Israelites in their forty years of wandering.

In this world, the state of perfect innocence (as it later seems) comes only at the beginning of life. It is also held out as a hope for the future in such myths as those of the coming messianic age or of a heavenly afterlife. The reconciliation and solace offered by the Torah myth is different. No one gets to cross the Jordan. Instead, on the day of Shemini Atzeret, the weekly portion is read that contains the death of Moses. But so is the beginning of the first chapter of Genesis. As soon as the myth ends and Moses dies, the story starts all over again. Moses may never reach the promised land, but he is destined to relive his myth every year, forever. He himself never enters Canaan, but while history goes forward—Joshua crosses the Jordan and historical time moves on—the myth persists unchanging, in an eternal, cyclical present, creating the meaningful cosmos against which history itself is experienced. In the myth, there is no "history," no straightforward motion of time, but rather a cycling from creation and birth through life, struggle, disappointment, death, and then re-creation and rebirth.[9]

The promised land of innocence, experienced by each of us in the presocialized state of childhood, follows death: a new year follows the old, a new cycle of Torah readings begins, and while one generation dies in the wilderness, a new generation of children experiences the pure state of innocence, symbolized in the myth by the pre-Sinaitic period and especially by the period of Jacob and his sons. In contrast with the solemn tone of Shemini Atzeret, then, comes the joyful outburst of Simchat Torah, marked by a mood appropriate to the rebirth. Men dance joyfully with Torah scrolls on their shoulders, and children figure prominently. The happiness of the childhood state of innocence is realized after the reconciliation achieved through the atonement of the Days of Awe; not by us, it is true, but by our posterity. The Jewish tradition is thus one in which the finitude of the life of the individual is redeemed by the higher value of ongoing reproductive success. The myth starts over with undiminished vitality, new generations are born, and the tradition is re-created as the children are inscribed in the myth and vice versa.

VI

Freud's description of the totemic sacrificial feast focuses on its expression of markedly contrasting affective moods. First there is mourning and lamentation: "When the deed is done, the slaughtered animal is lamented and bewailed. The mourning is obligatory, imposed by a dread of threatened retribution." This somber mood leads to its opposite: "But the mourning is followed by demonstrations of festive rejoicing: every instinct is unfettered and there is license for every kind of gratification" (1913b, 140). Freud explains this phenomenon by reasoning that, if the sacrificed totem animal represents the primal father, the festive mood swings express the ambivalence inherent in the relationship between the senior and junior males. There is joy at being free of the tyrant, balanced by grief at having lost a beloved parent.

While no single holiday in the Judaic calendar exhibits this clear emotional ambivalence, the annual cycle as a whole is punctuated by decompositions of it. The epitome of the carnivalesque festive feeling "produced by the liberty to do what is as a rule prohibited" (Freud, 1913b, 140)—along with Simchat Torah—is Purim, an unbridled expression of triumph and glee at the story (in the book of Esther) of the foiling of a threat of extermination against the Israelites issued by a non-Israelite king (by way of his evil henchman Haman).

The mournful mood predominates at various points throughout the year, of which perhaps the best example is Tisha b'Av, the commemoration of the destruction of the Temple. While the reading of the book of Esther at Purim becomes the pretext for a raucous theatrical burlesque, the reading of the book of Lamentations at Tisha b'Av is an occasion for an outpouring of grief and despair.

The opposition between the two affective tones is symbolized in the holiday celebrations by the opposition between feasting and fasting. On the days of grief, one eats nothing, on the days of celebration one feasts or prepares special culinary treats. The clearest hint the tradition gives us that this eating or not eating is connected to the fantasy of devouring the body of the slain primal father comes at Purim, where the distinctive seasonal treat is a pastry concoction referred to as "Haman's hat." I leave the rest of the analysis up to the reader.

VII

Let us now look at the dominant symbol of the cultus, the Torah itself, not only as a text that tells a story but as a multivalent symbolic object redolent with meanings that help reinforce the experience of the myth as a felt reality. I turn first to a consideration of how the Torah is itself like the primal father

The primal father, according to Freud, was a supreme narcissist, dependent upon no one, maker of his own rules, sole authority over his own existence. He was also the political authority over the junior males; as their father, he was also, genetically speaking, their source—or half of it anyway (and, in the ideology of a patrilineal system, much more than that). The relationship between the primal father and the junior males is asymmetrical. They obey his rules, depend upon his protection, derive their existence from him and his continued goodwill. He, by contrast, is independent.

In this asymmetry does his authority consist, and, semiotically speaking, we could do no better than to describe the nature of a dominant symbol in the terms I have just used to describe the primal father. Just as, in the primal horde, the junior males (and the females) derive their place in the system by virtue of relationship to the senior male, while he himself defines his own authority, so in a semiotic system, all terms take their meaning from reference to each other—but they derive their ultimate meaning from their collective reference to one or more central, orienting signs. These latter, however, are not themselves determined in relation to anything else. Lacan's image of such signs as *points de capiton,* upholstery buttons by means of which the slippery fabric of semiosis is attached to the furniture so it will stay in place, is remarkably apt and evocative.[10]

In the Bible, the search for a final genetic cause leads, by way of patrilineal descent, to God: if each paternal ancestor has himself been begotten by an ancestor of his own, he is still not the uncaused causer, the self-created creator. Even Abraham had a father, and his father too had a father, and the line of descent can be traced back through Shem, Noah, and finally to Adam. But with Adam we finally reach the stopping place. Adam, the ancestor of all humans but Eve, was created by God, who was not himself created by anything but has the power to create everything.

In the practice of Judaism, the Torah is the material representation of the ultimate authority of God. It is, indeed, treated like a king, just as God is addressed as "Our Father, Our King" during the Days of Awe. Torah scrolls are traditionally adorned with royal crowns and breastplates. They are surrounded by the taboos that pertain also to royalty, and one must stand when they enter the room (that is, when the ark in which they are stored is opened and they are brought out for reading). The authority of the Torah is supreme, and it itself contains the commands and instructions of an eternal ruler whose laws are for all time.

And just as the mythical primal father derives his authority from the fact that all other men in the group are his sons, genetic copies of himself, so the Torah is suited to play the part of the dominant symbol, the anchoring point of the entire meaning system of Judaism, and hence of Western civilization in general, because of *its* power of replication. While the primal father is the source of all *genetic* reproduction, the Torah is a source of *semiotic* replication. It is capable of producing copies of itself, as well as of men, who are themselves "copies" of it, its metaphorical "sons," insofar as they are informed by and exemplify in their being and actions the instructions imparted to them by the Torah.

Richard Dawkins (1976, 1982), atypically among evolutionary theorists, asserts that genes are themselves members of a wider class of "replicators," whose members include "anything in the universe of which copies are made. Examples are a DNA molecule, and a sheet of paper which is xeroxed." He recognizes the independent existence of a cultural or semiotic replicator, which he calls a "meme," and which he thinks follows an independent course of reproduction: "A meme has its own opportunities for replication, and its own phenotypic effects, and there is no reason why success in a meme should have any connection whatever with genetic success" (1982, 83). This claim for independence is, of course, stretched a bit far: memes can be produced and used only by organisms that have, in turn, first been constructed according to genetic instructions. But the essential point remains that traits transmitted by means of memes, according to the laws of the evolutionary process, need work only for the survival of the memes themselves, not for the genes of the organisms that use them.

A "memic" or cultural replicator accomplishes its work by channeling the motivations and capacities of human actors into activities that result in the reproduction of copies of the meme. By giving instructions to human actors, a successfully replicating meme produces two kinds of effects. It produces a population of humans who are "like" it, in the sense that they actualize its instructions. And through the instructions it gives these people, it also motivates and directs them to produce more copies, so that the instructions can be disseminated and transmitted over generations. People who have been significantly informed by the same memic instructions can be said to be like each other and, indeed, to be related in a way directly analogous to the way people are genetically related: that is, by being realizations of, and providers of future copies of, the same instructions.[11]

As I have been at pains to show throughout this book, the principal way the Torah attracts to itself and is enabled effectively to instruct the community of people for which it is a dominant symbol is in containing the narration of a myth that corresponds to and thus activates the personal unconscious fantasies of individual actors.

The Torah has characteristics that suit it to strike participants in its cultus as an uncaused cause of replication at the memic level, just as the primal father is the (apparently) ungenerated genitor of his sons. It is a symbol whose meaning, and ability to instruct authoritatively, comes from its own status as a self-created, self-referential symbol, or meme, and thus as a fixed point in relation to which all other symbols derive meaning, that derives its own meaning from nothing except itself.[12]

The Torah, being a set of instructions, is clearly a replicator, insofar as it produces a community of individuals "similar" to it and to each other, in the sense that they all, as individuals, embody the Torah by enacting the instructions within it.

In addition, the Torah not only enjoins those under its influence to practice the laws it gives but it also insists repeatedly that it be transmitted across generations and that it itself be copied. Exemplary of these points, I shall take the sixth chapter of Deuteronomy, one of the most magnificent in the entire Bible and certainly the most central in the practice of Judaic worship, prayer, and liturgy, containing as it does the call "Hear O Israel . . ." that, by synechdoche, stands for the entirety of Jewish faith. The passage continues: "Take to heart these instructions with which I charge you this day. Impress them upon your children. Recite them when you stay at home and when you are away, when you lie down and when you get up. Bind them as a sign on your hand and let them serve you as a symbol on your forehead. Inscribe them on the doorposts of your house and on your gates" (vv. 6–9).

What is the referent of the phrase "these instructions with which I charge you this day"? At one level, it may be understood to refer to the Ten Commandments, which have just been revealed in the previous chapter (repeating, as Deuteronomy often does, something that has gone before in a slightly different version). But we may also understand by "these instructions" the whole of the Torah itself, and all the commandments conveyed prophetically through Moses as recorded therein.

On the other hand, "these instructions" can also refer, in a literal way, to "these instructions," that is, themselves. Judaic practice has taken the passage in just this way. Thus the prayer "Hear O Israel, the Lord is our God, the Lord alone" is, in fact, repeated every day by every observant Jew. Further, "these instructions," that is, this passage, together with a few other verses, is inscribed on parchment and inserted in *tefillen*, or phylacteries, as the passage instructs, as well as in *mezuzot,* small casings attached to the doorframes of houses, also according to a (literal) reading of the instructions.

On a more general level, the command to recite, take to heart, and teach one's children "these instructions" is a basis for the entire practice of the reading, study, and teaching of the Torah itself.

Imagine a computer instruction (or virus, perhaps) worded as follows: "Make a copy of these words." One can see at once that an appropriately programmed computer would proceed to make an infinite number of copies of the words "Make a copy of these words." While the content of this message in terms of new information would be nil—an attribute that, as Roy Rappaport (1979) argues, is really an advantage in sacred liturgies— the actual process of replication exemplifies enormous, indeed infinite, creative or self-recreative power. This recursive power, enacted in fulfillment of the commandment to reproduce "these instructions," intimates to the practitioner an infinity of reproduction and thus a vast fecundity suitable to produce a sense of the infinity of the Deity himself: a Deity who introduced himself to Moses with that most self-referential and recursive of statements: "I am that I am."[13]

Later in the same chapter of Deuteronomy, Moses speaks thus to the Israelites: "When, in time to come, your son asks you, 'What mean the exhortations, laws, and rules which the Lord our God has enjoined upon you?' you shall say to your son, 'We were slaves to Pharaoh in Egypt and the Lord freed us from Egypt with a mighty hand. . . . Then the Lord commanded us to observe all these laws, to revere the Lord our God. . . . It will therefore be to our merit before the Lord our God to observe faithfully this whole Instruction, as He has commanded us' " (6:20–25). The Torah thus commands its own transmittal across generations: specifically, from father to son. This mode of transmission will, as I pointed out in connection with Passover (whose liturgy traditionally contains passages from Deuteronomy 6), give immediate experienced reality to the mythic logic underlying the covenant between God and the Israelites. Because the senior male refrained from killing us after the primal crime, we must now keep his commandments, which entails teaching the myth and its implications to our sons.

The Torah embodies the idea of self-referentiality appropriate to an uncaused cause in other ways as well. Let us consider the question of where the Torah came from. The answer, of course, is that it was revealed to Moses on Mount Sinai. But, as I have been arguing at length, the whole Torah, as a narrative, is nothing other than the story of the revelation at Mount Sinai: what led up to it, what happened during the life of the prophet Moses who received the Law, and, of course, the Law itself.

Thus we may say that the Torah was "created" (in its earthly manifestation) at Sinai. But at the same time, the creation of the Torah is a story contained within the Torah narrative, inscribed in the scroll. The book is at once container and content.

If the book contains its own inception, what of its author? Once again, paradoxical self-referential recursion lies at the heart of the matter. The Torah, the Five Books of Moses, is "of Moses" in the sense that Moses wrote the books or at least transcribed them from God's dictation. But at the same time, they are about Moses, who is the protagonist of the entire Torah narrative. Thus Moses, is, as any ultimate authority must be to maintain his status, the author of his own existence, in quite a literal sense.

Finally, let us turn to Deuteronomy 31, in which Moses begins the preparations for his impending death: "Moses wrote down this Teaching and gave it to the priests, sons of Levi" (v. 9).[14] The biblical passage continues: "Every seventh year . . . at the Feast of Booths, when all Israel comes to appear before the Lord your God in the place which He will choose, you shall read this Teaching aloud in the presence of all Israel" (vv. 10–11). By this means, the Israelites' children, too, "who have not had the experience, shall hear and learn to revere your God as long as they live in the land which you are about to cross the Jordan to occupy" (v. 13).

Thus, the commands of the Torah, if faithfully executed, lead to behavior whereby not only is the Torah brought to "phenotypic" existence from "memotypic" existence as an instruction manual, but it is recited, copied, taught, studied, and otherwise infinitely replicated and disseminated. This capacity to replicate and disseminate itself as a memotype is underscored by its self-referential qualities, which make the experience of being instructed authoritative and, as Geertz says, "uniquely real." Thus does the Torah stand as an uncreated but creative point of reference in relation to which all other signs acquire significance, a Turnerian "dominant symbol," a Lacanian point de capiton.

VIII

I have so far considered the Torah in its symbolic connection with the senior male and his Law. To complicate matters, I conclude this chapter with a brief discussion of another important dimension of the meaning of the Torah as a polyvalent religious symbol. The Torah represents the senior male, but it also symbolizes what he has that makes him senior. In addition to supreme authority, that thing would be the mother. The Torah is thus not only the sign of the senior male's command but also, in a less explicit but real symbolic equation, it is the female he possesses by means of whom he procreates. It is in part by drawing on the symbolic equation of the Torah with the erotically desired mother of childhood that Judaic practice is able to enlist the powerful fantasies and wishes of the boys whom it turns into men by means of their relation to the Torah.

No less an authority on Judaism than Yosef Yerushalmi asserts the symbolic equation of Torah and the feminine/maternal: "Who, then, . . . is the mother? I would simply and brazenly answer—the Torah, the Teaching, the revelation, the Torah which in Hebrew is grammatically feminine and which is midrashically compared to a bride" (1991, 92).

No more elegant expression of the idea that the study of Torah calls upon the emotions of a youthful (oedipal) lover can be found than this passage from the Zohar, the classic of the Kabbalistic tradition:

> She [the Torah] may be compared to a beautiful and stately maiden, who is secluded in an isolated chamber of a palace, and has a lover of whose existence she alone knows. For love of her he passes by her gate unceasingly, and turns his eyes in all directions to discover her. She is aware that he is forever hovering about the palace, and what does she do? She thrusts open a small door in her secret chamber, for a moment reveals herself to her lover, then quickly withdraws it. . . . He is aware it is from love of him that she has revealed herself to him for that moment, and his heart and soul and everything within him are drawn to her. (Scholem, 1949, 89)

In this imagery, the Torah, locked away in the ark except on sacred occasions, is like the woman locked away in father's palace, after whom the aspiring young student/lover pines.

Jacob Arlow cites this same passage in his study of psychoanalytic aspects of the ritual of bar mitzvah, which initiates a boy at thirteen to the brotherhood of those entitled to read from the Torah and makes him, by definition, a man. After citing a number of specific clinical cases in which conflicts concerning the bar mitzvah appear in dreams and other material, Arlow proposes that the equation of the Torah with a desired woman has a general application:

It will be recalled that the Bar Mitzvah boy is ceremoniously called to the Torah as a bridegroom and that in orthodox communities a bridegroom customarily went through the ritual of being called to the Torah before his wedding. The association between Bar Mitzvah and marriage recurs repeatedly in popular as well as religious writing and thinking. At the festival which marks the termination of the reading of the Torah and its immediate reinauguration [Simchat Torah], the last person called to the Torah is referred to as the bridegroom of the Torah. (1951b, 367)

Harvey Goldberg also cites the festival of Simchat Torah to examine the metaphor of marriage in relation to the symbolism of the Torah. In addition to the fact that the readers on that day are called bridegrooms of the Torah, Goldberg notes that young boys, normally forbidden to participate, may be allowed to recite the blessing for the reading of the Torah: When all the children are gathered at the reader's lectern, "a large prayer shawl is spread over their heads by the men who surround them. This is the precise way that a bridal canopy (hupah) is formed in many traditional weddings" (1987, 118). On this occasion children are given a peek of the forbidden mystery of the marital chamber to whet their appetite for learning.

Goldberg's principal theme is the symbolic connection between Torah and children, or procreation. He cites various ethnographic vignettes to support the view that Torah is linked, in the thought of many Jews, to the themes of sexuality and procreation. Thus he points out that while it is traditional for men to dance with Torah scrolls in their arms on Simchat Torah, he has observed as well men dancing with male children in their arms, thus suggesting a symbolic equation between the two. He also demonstrates the metaphorical equivalence between learning or imbibing the Torah and its wisdom, on the one hand, and images of oral ingestion on the other: "In seventeenth century Germany, a Jewish male child, on his first day in school, would lick honey smeared across the verses of a book of the Pentateuch, from which he would be taught to recite. . . . In Kurdistan, the teacher would write letters of the Hebrew alphabet on a piece of paper, smear honey on them, and give them to a child to lick" (1987, 114). We have seen that the meaning of the Jewish word for honey includes a reference to the maternal breasts, and the imagery of sucking wisdom from the breasts of the Torah is by no means alien to the Jewish tradition.

As Goldberg shows, the scene of imbibing the maternal Torah's essence can also be transposed into a male register, whereby it is symbolically semen, or phallic power, that is ingested through the study of Torah. The upward displacement from sexuality to the intellectual love of Torah, notes Goldberg, is facilitated by a belief, shared by the Jews with many other peoples, linking semen and the brain, or cerebrospinal fluid.[15]

These facts, combined with the significance of the great Jewish festivals as simultaneous celebrations of fertility and of the story of the Torah, indicate that the erotic oedipal strivings of the growing boy are directed by a symbolic maneuver away from literal sexual success and procreation to mastery of the Torah. In this way, a conceptual link is forged between the domains of genetic sexual procreation and memic textual reproduction, and the energy mobilized in the service of the former is diverted to and used to motivate the transmission of the latter.

For the young student, the Torah is the object of fervent desire, like the oedipal mother, but at the same time it embodies the voice of stern paternal prohibition. As such, it represents an ideal compromise formation, in which the wishes and fears of the oedipal complex each find expression in the impassioned love of the study of Law that proscribes the very love it calls forth.

When the bar mitzvah boy enters the moral community, he goes to the ark of the covenant, the sacred and secret inner chamber of the Torah/maiden. He parts the outer gates just as Moses cleft the sea. Then he opens the inner scroll, until that moment kept tightly rolled up in twin cylinders. He looks at what is there, but he may not touch it. And what he sees as he penetrates the innermost mystery is—the Law of the Father, inscribed on the flayed hide of a sacrificial sheep. In this image is elegantly condensed the richly multivocal meaning of the myth: the erotic desire, the paternal prohibition, and the threatened filicidal punishment that enforces it and transforms the originally transgressive wish into a love of and identification with the paternal Law itself.

10

Christianity and the Prophet

Like Moses

I

I have thus far put off a discussion of the obvious fact that, insofar as the Torah narrative is a master myth of Western civilization, this is not because it is the backbone of Jewish religion and the centerpiece of synagogue liturgy but rather because it became essential to the customs, ceremonies, and dogmas of that vast complex of practices known as Christianity. After all, few would dispute that Christianity has been, almost since its inception, the central ideological component of Western civilization. To stress that Western civilization is *Judeo*-Christian is simply to underscore that Christianity, which was originally invented in large measure by, for, and about Hellenized and Romanized Jews, has embraced, while also claiming to transcend, the Hebrew canonical writings. There cannot, after all, be a "new" testament, a "new" covenant central to Christianity, without there having been an "old" testament or an "old" covenant.

As Yosef Yerushalmi (1991) points out, this puts Christianity perpetually in the position of "younger brother" to Judaism in relation to God the father. We have already seen that the position of the older brother, the first-born, is a problematic one in the mythic paradigm and that the younger brother typically prevails. But the younger brother bears the anxiety of knowing he has usurped his older brother's birthright and so is required to justify his own favored position (as I think the parable of the prodigal son tries to do).

The ideological strategy of Christianity has thus been not to distance itself from Judaism and from the Hebrew canon and its myth but rather to subsume the Judaic tradition and to reinterpret it in such a way as to justify Christianity's own claim of having surpassed, resolved, and transcended it. The Christian myth is a transformation of the Hebrew one, in which the Hebraic myth is seen as posing a dilemma that is solved by the Christian. Christianity is thus incomprehensible without knowledge of the Judaic myth. Ironically, Christianity has therefore been the main agent in preserving and disseminating the doctrine and covenant it announces itself to have surpassed. I might, in a less-than-charitable mood, describe Christianity's key ideological move as being the equivalent of a "hostile takeover" of the Judaic tradition and its myths. (Of course, in the same mood I could point out that Judaism asked for it by ending its mythic system with a promise of a messiah.)

Why this appropriation? I contend that it is because Christianity, and its core myths and rituals centered around the life and death of Jesus, makes sense only in the context of the myths and rituals of Moses. Indeed, this was the fact that allowed me, following Freud's decisive move, to decipher the meaning of the Hebrew myth, by working backward from the Christian myth of the Passion and the ritual of the Mass. The implication, of course, is that the Christian myth can be so deciphered because it is itself a response to and further transformation of the myth that constitutes the Torah narrative. The Passion, in short, as story and as enacted drama in the Eucharist as well as in the yearly round of rituals, is a transformation of the myth of Moses and the Exodus.

Christianity is a salvation religion, and it defines what people need to be saved *from* as a fault inherent in Judaism. Therefore, before it can promise to save people, Christianity first has to convince them that they need to be saved, and to do that, it teaches them the "old testament" so that they too will find themselves in the state from which Christianity, by its design, is supposed to save them. What for the Jews has been the support for an ongoing social system has been reinterpreted through the lens of the Christian myth as an intolerable condition, one from which a person self-evidently needs to be rescued.

According to the Christian view, we all need to be saved from a state of "sin," a particular cultural construction of guilt. Because of universal guilt, under the old covenant of the Mosaic Law, Christians claim that the inevitable outcome for anyone and everyone is unredeemed death. But thanks to the new covenant, which announces the dispensation of grace, the way is opened to repentance, redemption from guilt, and eternal life. As I have so far interpreted the dynamics of the Hebrew world, the unconscious guilt generated by the core myth and the practices that surround it is not incapacitating nor even consciously felt. Rather guilt serves as the impetus to personal commitment to the norms and values that make the life of the society possible and reasonably harmonious. In this respect, the guilt operates similarly to guilt in the Kleinian "depressive position," as the beginning point of reparation and so of love, social solidarity, and the acceptance of the otherness of others.

The key move of Christian ideology has been to recast this guilt as a state of intolerable anxiety rather than creative instigation. I wish here to show specifically how the Christian myth has accepted, while at the same time transforming and seeking to transcend, the myth of the primal horde. My present investigation of Christianity must obviously be narrowly limited in scope. I address only those particular aspects of the Christian myth, as originally inscribed in the "New Testament," that explicitly confront, address, or use the story of Moses.

II

Let me begin with a disclaimer: As with my treatment of Judaic texts and practices, I discuss the Christian Bible as it has taken shape as a coherent whole. That this canon is an amalgam of different parts by different people from different places and periods and with different agendas is a historical matter that is beyond the scope or purpose of this book to examine. I aim only to look at certain dimensions of Christian belief and practice as these appear from the particular perspective opened up by my analysis of the myth of Moses.

Matthew's account of the life of Jesus contains the most explicit mythological echoes of the Moses myth, although it is the Gospel of John that specifically dwells on the idea that Jesus has come in fulfillment of a prophecy by Moses himself. (The Gospels of Luke and Mark, by contrast make little use of such parallels.) Christian exegesis employs the typological method, which entails finding in the Hebrew Bible a model repeated or paralleled in the Christian Bible. Excellent scholarship has established a number of well-recognized points where Moses serves as a type of Jesus and also, by contrast, instances in which the character and deeds of Jesus seem to refer to the myth of Moses in a condition of transformation: they recall some aspect of the Moses myth but negate, overcome, or surpass it, or in some way emphasize a key difference between Jesus and Moses.[1]

The prophecy of the coming of a messiah who will redeem Israel occurs throughout the works of the prophets of the Hebrew Bible. The Jewish messianic tradition had essentially three images and traditions concerning the expected messiah with which to work. The first was that the messiah would be a new Moses, a prophet who would lead a new, divinely inspired spiritual renewal.

Moses himself prophesied to this effect in a passage crucial to the Christian understanding of Christ's mission:

> The Lord your God will raise up for you a prophet from among your own people, like myself; him you shall heed. . . . The Lord said to me, . . . "I will raise up a prophet for them from among their own people, like yourself: I will put My words in his mouth and he will speak to them all that I command him; and if anybody fails to heed the words he speaks in My name, I Myself will call him to account." (Deut. 18:15, 17–19)

The second idea about the messiah was that he would be a king of Israel, descended from the Davidic line of kings, who would lead a resurgent Israel to independence from foreign domination, punish her enemies, and reestablish a just society governed by the Law. Moses had also enjoined this on all future kings: "When he is seated on his royal throne, he shall have a copy of this Teaching written for him on a scroll by the levitical priests. Let it remain with him and let him read in it all his life, so that he may learn to revere the Lord his God, to faithfully observe every word of this Teaching as well as these laws" (Deut. 17:18–19).

(For reasons of space, I shall not explore the tradition in Judaism which speaks of two messiahs, one from the house of Joseph and the other from the house of David. According to this tradition, the Josephite messiah would be a military leader who, subduing the enemies of Israel, would also die at their hands. The Davidic messiah would subsequently preside as king over a pacified world. Clearly, however, this tradition obeys the assumption, derived from the myth as I have analyzed it, that a death is owed for the slaying of the primal father and that only after this debt has been paid can there be an era of true social harmony.)

The third idea of the messiah derives from the prophecy of Isaiah, which describes him as a "servant" of God who suffers and is martyred on God's behalf. The Christian canonical writings interweave these three messianic themes, emphasizing now one, now the other, while adding their own conception of who this messiah is.

Matthew begins his Gospel in a clearly Davidic key by giving a genealogy demonstrating Jesus's direct descent from King David. But it is in the subsequent stories that the echoes of Moses appear most clearly. First, the names of the Holy Family—Joseph, Mary (Miriam), and Jesus (Yeshua: Joshua)—recall Egypt, the Exodus story, and Moses. Joseph was Moses's predecessor as leader of the Jews in Egypt, Joshua his successor and leader of the conquest of Canaan, and Miriam, of course, was his sister. This constellation, for Jews conversant with the Moses myth, might almost constitute a riddle asking, "Who is missing from this picture?" and thus by inference calling to mind the figure of Moses.

In Matthew 2, we learn that there is a wicked and infanticidal king, Herod, who, like the pharaoh who did not know Joseph, tries to foil his destined usurper by killing all the male children. Jesus, like Moses, is spared, in this case by a flight *into* Egypt. Moses, recall, avoided the wrath of Pharaoh after killing the overseer by a flight *out of* Egypt. This not only constitutes a parallel transformed by reversal but sets the stage for a more direct parallel: "This [the flight to Egypt] was to fulfil what the Lord had spoken by the prophet [in Hosea 11:1], 'Out of Egypt have I called my son'" (v. 15). That is, Christ first sojourned in Egypt so that, like Moses before him, he could later be said to have come out of Egypt.

When Herod dies, an angel informs Joseph that he may return from Egypt, saying, "'Rise, take the child and his mother, and go to the land of Israel, for those who sought the child's life are dead.' And he rose and took the child and his mother, and went to the land of Israel" (Matt. 2:20–21). This is a more-or-less verbatim reprise of a parallel episode in Moses's life: "The Lord said to Moses in Midian, 'Go back to Egypt, for all the men who sought to kill you are dead.' So Moses took his wife and sons, mounted them on an ass, and went back to the land of Egypt" (Exod. 4:19–20).

The transformation here, besides making Egypt exile in one story and home in the other, lies in making Moses parallel Jesus's father Joseph, not Jesus. Combined with the fact that Jesus's name is the same as that of Moses's successor, this detail suggests that Jesus is to be taken not just as a new version of Moses but as one who represents the junior generation to him, the one who will succeed and surpass him. Here we see presaged the idea that Moses is to Jesus as senior to junior male.[2]

This formulation requires a slight modification, however. Whereas Moses is destined forever to approach the promised land only to die, prevented from crossing the Jordan by the ultimate Divine prohibition—destined, as well, in the annual Torah cycle to return to the beginning—Jesus, like his namesake, Joshua, will cross the boundary of the (spiritual) Jordan and achieve the goal his predecessor is eternally denied. He will violate the paternal prohibition and be punished for it by death, but through resurrection he will achieve the ultimate apotheosis.

In Matthew 3, the emphasis on Jesus's sojourn in the wilderness parallels Moses's own passage through the wilderness. Jesus's fasting for forty days and nights recalls Moses's fast of forty days and nights on Mount Sinai; the number forty also corresponds to the number of years Moses spent in the wilderness.[3] The devil's temptation of Jesus to turn stones to bread after his fast can be seen as an indirect parallel to Moses's miraculous feeding of the Israelites in the wilderness with manna and water from stones. Likewise, when the devil takes Jesus up the high mountain and shows him all the kingdoms of the world (Matt. 4:8), there is an unquestionable echo of God taking Moses to the top of Mount Nebo to survey all the peoples of the land of Canaan.

Jesus delivers his first great sermon on a mountaintop (Matt. 5). This sermon consists in part of a commentary on the Law that Moses also promulgated from a mountain. Jesus specifically says, " 'Think not that I have come to abolish the law and the prophets; I have come not to abolish them but to fulfil them' " (v. 17). He goes on to show that his new covenant demands not only observance of the traditional laws, but also righteous attitudes and states of mind. In one important respect, however, Jesus directly challenges Mosaic Law: " 'You have heard that it was said, "An eye for an eye, a tooth for a tooth." But I say to you, Do not resist one who is evil. But if any one strikes you on the right cheek, turn to him the other also' " (vv. 38–39).

The overall impact of the Sermon on the Mount is continuity with, but also essential change from, the Mosaic covenant. The alteration offers perhaps the prime example of that intensification of guilt to which I referred that constitutes the central Christian move, for now we are supposed to feel guilty not just about what we have actually done but even about what we have simply thought of doing: "You have heard that it was said, 'You shall not commit adultery.' But I say to you that every one who looks at a woman lustfully has already committed adultery with her in his heart" (vv. 27–28).[4]

It would be a mistake, however, to look for the main content of the new and better covenant Christianity proclaims itself to be in any new teachings, or even in revisions of the Mosaic laws.[5] Insofar as Jesus has a codifiable rule, it can be summarized simply as the injunction to live up to the spirit as well as the letter of God's Law as given through Moses: to acknowledge and love God and to love one's fellows regardless of nationality

(Israelite or Gentile). This represents a widening of scope and intensification of what is already contained in the Mosaic Law but not a new set of rules as such.

The radical novelty that Christ has to offer is not a new code of laws, but rather himself. While the messianic tradition led people to expect some combination of king, prophet, and suffering servant, what was wholly unexpected and different was the proclamation that the messiah was the son of God, and as such authorized to speak not only *for* God but *as* God. His saving gesture is therefore not his teaching or his rule but his own self-sacrifice, which completely alters the nature of the relationship between humans and God.

For Matthew, the definitive proof of Christ's status as God's son is given in the scene of Jesus's transfiguration, a scene in which he explicitly both parallels and surpasses Moses. Jesus takes the disciples Peter, James, and John "up a high mountain" (17:1). He is transfigured so that his face shines like the sun and his garments like light. Moses and Elijah appear and talk with him, and just as Peter is offering to build "booths" for them, God's voice proclaims, "This is my beloved Son, with whom I am well pleased" (v. 5). Jesus, resuming his normal appearance, explains to the disciples that Elijah has indeed reappeared, as was prophesied would happen before the coming of the messiah, in the form of John the Baptist.

In this episode, the direct reference to Moses, the scene atop a mountain where God speaks directly to humans, the booths, and the radiance of Jesus's face (echoing the shining of Moses's face after talking with God on Mount Sinai, as described in Exodus 34:29–30) all point to explicit Mosaic prototypes. At the same time, God clearly shows the disciples that Jesus outranks Moses in a direct comparison.

While Luke and Mark make some reference to Jesus in relation to Moses, it is John who most fully develops the continuity and contrast between the two figures and the covenants they represent. John's prologue sets forth the following crucial contrast between Moses and Jesus in New Testament Christian thought: "For the law was given through Moses; grace and truth came through Jesus Christ" (1:17). The implication is that grace is in some sense opposed to law. According to the law, humans, or at least the Israelites, deserve to be obliterated in punishment for their sins against God. But God also proclaims himself a God of love and forgiveness (Exod. 34:6–7). How can these two views be reconciled? Only through grace, that is, a free gift from God of his own son, who alone, by his death, constitutes adequate ransom to satisfy God's demand for just vengeance against the Hebrews, thereby allowing those who accept the validity of the sacrifice to be freed from sin and guilt. The gift of grace contrasts with the gifts under the social regime of balanced reciprocity: it purports to be a gift that expects no return, flowing from a bounteous source that never needs to be replenished or repaid.

Jesus's first miracle in John's Gospel, the conversion of water to wine at the marriage feast at Cana, has been seen by some as an echo of the changing of the waters of the Nile into blood, the first of the ten plagues preceding the Exodus. Much more explicit as a Mosaic parallel is the passage in which Jesus says to the Pharisee Nicodemus: " 'No one has ascended into heaven but he who descended from heaven, the Son of man. And as Moses lifted up the serpent in the wilderness, so must the Son of man be lifted up, that whoever believes in him may have eternal life' " (3:13–15). If one takes this passage literally, Jesus may (or may not) be asserting his superiority over Moses, inasmuch as he, unlike Moses, can actually ascend to heaven. In the figure of the snake, echoing an episode in Numbers 21:6–9 where Moses lifts a bronze snake on a pole to cure snakebite, it is implied that while Moses is the lifter up, Christ himself is the one lifted, the one who can cure the deadly poison of sin and, like the snake, shed an old life and begin a new one. Moses is placed in the ambiguous role, on the one hand, of "raising up," that is exalting, his mythic successor as a savior, and on the other, of sacrificing—crucifying—him (raising him on a "rod"/cross).

Later in John, when the Jews seek to kill Jesus for the offense of having cured a lame man on the Sabbath, Jesus calls, among his many witnesses, both the Hebrew Scriptures and Moses himself. In responding to the Jews who seek his life, he first declares, " 'You search the scriptures, because you think that in them you have eternal life; and it is they that bear witness to me; yet you refuse to come to me that you may have life' " (5:39–40). Then he calls Moses as a witness for himself: " 'Do not think that I shall accuse you to the Father; it is Moses who accuses you, on whom you set your hope. If you believed Moses, you would believe me, for he wrote of me' " (vv. 45–46).

In this episode, Jesus clearly regards the Torah, if understood rightly, as pointing the way to his own mission. He is no doubt referring to the verse in Deuteronomy 18 that I have already quoted, in which Moses predicts the future coming of a prophet like himself. For John's Jesus, the Jews cannot escape the Law, under whose sentence of guilt they remain, unless they are willing to believe that its message requires them to accept the grace Christ claims to represent.

The most detailed and extensive comparison between Jesus and Moses in the Gospel of John is certainly the one found in the remarkable chapter 6. This chapter begins with the miracles of the loaves and fishes and the walking on water. In both of these it is possible to recognize echoes of miracles performed by Moses. In the first case, miraculous feeding recalls the provision of manna, quails, and water in the wilderness. The walking on water could almost be read as a deliberate "trumping" of Moses's parting of the Red Sea (as well as of Joshua's similar miracle in crossing the Jordan, in Joshua 3), as if Christ were saying: "Moses had to part the waters and walk on dry land, but I can walk directly on the water."

Would-be disciples flock to Jesus after these feats, and those who have not witnessed the miracles ask for a sign, suggesting as an example Moses's giving of manna in the wilderness. Jesus answers thus: " 'Truly, truly I say to you, it was not Moses who gave you the bread from heaven; my Father gives you the true bread from heaven' " (v. 32). Jesus then makes it clear that he himself is the bread of heaven. When the Jews murmur among themselves (replicating the grumblings about food in the wilderness under Moses), Jesus makes it plain that he means quite literally that he is the equivalent of manna, and that he must be eaten by those who would be saved. I quote this passage at length, so as not to lessen its still scandalous impact:

> The Jews then disputed among themselves, saying, "How can this man give us his flesh to eat?" So Jesus said to them, "Truly, truly, I say to you, unless you eat the flesh of the Son of man and drink his blood, you have no life in you; he who eats my flesh and drinks my blood has eternal life, and I will raise him up at the last day. For my flesh is food indeed, and my blood is drink indeed. He who eats my flesh and drinks my blood abides in me, and I in him. As the living Father sent me, and I live because of the Father, so he who eats me will live because of me. This is the bread which came down from heaven, not such as the fathers ate and died; he who eats this bread will live for-ever." (vv. 52–58)

This passage, which serves as a scriptural foundation for the ritual of Communion, makes explicit, first, that God, not Moses, is responsible for the miracle of the manna, and second and more important, that Jesus is himself the gift of God—not manna, not miracles, not a code of laws, or a book, but a live human being who is to be eaten and drunk. (One gets an idea from this passage of why Freud was right to insist on the central importance of what he called the totemic feast as the key to understanding the system.)[6]

Once again, the Christian myth juxtaposes Christ to Moses in a particular way. Moses, as intercessor and prophet, can represent God to the Israelites; he can thus direct and oversee, though not himself cause, miraculous gifts like the manna on which the Israelites fed. Christ *is* this manna and as such *is* the food Moses serves to the people that gives them life in the midst of the wilderness.

John has more to say about Christ and Moses, but for my present purposes, let me turn briefly to the Acts of the Apostles. In the discourses of Saints Peter and Stephen to the skeptical Jews, we may find answers to the question of what exactly the Jews are supposed to feel so guilty about that they require the salvation available only through Jesus.

Peter, having cured a lame man, wins the admiration and attention of the people, to whom he addresses a speech from Solomon's portico (Acts 3:11–26). According to Peter, who is speaking after Jesus's crucifixion, the sin for which the Israelites bear guilt, and from which they require salvation through Christ, is their failure to accept Christ in the first place and their crime of putting him to death. They acted in ignorance, it is true, but they should have known better, because of the prophecy of Moses contained in Deuteronomy 18: " 'But what God foretold by the mouth of all the prophets, that his Christ should suffer, he thus fulfilled. Repent therefore, and turn again, that your sins may be blotted out. . . . Moses said, "The Lord God will raise up for you a prophet from your brethren as he raised me up. You shall listen to him in whatever he tells you" ' " (Acts 3:18–22).

This is something of a Catch-22, since, as Jesus makes clear (especially in the Gospel of John), although he is destined to die a sacrificial death and dies of his own free will, nonetheless those who bring that death about are guilty of having killed him. By dying, Jesus thus *inflicts* on the Jews the same guilt from which his death is supposed to save them.

Peter refers to Jesus in this chapter as a "servant": " 'The God of Abraham and of Isaac and of Jacob, the God of our fathers, glorified his servant Jesus' " (3:13). This title alludes to Moses, who was regularly referred to in this way. It also emphasizes the role of the messiah as the one who fulfills the prophecy of Isaiah concerning the "suffering servant." The exhortation, addressed to Jews, is designed to point out to them that if they believe their own Scriptures and prophets, they will recognize their sin in rejecting Jesus and handing him over to crucifixion, and they will repent.

In chapter 7 of Acts, Saint Stephen, too, discusses at length the fore-shadowings in the Hebrew Bible of Jesus as the messiah. Chapter 6 relates how Stephen has preached with such spirit and persuasiveness that those who disputed with him but could not refute him have arranged to have him falsely charged: "Then they secretly instigated men, who said, 'We have heard him speak blasphemous words against Moses and God' " (v. 11). These "men" go on to specify the misdeeds they allege Stephen has claimed Jesus will do: " 'We have heard him [Stephen] say that this Jesus of Nazareth will destroy this place [the synagogue], and will change the customs which Moses delivered to us' " (v. 14). Stephen, in reply, launches into a disqui-sition summarizing the essential points of the history of the Israelites from the time of Abraham up to the Exodus and beyond. What is distinctive in Stephen's narrative, which occupies most of chapter 7, is the effort to por-tray Moses as a man who, though appointed to lead Israel, was constantly rejected, rebuffed, and persecuted by the stiff-necked people God was try-ing, through him, to bring to holiness. In this way, Stephen makes Moses the type of Jesus as the suffering redeemer-prophet whom the Israelites incur guilt by persecuting. Thus, for example, in recounting the story of the slaying of the Egyptian overseer, Stephen offers this bit of exegesis: " 'He [Moses] supposed that his brethren understood that God was giving them deliverance by his hand, but they did not understand' " (7:25). This inter-pretation makes it possible to understand the remarks attributed to the quarreling Israelites who question Moses's right to judge them as a willful defiance of their deliverer and, through him, of the God who empowered him. Stephen rhetorically underscores his point with phrases such as: " 'This Moses whom they refused, saying "who made you a ruler and a judge?" God sent as both ruler and deliverer by the hand of the angel that appeared to him in the bush' " (v. 35).

Stephen goes on to remind his audience that this was the Moses who prophesied that God would raise up another prophet like him, alluding to the familiar passage in Deuteronomy 18. He then launches into a scathing indictment of the Jews, past and present, for disobeying God and his ap-pointed prophets: " 'Our fathers refused to obey him [Moses], but thrust him aside, and in their hearts they turned to Egypt, saying to Aaron, "Make for us gods to go before us; as for this Moses who led us out from the land of Egypt, we do not know what has become of him" ' " (vv. 39–40). For Stephen, then, the deed that most clearly epitomizes the Israelites' disobedience and declares them sinners deserving of death is the episode of the Golden Calf. He concludes thus: " 'You stiff-necked people, uncircumcised in heart and ears, you always resist the Holy Spirit. As your fathers did, so do you. Which of the prophets did not your fathers persecute? And they killed those who announced beforehand the coming of the Righteous One, whom you have now betrayed and murdered, you who received the law as delivered by angels and did not keep it' " (vv. 51–53). Not too surprisingly, this speech fails to placate his accusers, and Stephen is stoned to death.

For Peter, as we have seen, the sin from which stems the universal guilt requiring salvation through the sacrificed Jesus is the sacrifice of Jesus itself; Stephen amplifies this theme to make that episode a repetition of an overall pattern of defiance of and disobedience to God and his messengers. The main type of this is the episode of the Golden Calf.[7] As we know from the Exodus account, God is on that occasion only with great difficulty prevented by Moses from exterminating the Israelites, being mollified in part by Moses's own offer to die on behalf of his sinning people, as well as by sending a plague and by the execution of three thousand of the sinners. In the wake of that disastrous event, God, passing before Moses with the second set of tablets of the Law, makes the following problematic proclamation: " 'The Lord! The Lord! a God compassionate and gracious, slow to anger, abounding in kindness and faithfulness, extending kindness to the thousandth generation, forgiving iniquity, transgression and sin; yet He does not remit all punishment, but visits the iniquity of fathers upon children and children's children, upon the third and fourth generations' " (Exod. 34:6–7).

The tension in this passage between a God who judges strictly and surely according to his stern Law and one who forgives and grants mercy, remains unresolved; but it is clear from Stephen's speech in Acts that for him the guilt from the sin of the Golden Calf, and others like it, has not been and cannot be forgiven according to the Law of the Mosaic covenant. Therefore a special dispensation of grace on God's part is required. Jesus is the actualization of this divine grace, but he is also the just payment required by the Law. In this way Jesus simultaneously fulfills the Law, paying the debt required by the principle of reciprocity, and claims that the principle has itself been superseded by him and the gift of pardon he represents.

It is Saint Paul who most systematically develops a theological position based on the contrast between law and grace. The great advantage of the new covenant is, in his view, that whereas under the regime of the Mosaic Law everyone stands under an as-yet unfulfilled sentence of death and damnation, the new covenant allows for an abrogation of the Law itself, so that God's grace can work to save the condemned from their deserved fate.

In Acts, Paul preaches thus to the Jews: " 'Let it be known to you therefore, brethren, that through this man [Jesus] forgiveness of sins is proclaimed to you, and by him every one that believes is freed from everything from which you could not be freed by the law of Moses' " (13: 38–39). The proclaimed superiority of the new covenant leads to Paul's valuation of faith, rather than works, as the way to salvation. "Works" implies performing acts in keeping with the Mosaic Law; but according to this same Law, as far as Paul is concerned, everyone is irrevocably condemned already by the misdeeds of their forefathers. Jesus, by contrast, offers no law, but only himself and his death and resurrection. What can be achieved by this deed is not a new set of rules to act upon but rather an attitude of faith that one has indeed been forgiven through Jesus: "Since all have sinned and fall short of the glory of God, they are justified by his grace as a gift, through the redemption which is in Christ Jesus, whom God put forward as an expiation by his blood, to be received by faith" (Rom. 3:23–25). Paul goes on in this passage to argue that Abraham and David were themselves exemplars of the fact that righteousness abides in faith, not works.

The writer of the Epistle to the Hebrews goes so far as to make Moses himself a paragon of faith in Jesus, whose future coming Moses, as God's greatest prophet to that time, presumably foresaw:

> By faith Moses, when he was born, was hid for three months by his parents, because they saw that the child was beautiful; and they were not afraid of the king's edict. By faith Moses, when he was grown up, refused to be called the son of Pharaoh's daughter, choosing rather to share ill-treatment with the people of God than to enjoy the fleeting pleasures of sin. He considered abuse suffered for the Christ greater wealth than the treasures of Egypt, for he looked to the reward. By faith he left Egypt, not being afraid of the anger of the king. . . . By faith he kept the Passover and sprinkled the blood, so that the Destroyer of the first-born might not touch them. (Heb. 11:23–28)

We may conclude from this survey that for the writers of the Christian Scriptures, Moses was a great type and predecessor of Jesus, but he fell short of Christ's stature in a number of ways. He is the first of a line of prophets to predict the coming of another prophet like himself, who will be, as Jeremiah predicts, the bringer of a new and better covenant (31:31–34). Insofar as he is the servant of God, and to a greater or lesser degree the prototype of the suffering servant prophesied by Isaiah, Moses presages Jesus as a rebuked martyr, a redeemer reviled and persecuted by those he has been sent to lead to righteousness.

As a servant of God, Moses stands in an unalterably inferior position to God. In this respect, he ranks below Jesus, who is the son of God and thus partakes of the divinity of his father. A servant rarely becomes master, but a son usually becomes a father. In the same way, Moses stands as one who mediates divinity for humans to Jesus, who is that divinity itself. Whereas Moses can call upon God to provide food miraculously, Jesus *is* the food that God provides, a food that is both carnal and spiritual.

Ultimately, Moses's inferiority to Jesus, for the Christian writers, is embodied in the imperfect covenant he delivers. For after all, as the Epistle to the Hebrews argues, "if that first covenant had been faultless, there would have been no occasion for a second" (Heb. 8:7). The great failing of the first covenant, as the New Testament portrays it, is that according to its laws everyone is guilty. Indeed, in the very moment of its being enunciated, those for whom it was intended were engaged in actions that violated it so profoundly as to make it a sentence of death from the instant it was revealed. The new covenant, by contrast, is sealed, not with the sacrificial blood of animals, as was the Mosaic covenant, but with Christ's blood: "He [Jesus] entered once for all into the Holy Place, taking not the blood of goats and calves but his own blood, thus securing an eternal redemption" (Heb. 9:12).

This second covenant will not consist of a set of laws to be enacted but will result in a change of spirit, which, needing no particular instructions, will act spontaneously in the spirit of God, as Jeremiah had prophesied: " 'I will put my laws into their minds, and write them on their hearts, . . . And they shall not teach every one his fellow . . . for all shall know me' " (Jer. 31:34–35, cited in Heb. 8:10–11). The author of Hebrews summarizes the gist of the argument pithily: "Therefore he [Jesus] is the mediator of a new covenant, so that those who are called may receive the promised eternal inheritance, since a death has occurred which redeems them from the transgressions under the first covenant" (9:15). What now remains to be seen is the nature of that death that has occurred, what were the transgressions under the first covenant, and how is it possible for the former to redeem the latter?

III

Christ's sacrificial death has the specific significance of being a transmutation of the Passover sacrifice. As Saint Paul says, "Cleanse out the old leaven that you may be a new lump [of dough], as you really are unleavened. For Christ, our paschal lamb, has been sacrificed" (1 Cor. 5:7). My own task in arguing for a direct correspondence between Passover and the Passion of Jesus is considerably lightened by the fact that Gillian Feeley-Harnick has devoted an admirable study to documenting and supporting just such an assertion. Feeley-Harnick, after extensive consideration of the various scriptural accounts of the Last Supper, puts forward this ingenious hypothesis:

> I would like to suggest an interpretation relating the passover to the last suppers described by early Christian writers in which the last supper is simply the preliminary, including the benediction over the wine (the kiddush) and the benediction over the bread, the grace before meals. The crucifixion is the main part of the meal, the *shulhan arukh* or "prepared table." The cross is the table of the Lord where the bitter herbs and the paschal lamb are consumed. (1981, 129)

Examining the entire sequence of events from the Last Supper through the Crucifixion as described in the Gospels, Feeley-Harnick shows a point-by-point correspondence with the prescriptions for the Passover seder set forth in the Mishnah, which represents Jewish practices from the time of the very early Christian era. The Mishnah seder, for example, calls for the drinking of four cups of wine; as Feeley-Harnick explains, "The first cup of wine accompanies the kiddush [at the Last Supper]. The second cup is offered in the Garden of Gethsemane, the third immediately before the crucifixion, and the fourth, the one that the host finally takes, is offered at the end" (130). Supporting her position—which I share—that "the story of Jesus . . . can be viewed as a midrash on the story of Moses" (127), Feeley-Harnick concludes: "The Eucharist, commemorating the last supper in which Jesus prefigured the crucifixion and resurrection, is a symbolic representation in food patterned exactly after the passover." Putting the crux as succinctly as possible, she writes: "The passion narrative is the passover haggadah" (130).

But in transforming the Passover ritual and story into the story of the Passion and its enactment in the Eucharist, the Christian myth has consistently inverted aspects of its Mosaic prototype. Thus, as Feeley-Harnick shows, whereas the slaughter of the first-born and the apotropaic Passover sacrifice occurred in the middle of the night, the Crucifixion occurs in the middle of the day, when a mysterious darkness descends on the land. Instead of remaining indoors, as the Passover regulations require, Jesus goes out into the Garden of Gethsemane and the disciples disperse. And while the Passover separates the Israelite from the non-Israelite, Jesus's sacrifice of himself as the Lamb of God embraces Jews and Gentiles together. We may conclude, then, that in the central Christian myth, and its ritual enactments at communion as well as in the calendrical cycle culminating in Easter Week, the Passover myth and ritual are simultaneously both repeated and undone by symbolic reversals.

IV

Freud's psychoanalytic understanding of Christianity is not, in the end, very different from the self-understanding of the New Testament authors. It is hard to see what there might be for a Christian to argue with in this formulation of Freud's: "Original sin and redemption by the sacrifice of a victim became the foundation stones of the new religion founded by Paul." It might be supposed that Freud's account of the source of original sin could lead to a dispute; but on this score too one finds, perhaps surprisingly, that the Christian Scriptures are even more explicit than Freud. For Freud, the great insight of Saul of Tarsus—Saint Paul—was this: " 'The reason we are so unhappy is that we have killed God the father' " (1939, 135). One might paraphrase Freud's understanding of the historical truth underlying this insight in this way: "We are unhappy because we killed the father, who has become God by virtue of our having killed him, and whose justifiable persecution of us makes us feel anxious and guilty."

Freud supposed that this direct grasp of the truth would have eluded Paul, who would instead have apprehended it under the "delusional disguise of the glad tidings: 'we are freed from all guilt since one of us has sacrificed his life to absolve us.' In this formula, the killing of God was of course not mentioned, but a crime that had to be atoned by the sacrifice of a victim could only have been a murder" (1939, 135). But Freud is here not giving the Christian thinkers enough credit. In fact, while it was not Paul but Peter who said it, Freud's formulation is stated explicitly and quite undisguised, delusionally or otherwise, in the Christian Scripture, as this quotation attests: " 'But you [men of Israel] denied the Holy and Righteous One, and asked for a murderer to be granted to you, and killed the Author of life, whom God raised from the dead' " (Acts 3:14–15). The phrase that Peter uses here, translated as "Author of life," relies on a Greek word which may be rendered as "pioneer," "originator," or "leader," implying one who goes first.[8] That phrase could surely be applied both to the Mosaic God and to the Freudian primal father, albeit in different ways.

Peter's statement thus carries not only the accusation that the Jews have killed the Son of God, who was also God's prophet and servant, but also that they have killed God the father himself. This understanding is, of course, ratified in the postscriptural doctrine of the Trinity, whereby it is claimed that God the Father and God the Son are identical. According to this Christian doctrine, then, in killing Jesus, the Jews are guilty of having killed God.

For Freud, the truth of this accusation lay in two historical realities. The first is that all humans have some share in the sense of guilt deriving from the primordial murder of the father by the band of brothers. The second is that the Jews, in particular, experienced a particular malaise or "discontent" (Unbehagen) during this period, ostensibly owing to political setbacks of which the Roman conquest was the final, catastrophic ignominy, but at a deeper, unconscious level because of their guilt over having in former times been party to the murder of Moses.

My own argument does not rest on historical events but on events created and re-created in the present by means of the customs, ceremonies, and dogmas constituting the religious life of society. According to my view, the original sin for which Jesus sacrificed himself and thus redeemed humanity is Moses's rebellion within the mythic primal horde that culminated in the deaths of the Egyptian first-born, army, and pharaoh. This scenario is told through the teaching of the Torah and in addition is enacted annually through the rite of Passover and in transmuted form through the performance of the Christian rituals based on the Passion story.

In the original Passover, Moses, though almost entirely absent in the haggadah that accompanies the ritual, is nonetheless, according to the sacred narrative of the Torah, the sacrificer who orders the killing and eating of the Passover lamb to protect the Israelites from the death and destruction visited by God on Egypt.

But this destruction of Egypt is, at the same time, a crime on Moses's hands. As we have seen, Moses's rebellion is at once a patricide, since Pharaoh is Moses's father; a deicide, since Pharaoh is a living god; a regicide, since Pharaoh is the ruler of the Egyptian empire; and a revolt of the servant against the master, since Moses leads the enslaved Israelites against their overlord and taskmaster.

Because of the guilt engendered by this deed the covenant on Mount Sinai is instituted, and from that guilt the Law gains its compulsory force. According to the Mosaic Law—which is, however, a statement of the more general human social principle of reciprocity—justice demands like for like: punishment, in talionic fashion, must match the crime. By this reckoning Moses, and by extension all the Israelites for whom he acted and who participated in the events, stand under sentence of death for having committed the deed by which they liberated themselves.

Because this debt remains uncollected, the Israelites are violators of the Law by virtue of the very events that led to its promulgation. The Law itself, no matter how restrictive it may seem, protectively wards off the as-yet unexecuted and dreaded talionic punishment for the original crime. But, as we have seen, only retrospectively, according to the Sinaitic Law, is the original deed a crime. Looked at from the post-Sinaitic viewpoint the primal rebellion of Moses has violated almost every one of the Ten Commandments: The son rose against his father, god, and king to take for himself what the father had (abusively) held for himself; he thus denied the deity of his father, took his name in vain, failed to honor his father and mother, murdered, committed adultery by conspiring to take the father's wives, stole, and coveted his father's possessions.[9]

Saint Paul recognized that it was the Law itself that, paradoxically, gave rise to sin: "If it had not been for the law, I should not have known sin. I should not have known what it is to covet if the law had not said, 'You shall not covet' " (Rom. 7:7). What Paul here points to is that in the state before the Law, that is, in the primal horde, there was no sin, because there was no law to violate. The impulse to desire freedom, including freedom of sexual expression, denied by the father/pharaoh, as well as the impulse to fight for such freedom, were not crimes but the assertions of innocent, uncomplicated and "conflict-free" strivings on one's own behalf.

The Law, then, rests on the presupposition of the guilt of those to whom it applies, and it constitutes a sentence of lifelong penance for the crimes of which one is perforce already guilty. Yet the Law cannot obliterate the sense of being made to suffer unjustly for crimes that were not crimes at the time they were committed. Consequently, the Law itself gives rise to a rebellious impulse to violate it. These feelings, in turn, reinforce the sense of guilt that lends to the Law its severity and its peremptory effectiveness.

Moses, as we saw, never suffered the death he owed for his crime. He did die, of course, with his life's goal unachieved, but he was luckier than most, dying after a long life, with many great deeds accomplished. Moses imposed on himself and his people the Law as a defense against God's impending judgment—a judgment that would have to be terrible, given what they did to him in his decomposed "bad" guise as the wicked pharaoh. This Law has the adaptive effect of making possible harmonious life in society, based on a common sacrifice of some, at least, of what was originally desired, a compromise gratefully accepted in lieu of the far worse fate held in the background as an ever-present threat.

But the talionic principle demands that the covenant be ratified by a sacrifice. For this purpose, Moses institutes a set of animal sacrifices as substitute offerings. These sacrifices include the sacrifice of bulls by which Moses seals the Sinaitic covenant with blood, the Passover sacrifices, and the guilt and sin offerings meticulously described in Leviticus.

Among these, the Passover sacrifice is the most important because unlike the others, it serves as the focus for an annual ritual that combines the eating of a festival meal, the telling of the Exodus story, and the activation of the dynamic relationships between fathers and sons. It thus perpetuates and brings to life the overt commemoration of joyous liberation, together with the more covert acknowledgment of the guilt entailed thereby and the obligation to make sacrifices for it.

As we have seen, Moses acts as sacrificer of the father, the first-born sons, and the sacrificial lamb that serves as a substitute for the Israelites. If Moses is the sacrificer, continually incurring more guilt by the deeds intended to appease the persecuting wrath of the Deity in his role as avenger of the slain father, then Jesus is the sacrifice. And as the Christian Scriptures keep pointing out, only Jesus, as God, constitutes an adequate talionic sacrifice sufficient to erase the guilt for having killed God, the guilt that sustains the Law.

In the Christian myth, Jesus is able, unlike Moses, to satisfy God's demand for justice because he matches the original victim, like for like. Just as Pharaoh was father, king, master, and god, so Jesus is son, citizen, servant, and man—but at the same time (especially by the Trinitarian doctrine) he is father, king, master, and God. The blood of such a victim can erase the sin and wipe clean the guilt of the Israelites—and by extension all humanity—in a way that, as the Epistle to the Hebrews stresses, the blood of goats and lambs cannot.

Having offered himself as a proper ransom and having survived his own death, Jesus can now address the other side of the ambivalent relationship of junior and senior male. The jealous wrathful senior male who demands satisfaction has been appeased, the junior male has been duly punished for his rebellion. Now the side of the senior-junior relationship that emphasizes love and union can come to the fore. Seated at the right hand of his father, with whom he is, in some mysterious sense, identical, Jesus offers clemency and freedom from sin and guilt as a gift to those who will accept it.

Christ's sacrifice, thus, does not so much abrogate the Mosaic Law as it undoes the deed that gave rise to both the guilt and the Law. Without the threat of punishment, the brothers can now live without rules, their social harmony ensured by the same spirit of brotherly love that ruled among them during the days when, under the regime of the primal father, they banded together, converted their jealousy and envy of each other into aim-inhibited love, and planned their liberating deed. Societies animated by this spirit, whether created by a ritual or in ongoing communities, bring with them, at least for a while, the pleasurable and exhilarating experience of liberation from guilt and obligation, as well as from the obsessional defenses called forth by them. Herein lies some of the intoxicating appeal of the "good news."[10]

The distinction between Law and spirit is neatly exemplified in the Christian transformation of Shavuot, the Hebrew Feast of Weeks celebrated on the fiftieth day after the second day of Passover. Originally this was a harvest festival. For the Jews under the rabbis in exile, it became redefined as the day on which the Torah descended from heaven; it is the celebration of the bestowal of the Mosaic Law.

In Christianity, Pentecost, "the fiftieth day," takes on a meaning that crucially matches and also transforms the Jewish festival: "When the day of Pentecost had come, they [the apostles of Christ] were all together in one place. And suddenly a sound came from heaven like the rush of the mighty wind, and it filled all the house where they were sitting. And there appeared to them tongues as of fire, distributed and resting on each one of them. And they were all filled with the Holy Spirit and began to speak in other tongues, as the Spirit gave them utterance" (Acts 2:1–4). As Christ's death was his transfigured Passover, so the fiftieth day for the Christians, a transformed Shavuot, marks the descent not of the Law but of the Holy Spirit, the third member of the Christian Trinity. This spirit fills each member of the Christian community and imbues each with divine enthusiasm, prophetic power, grace, and brotherly love.

For Paul, the letter of the Law kills, but the spirit brings life. The Mosaic covenant is associated, for him, with death, the flesh, sin, guilt, and damnation to eternal separation from God. The spirit, by contrast, which Christ liberates in the second covenant by his self-sacrifice, replaces these with life, love, redemption, purity of spirit, and eternal salvation.

V

The Christian transformation of Passover, as narrative in the Gospels and as enactment in the ritual of communion, as well as in the annual celebrations of the sacred moments of Christ's life (which focus chiefly on his death and resurrection), both retains and counters the meaning of the Passover myth and ritual. Like Passover, the Passion is at once a reenactment and an expiation of the primal crime. It holds out the promise, however, that a time will come in which the crime that underwrites the social contract, making that contract necessary and inescapable, will be adequately atoned for, and social life will proceed in harmony, with the destructive mutual hostility between the junior and senior generations of males abolished or held in check and reconciled so that amity among brothers, and between generations, can prevail.

What would this promised society be like? The answer, in biblical terms, I think, is that it would resemble the original society of the Israelites, when they were a band of twelve brothers, their sister, and their families. They lived at peace (by and large), with the blessing of their father, Jacob. Although they were jealous of and tried to kill one of their number, Joseph (himself a type of Jesus), he forgave them and ultimately established them in prosperity and honor in Egypt. There the ruling pharaoh honored Joseph as a father, and protected the band, while God himself clearly smiled on the enterprise.

We have, then, a narrative, conveyed in the combined Judeo-Christian biblical myth comprising the Pentateuch and the Gospels, in which a harmonious state of society exemplified in the situation of the twelve Israelites under the good pharaoh gives way to the regime of a bad pharaoh, who transforms the situation into the paradigm of the "bad" primal horde as envisioned in Freud's myth. Moses leads a rebellion against this regime, and establishes a covenant based on shared guilt in the rebellion. Christ leads a second rebellion and establishes a new covenant, which takes as its model of society the oppressed but united band of brothers living in harmony and love. We have seen, however, that this harmony can flourish only when the hostility of the group is projected outward onto persecuting enemies. This accounts for the rise of Satan to the status of God's evil double in Christianity and for the hope of a final showdown beween them. (See Cohn 1993 on the apocalyptic tradition.)

We may analyze the biblical narrative, in summary, as a succession of four defining moments, organized as stories, each of which is a variation on the same theme. The first is the story of Jacob and his brothers; the second, the story of the wicked pharaoh and the bondage in Egypt; third, Moses and the liberation from slavery; and fourth, the Passion and Resurrection of Jesus. These four moments may also be understood as themselves constituting a larger narrative, and this overarching narrative matches precisely the more general mythic schema that I have called the succession scenario.

In my previous discussion of that scenario, I noted that the succession of the junior male to senior status requires four moments featuring four different characters. The first moment is the reign of the legitimate senior male who is to be displaced. This is followed by the reign of the bad, illegitimate senior male who deserves to be replaced. The avenger, a junior male who, on behalf of the deposed "good" ruler kills or otherwise disposes of the bad usurper, appears next. The fourth moment is the advent of the innocent heir, often decomposed into the innocent who inherits and the innocent who atones through his martyrdom for the rebellion of the avenger.

In the story of the kingship in Ethiopia, we saw the scenario played out in full. King Chichanos is the rightful king of Ethiopia, Balaam the usurper. Moses plays the role of avenger, who, however, does not achieve full senior status himself but prepares for the rightful, innocent heir, Monarchos. We can now see that this story shows in miniature the part played by Moses in the much vaster story encompassing the Torah narrative and the Christian Gospels. The part of rightful ruler is played by the good father, Jacob/Israel. His regime is displaced by that of the bad father, the wicked pharaoh. Moses again becomes the avenger, though in the Bible story he actually commits the murder that in Ethiopia is rendered unnecessary by the fortuitous death of Chichanos. Jesus, finally, having first played the martyred victim, reigns as innocent heir and new legitimate ruler, co-equal with the "father" who has been displaced and is now represented by God.[11]

The combined Hebrew and Christian scriptural myths, then, present the full range of possible transformations of the primal-horde paradigm. But any one of them also contains within itself the possibilities of the others and thus, like the fragments of a hologram, has the potential for generating the whole array (and thus allowing me, following Freud, to reconstruct the schema by undoing the transformations).

Freud was right to see that one can "reconstruct" the myth of the primal horde from the myth and narrative performed in the Christian communion, especially in the Catholic form in which he encountered it. The image of an innocent son, devoid of sinful sexual or aggressive impulses, surrendering to torture and offering his body to be eaten and his blood to be drunk, generates its opposite and complement: a guilty father, driven by violent and lustful appetites, sadistically persecuting (and cannibalizing?) his victims. Freud, as we have seen, thought this meant that he could posit the transgenerational memory of a historical moment in which these images had been a reality. In my own view, the image of the primal father is itself (re)created in the process of enacting the symbolism of Christ's Passion.

The primal horde scenario is thus implicit *within* the symbolism of the Eucharist. But just as we recognize in the image I have conjured of the primal father a recurrent Christian caricature of the Jew, we recognize that the referent is not the bad pharaoh, as I have shown it to be in the case of the Torah narrative, but rather Moses himself. It was he who brought the Law whose letter kills and by which all of us are damned, as Christians interpret it. And he himself, the liberator of the Jews, is now transformed into the guilty sacrificer of the innocent sacrifice/martyr.

Jesus is thus "like Moses" in the sense that he is the leader of a rebellion against the death-dealing oppression of a senior tyrant. But he is antithetical to Moses in the sense that the Mosaic Law has become, in the New Testament, the embodiment of the paternal tyranny that is to be overthrown. Unlike Moses, Jesus is understood to absorb and thus banish the guilt of his rebellion by means of his own martyrdom.

Christian practice can thus be seen to repeat and intensify the dynamics that produced the Torah and Jewish practice. It contains within itself the whole story. But it has been necessary, especially since Christianity is addressed to non-Jews not already under the sway of the Mosaic Law, to make sure people know they are in the guilty condition from which Christianity promises to save them. Ironically, it has thus been in the interests of Christianity, for its own success, to insist on the authority and the truth of the Torah narrative and to uphold the legitimacy of the Mosaic Law and covenant. Only in the context of this myth do people feel guilty enough to desire Christian salvation. In its tireless evangelical mission, then, Christianity has exported and universalized the Torah, its story and its moral force, in a way unimaginable to that tiny and short-lived state whose national myth it once was.

VI

In one of his earliest writings on the dynamics of obsessional neurosis (1896), Freud distinguished between the "primary" and "secondary" defenses characteristic of this pathology (a distinction he later modified [1909, 221 ff.] but did not discard as his understanding of mental life advanced). According to this view, the origin of the obsessional neurosis lies in the unconsciously preserved memory of an act, performed with pleasure during the infantile "period of immorality," which, when viewed in retrospect, after childhood "immorality" has been replaced by society's morality and other measures of self-control and self-reproach, appears reprehensible to the now conscientious ego. Consequently, an affect of self-reproach attaches to the memory of the original deed, and the psyche, during latency, replaces the memory itself in consciousness with primary operations of defense, among which are conscientiousness, shame, and self-distrust.

The setting up of these primary defenses ushers in a period of what appears to be psychic health but is actually simply the work of successful defense. In many people this process leads to no later pathological or social maladaptive result. In those destined to fall ill from an obsessional neurotic disorder, however, the illness sets in when, perhaps in response to renewed intensification of sexuality at puberty, the repressed memories return in disguised form.

The return of the repressed in turn stimulates the elaboration of a system of secondary defense, aimed at preventing *both* the original repressed memory *and* the painful self-reproaches proper to it from emerging into conscious awareness. Secondary defense against the obsessional ideas "may be effected by a forcible diversion on to other thoughts with a content as contrary as possible" (Freud, 1896, 173). Hence one such typical class of secondary defenses entails intellectualization and concentration on elevated and abstract thoughts; this is why "*obsessional brooding,* if it succeeds, regularly deals with abstract and *suprasensual* things; because the ideas that have been repressed are always concerned with *sensuality.*"

The secondary defenses against the original self-reproaches attached to the unconscious memory include: "*penitential* measures (burdensome ceremonials, the observation of numbers), *precautionary* measures (all sorts of phobias, superstition, pedantry, increase in the primary symptom of conscientiousness); measures to do with *fear of betrayal.* . . or to insure *numbing* (dipsomania)" (1896, 173).

Framing this early formulation in the more familiar language of the later theory, we might say that in early childhood, impulses arise involving incestuous, sadistic, and hostile wishes toward the parents. With the resolution of the Oedipus complex, the superego emerges as an internal institution of self-reproach. If the original repressed impulses, and the memories and fantasies attached to them, threaten too strongly to emerge again, as happens with the maturational transformations of puberty, the superego recriminations are likewise increased. The ego thus faces two different threats, one from the repressed impulses, the other from the harshly punitive superego responding to them. It is the latter that represent the greater danger; the former are felt as unacceptable only because of them.

As a consequence, the system of secondary defense is driven to defend itself first and foremost against the ferocity of the superego attacks that threaten to erupt whenever the underlying impulses or memories are stirred. The precautions, penances, and so on are designed to ward off painful superego punishments, while at the same time providing the ego with enough unhappiness and suffering to mollify the superego's demand for punitive retribution.

If we examine this scheme in the context of the biblical myth, the parallels that emerge are these. In the "period of immorality" (that is, the era before Sinai) the Israelites and their mythic hero Moses act on incestuous, defiant, and hostile impulses climaxing in an oedipal patricide. In response to the fear of retaliative castrating punishment, Moses institutes a set of self-reproaches, namely the Law, according to which, retrospectively, the deeds preceding and indeed motivating it are judged negatively. The Torah and its covenant thus correspond to the primary defenses postulated by Freud and to his later concept of the superego itself.

Christianity, then, corresponds to a system of secondary defenses, in the sense that the first self-reproaches—the Mosaic Laws—now themselves seem to be the primary danger, since they accompany the impulses that led to the original deed with a need for inexorable and dreadful punishment. The ceremonials and penances to which Christianity is driven may be understood as defenses against Judaism, its prophet, and his Law. These, in turn represent a level of primary defense against the patricide I have identified.

Secondary defense involves a "forcible diversion on to other thoughts with a content as contrary as possible" to the ones being defended against. We can thus understand why and how Christianity represents the original memory, as it were, in the negative, substituting a passive sacrifice of an "innocent" son for the active patricide performed by a "guilty" son, and why and how it resolutely concerns itself with abstract, suprasensual thoughts about the spirit and otherworldly matters and places a negative value on the flesh and sensuality.

Epilogue

Freud's myth of the primal horde has not, for the most part, been taken very seriously. The discipline of psychoanalysis has done very well without it, and in the fields of history, religion, anthropology, and the humanities it has been treated more as a curiosity than as a useful theory. For Freud's admirers it has often been an embarrassment, and for his detractors it has provided yet another cudgel with which to beat him. His attempt to rework it in a biblical setting in *Moses and Monotheism* and thus establish it at the root of Judeo-Christian civilization has fared no better.

In retrospect we can see the logic underlying his thinking. He was attempting to offer his readers an insight comparable to the kind of interpretation he thought essential in a psychoanalytic treatment. He perceived that many people are unhappy in civilization, burdened with guilt and inhibited in their ability to enjoy life. His diagnosis was that our society suffers from an obsessional neurosis and that the practices of Judeo-Christian religion are its symptoms. We know that throughout his career he held to the view that neurosis could be cured by helping the patient remember a forgotten trauma from childhood. And, since people in fact rarely do remember such things, he regarded it as necessary for the analyst to reconstruct the trauma from the clues offered by the symptoms and to present that trauma to the patient. Treating Western civilization as his "patient," Freud constructed the supposed historical event of the rebellion of the brothers against the jealous sire of the primal horde.

This intervention largely went unnoticed because its weaknesses are only too visible. It mistakenly treats a civilization as if it were a person; it appears to assume a transgenerational collective unconscious containing repressed memories on the part of that civilization; and it proposes as real historical traumas a deed and a replay of it in the murder of Moses that have no basis in fact and have never been corroborated with any independent evidence.

Contemporary psychoanalytic therapy is, however, no longer focused on the goal of recovering repressed memories, on making the unconscious conscious, or even on letting ego be where id was. The current analytic goal is, rather, as Jacob Arlow succinctly puts it, "to demonstrate to the patient how his or her mind works. . . . The governing paradigm is to demonstrate how present-day experience may be misinterpreted in terms of derivatives of persistent unconscious fantasies from the past" (1995, 222).

If we approach the interpretation of Western culture in light of this somewhat different strategy, we see that we should be seeking to discover what persistent unconscious fantasy, or, as it would be constituted in social life, what persistent myth inherited from the past, continues to determine aspects of our thought and action in ways of which we might not be fully aware. Using the primal horde story as this sort of mythic paradigm or scenario, some contemporary scholars of cultural and social history have begun to notice that Freud's myth is indeed a useful interpretive construct.

Thus, for example, Lynn Hunt, in her perceptive study of the French Revolution, writes, "I find Freud's analysis in *Totem and Taboo* suggestive because it sees a set of relationships as being critical to the founding of social and political authority: relationships between fathers and sons, between men, and between men and women. In addition, Freud's own need to write a myth of human origins demonstrates the centrality of narratives about the family to the constitution of forms of authority, even though Freud's account cannot fruitfully be read as an analysis of an actual event in prehistory or as a rigid model for social and political relationships" (1992, 7–8).

Hunt's caution in the last clause indicates that while she finds the myth useful as an interpretive paradigm, she realizes that it has no positive standing on its own, except perhaps as Freud's myth of his own authority. Ann Douglas, who also uses Freud's model productively, in her study of the intellectual culture of New York in the 1920s, makes it even plainer that Freud's myth is useful precisely because it is an expression of his (and our) cultural milieu: "Few scholars in Freud's day or since have believed that *Totem and Taboo* is an accurate re-creation of any primitive society, as Freud claimed it was, but fewer have realized that it does offer a fairly accurate picture of the society and era in which Freud lived, a picture, moreover, with specific relevance to America, his least welcome but most assiduous and powerful ally" (1995, 239).

If Freud's myth is a valuable guide to understanding the interplay of family fantasies and sociopolitical reality in revolutionary France and 1920s America, might we not suspect that it encapsulates some central enduring themes in Western civilization? And might we not ask where, within this civilization, it is itself grounded, if not in the collective memory of the speculative prehistory Freud proposed?

This book provides the answer to those questions, by demonstrating that what Freud reconstructed as ancient history, while not that, is an almost perfectly accurate model of the myth that we already know to be the central organizing master narrative of the Judeo-Christian tradition, namely the Bible.[1] The mythic paradigm of the primal horde is not, then, something that hovers in the air structuring the zeitgeist or a ghostly skeleton hidden away in the unconscious collective memory of the West. It is, on the contrary, the most widely known, read, and performed sacred story we have, whose influence on the West, and through it on life on this planet, has been incalculable.

This consideration opens up, I believe, horizons for new understandings of the Bible, of Freud, of Western civilization, and of the primal-horde paradigm. My hope is to have demonstrated that Freud's myth of the primal horde and the story of Moses as told in the Torah are one and the same, to have drawn out some of the implications of this identity, and to suggest that inquiry based on the recognition of it will lead toward a richer understanding of who we are and what we are doing.

Notes

1
Beyond Freud's Moses

1. I have covered some of this ground in my essay "Freud's Anthropology" (1991).

2. There has been a steady stream of literature on *Moses and Monotheism,* the book whose subject is also my own here. The continued interest in this work is not the result of the persuasiveness of its arguments but because it is so generally accepted that the book's scholarly content is without merit that one can safely dismiss it and read the text for what it reveals about Freud: his personal conflicts and fantasies, his Judaism, and his cultural and historical milieu. What engagement scholars give to the argument seems largely involved with issues that seem to me marginal to the main point of the book: whether Moses was an Egyptian, or why Freud considered this important, for example, or whether patrilineal descent represents an advance in the intellectual life of civilization.

A partial review of the literature devoted wholly or in considerable part to *Moses and Monotheism* would include Ater (1983); Bakan (1958, part 3); Baron (1969); Bennington (1994); Bergmann (1982); E. Blum (1956); H. Blum (1991); Carroll (1988, 1989); Certeau (1988); Christen and Hazelton (1969); Day (1988); Desmonde (1950); Doria-Medina (1991); Eilberg-Schwartz (1994b); Goldstein (1992, chap. 4); Handelman (1987); Jones (1953–57, 3:367–374); Koret (1986); Krüll (1986); Lévi-Valensi (1984); Meissner (1984b, chap. 5); Oelschlegel (1943); Oring (1984, chap. 7); Reid (1972); Reik (1958, 1959); Rice (1990, 1994); Ricoeur (1970, chap. 3); Robert (1976); Robertson (1988, 1994); Roith (1987); Schorske (1993); Schur (1972); Van Herik (1982); Vitz (1983, 1988); Wallace (1977); Weiss-Rosmarin (1939); Wulff (1950); Yerushalmi (1989, 1991); and Zeligs (1986).

On Freud's Judaism more generally, see Bakan (1958); Balmary (1982); Frieden (1990); Gay (1987); Gilman (1993); D. Klein (1985); Krüll (1986); Loewenberg (1977); McGrath (1986); Miller (1981); Rice (1990); Robert (1976); Roith (1987); Schur (1972); Velikovsky (1941); Vitz (1988); and Yerushalmi (1989, 1991), to name only a few.

On the general topic of psychoanalytic interpretations of the Bible, see, for example, Chasseguet-Smirgel (1983); Eilberg-Schwartz (1994a); Y. Feldman (1989); Forsyth (1991); Ingham (1992); Lacan (1990, 1991); J. W. Miller (1983); Ostow (1982); Paul (1977, 1980, 1985a, 1987c, 1994a); Zeligs (1974).

3. I include a bibliography of the critical response to *Totem and Taboo* in my "Did the Primal Crime Take Place?" (1976). Wallace (1983) also reviews the recep-

tion of this work. Among the scholarly considerations of *Totem and Taboo* that have appeared since my article, Mahony's (1982, 1989) are particularly interesting.

4. See Dulaney and Fiske (1994) for a thorough exploration of the close connection between ritual and obsessional and compulsive symptoms.

5. See my "Psychoanalytic Anthropology" (1989) and "My Approach to Psychological Anthropology" (1994b) for my view of the field. Ambitious attempts to unite the cultural and the psychodynamic may also be found in works by Obeyesekere (1981, 1990), whose efforts parallel mine in many ways. Both of us owe a major debt to Melford Spiro, some of whose most influential papers are collected in his *Culture and Human Nature* (1987a).

6. See Freud's "Constructions in Analysis" (1937). The analyst's task, Freud writes, is "to make out what has been forgotten from the traces which it has left behind or, more correctly, to *construct* it" (258–59).

7. For a closer examination of Sellin's role in the composition of *Moses and Monotheism,* which is by no means as simple as is usually believed, see my article "Freud, Sellin, and the Death of Moses" (1994a).

8. Freud's evaluation of the status of his hypothesis of the primal horde fluctuated wildly. He seems to have told Abram Kardiner (1977:75) that it was something he dreamed up to while away a rainy Sunday afternoon. But in his *Autobiographical Study* (1925) Freud gives it the status of an almost mystical "vision" into the nature of things. I think he recognized that he was dealing with a myth, not a historical or scientific fact, but was prevented by certain prejudices from recognizing just how important a thing a myth really is. Compare Norman O. Brown's opening paragraph in his own quite visionary *Love's Body* (1966, 3): "Freud's myth of the rebellion of the sons against the father in the primal, prehistoric horde is not a historical explanation of origins, but a supra-historical archetype; eternally recurrent; a myth; an old, old story."

9. I should, for complete accuracy, exempt from my statement those early psychoanalysts who believed almost anything Freud said, including his theory of the primal horde. Among these are Reik (1958, 1959) and Róheim (1985 [1923]).

10. A short but typically masterful treatment of the role myths play in social life can be found in Durkheim's *Pragmatism and Sociology* (1983).

11. For a subtle discussion of the issue, see Lyotard's "Jewish Oedipus" (1977).

12. Those who have argued that in stressing patricide Freud overlooked the

theme of fratricide or fraternal strife in the Hebrew Bible include, to name only three, such diverse writers as Y. Feldman (1994); Rieff (1979); and Yerushalmi (1991).

13. On the sources other than Sellin for Freud's ideas in *Moses and Monotheism,* see Rice (1993) and Robertson (1994).

14. For an extensive and insightful psychoanalytically informed discussion of fraternal rivalry and the victory of the younger brothers in Genesis, see Forsyth (1991). See also Goldin (1988b).

15. I take the term *conscientious personality* from Oldham and Morris (1990). I shall discuss the relations and differences between obsessional neurosis, Obsessive-Compulsive Disorder, and the conscientious personality more fully in Chapter 8.

16. The question of the universality of the Oedipus complex is too complicated and important to be resolved here; for purposes of this book I shall simply note that if the Oedipus complex exists anywhere, it is in the Judeo-Christian West.

I believe that while the Western Oedipus complex represents a distinct cultural form, the oedipal phase of childhood, oedipal fantasies, and oedipal conflicts are present in humans everywhere and are manifested in one guise or another, though these forms may vary widely. One can view different cultural outcomes of oedipal conflict as varying solutions to the task of mediating such oppositions as good-bad, active-passive, me/not me, male-female, adult-child, and so on, as proposed by T. Shapiro (1977), and as involving a triadic rather than a dyadic structure.

For arguments supporting the idea of the universality of the Oedipus complex, see Spiro (1982) and Paul (1985b). For evidence of the wide distribution of oedipal stories, see Edmunds (1985); Edmunds and Dundes (1983); Johnson (1992); and especially Johnson and Price-Williams (1995), whose data argue strongly in favor of the universality of oedipal narratives. For an overview of current psychoanalytic thinking about the status of the Oedipus complex, see Pollock (1988); Pollock and Ross (1988); Steiner (1989); and Simon (1991).

17. I give a more extended presentation of my theoretical views about the nature of the interaction between individual persons and cultural symbolic systems in my "What Does Anybody Want? Desire, Purpose, and the Acting Subject in the Study of Culture" (1990b).

2
The Primal Horde

1. We cannot completely rule out Bakan's idea (1958) that Freud spoke allusively and in riddles on important matters, especially those having to do with Judaism.

2. "Not only Sophocles, but Freud himself, should be included among the recorded versions of the Oedipus myth" (Lévi-Strauss, 1967b, 215). Lévi-Strauss addresses Freud's myth of the primal horde at some length in *The Elementary Structures of Kinship* (1969) and again in *The Jealous Potter* (1988b). It would be possible to argue that his whole four-volume *Mythologiques* (1969–1981) represents an attempt to deconstruct the Oedipus myth, represented by his M1, the birdnester myth of the Bororo, which, as Spiro has shown (1987d), is manifestly about Oedipal themes. Lévi-Strauss's ambivalent wrestling with the Freudian myth has, to my mind, been very productive. My own deep debt to his method of myth interpretation should be self-evident.

3. I have elected to use the pronoun *his* not only here but in some less gender-specific contexts to emphasize that the prototypical assumed "ego" of both the Freudian and the biblical myth is male, and that the "hero" in the Western, Judeo-Christian narrative tradition is the junior male seeking to become a senior male. This is an empirical observation about and analysis of the ethnographic material under discussion, not an expression of my own views.

4. Robin Fox is one of the anthropologists who has explored many of the topics I examine here with subtlety and a wide-ranging theoretical perspective. His *The Red Lamp of Incest* (1980) contains a valuable consideration of Freud's primal horde theory from a sophisticated contemporary anthropological point of view.

For overviews of primate social organization, see Dunbar (1988); Hinde (1983); and Smuts et al. (1987). On human social organization as a form of primate social organization, see Rodseth et al. (1991).

5. For my views on the place of Darwinian thinking about inclusive reproductive fitness and its importance for and relation to cultural and social theory, see my "The Individual and Society in Cultural and Biological Anthropology" (1987a; see also 1994b). Briefly, I subscribe to a dual-inheritance model, which grants to both genes and the cultural symbols relative autonomy, and allows us to explore the empirical relations between their differing and often conflicting implications. For a particular ethnographic case that uses this model, see my "Symbolic Reproduction and Sherpa Monasticism" (n.d.).

6. The famous "Lordship and Bondage" chapter of Hegel's *Phenomenology of Spirit* (1967) was influentially interpreted by Alexandre Kojève (1969), whose reading I partly follow here. Jacques Lacan attended Kojève's Paris seminars, and his distinctive psychoanalytic theory in large measure reflects his application of Hegelian-Kojèvian concepts to Freudian subject matter. For valuable attempts to integrate Hegelian and Freudian thought, see Benjamin (1988) and Wolfenstein (1993).

7. Lévi-Strauss's theory about the centrality to society of the exchange of

women in marriage systems is to be found in *The Elementary Structures of Kinship* (1969). It represents an extension of Marcel Mauss's ideas about reciprocity (1967), which I explore in greater detail in Chapter 5. An influential feminist rereading of Freud and Lévi-Strauss on the circulation of women can be found in Rubin (1975).

8. Lévi-Strauss presents his "atom of kinship" in "Structural Analysis in Linguistics and in Anthropology" (1967a). I originally explored the ideas in this section in my article "Did the Primal Crime Take Place?" (1976), to which the reader may turn for further exposition of arguments given here perforce in a rather condensed way. Robin Fox gives a clear explanation of Lévi-Strauss's ideas in "Sisters' Sons and Monkey's Uncles" (1993).

9. The importance of splitting in the building up of psychic structure has been explored by Kernberg (1984); the concept was developed by Fairbairn (1952) and M. Klein (1948, 1984) after originally being suggested by Freud (1940). A good psychoanalytic discussion of the general idea of "decomposition" may be found in Rogers (1978). In my article "What Does Anybody Want" (1990b), I show the close similarity between Kernberg's idea that the building blocks of the psychic world are positively or negatively toned affective interpersonal dyads and Lévi-Strauss's idea that the building blocks of myth (and hence presumably also of fantasy) are also affectively charged dyadic relationships, which can be combined into more complicated structures. This similarity provides a welcome bridge for uniting structural theories of myth and culture and psychoanalytic theories about fantasy and the representational world of individuals.

10. The most complete source for the myth of Isis and Osiris is Plutarch, for a text and translation of which, along with commentary, see Griffiths (1970). Other sources include Budge (1904); Clark (1959); Frankfort (1948); and Robins (1993).

11. The concept that a hero deserves punishment for his heroic deeds and that this dilemma is at the heart of many myths, including the story of Moses, rests on the principle of the talion—like for like—which itself is a particular instantiation of the more basic principle of reciprocity. These ideas are central to my argument; I present them in fuller form in Chapter 5.

12. In searching for a "source domain" for the primal-horde model, I am following the lead of Lakoff and Johnson (1980) in their fruitful approach to the study of metaphor.

13. For a detailed description of pastoral techniques and practices in the biblical lands in ancient and recent times, see Dalman (1928).

14. A number of recent works explore the role of carnality, the opposition

between spirit and flesh or mind and body, and the place of procreation and sexual desire in the Judaic tradition; among these are Biale (1992); Boyarin (1994); and Eilberg-Schwartz (1992, 1994a).

3
Israel in Egypt

1. In citing the Torah, I have used the translation by Plaut (1983) for consistency's sake. My choice does not indicate that I prefer Plaut's interpretations to others in any particular case. I have also consulted the *Anchor Bible* commentary series (1964–94), the *JPS* commentary series (1989–91), and Rosenbaum and Silverman's edition (1963) of the Pentateuch with traditional Hebrew commentary.

2. The difference hinges mainly on substituting a *dalet* for a *resh,* so that "he'eviyr 'oto le'ariym" becomes "he'eviyd 'oto la'avdiym."

3. While I would not describe myself as a structuralist, my own thinking about the interpretation of myth and fantasy has developed under the influence of deep immersion in Lévi-Strauss's method (see 1967b, 1969–1981, 1988b). Leach (1969, 1970, 1982, 1983, 1986) is the interpreter of Lévi-Strauss who has most directly addressed himself to biblical myth using a structural approach. My own way of combining psychoanalytic and structuralist interpretations of cultural symbolism can be seen in Paul (1979, 1982, 1987b, and, with particular regard to biblical symbolism, 1980, 1985a, and 1987c). See also Barthes's *On Racine* (1983) for an admirable model of the structural method of analysis. Barthes shows in detail how the eleven tragedies of Racine, different though they are on the surface, reveal themselves to be transformations of the paradigm of the primal horde.
I do not address the issues of literary style dealt with in such influential works as Alter (1981) or Sternberg (1985).

4. I discuss these methodological issues in "The Question of Applied Psychoanalysis and the Interpretation of Cultural Symbolism" (1987c). Of course, the reader of a finished analysis, such as the present one, does not see the process but only the product of the analysis, which may give a misleading impression of the methodological approach, and the experimentation, trial and error, and reworking that go into it.

5. See especially chapter 6 of Boyarin (1990), "The Sea Resists: Midrash and the (Psycho)dynamics of Intertextuality," 93–104. Zeligs (1960, 1974, 1986) also uses the midrash as free association to the Bible.
I must cite in addition here a passage from Lacan, who anticipates my current project in a typically uncanny way. Asking himself what it was in Judaism that Freud admired most, Lacan answers that it must have been the tradition of midrash, which so closely parallels Freud's own method of interpretation. If the

midrash takes the Book literally, he writes, "It is not in order to make that letter support more or less obvious intentions, but in order to pull a speech that is other from the text, through a signifying collusion . . . such that this combination of colluding signifiers, taken together in their materiality and (even unwanted) proximity, necessitates that grammatical variations impose inflected choices, indeed goes so far as to implicate that which it neglects (as reference)—Moses's childhood, for example" (Lacan, 1970, 81). (I am grateful to my colleague Elissa Marder for her invaluable aid in translating Lacan's convoluted prose; I take responsibility for any errors in the text.) I shall use midrash to fill in the gaps in Moses's neglected childhood in Chapter 5.

6. The essential English source for the midrash is *Midrash Rabbah* (1939). Ginzberg (1911) offers an ambitious attempt to weave the tales and legends from the midrash and elsewhere into an artful literary narrative; I find it particularly charming. Other authoritative collections of midrash include Bialik and Ravnitzky (1992) and Bin Gorion (1976). In addition, I have consulted collections and works by Cohen (1993), Frankel (1989), Glatzer (1962), Miller (1965), Patai (1981), and S. Rapaport (1968). These are of varying quality and reliability. Many of the stories I cite can be found in several or all of these sources. I have also consulted the Hebrew versions of most of them in the edition of Bialik and Ravnitzky.

Goldin (1971) is an excellent scholarly study of the midrash to the Song at the Sea, Exodus 15, as is his article on the midrash concerning the death of Moses (1988a). An excellent guide to the literature of and about midrash, as well as about the classic Judaic literature generally, is to be found in Holtz (1984).

7. Cohen (1993, 84ff.) provides a thorough treatment of the question of how Pharaoh's commands are to be understood as "dealing shrewdly (or 'wisely')" with the Israelites. As he writes, "Jewish legends had difficulty understanding the connection between the fear lest the people multiply and the means used against them: hard labor" (87–88). Cohen cites, for example, a midrash according to which the Egyptian plan was supposed to work by placing such a heavy quota of bricks on the Hebrew slaves that they had to sleep at the work site in order to fulfill it. But the wives of the workmen brought their husbands hot lunches and used the opportunity to have intercourse, thus outwitting Pharaoh and fulfilling God's intention that the Hebrews be fruitful and multiply.

8. I discuss and illustrate the idea of there being two simultaneous levels in at least some kinds of narratives, one on the surface following an apparent plausible historical chronology of events, the other less obvious and following a logic of its own, in Paul 1987b. As I show there, the hidden structure is more easily discovered in those works in which the two fit together only imperfectly, leaving enough gaps and inconsistencies to make the structure of the underlying fantasy schema at least partially visible. The rest is then discoverable by means of the techniques of analysis I am using here.

9. On decomposition as a literary device, examined from a psychoanalytically informed perspective, see Rogers (1978).

10. I must presume the pervasive influence here of the principle of the talion, both in human social and psychic life generally and in the Judeo-Christian tradition in particular, although I have not yet established its central importance. I take up the issue at greater length in Chapter 5.

It may be wondered whether the death of Pharaoh's first-born son is exact retaliation for the wholesale murder of the Hebrew boys. My structural paradigm makes no requirement about whether the different roles are filled by one or more characters; simply, a senior male or males must kill a junior male or males. This is achieved alike by Pharaoh's killing a great number of young Hebrew boys and by those of his actions that result in the death of his own son. In any event, his action actually results in the death of his whole army, who are of course "junior" to him along a hierarchical "lord and bondsman" dimension. There is in addition the tradition of the intergenerational war between the Egyptian first-born and their fathers, in which Egyptian fathers kill their sons.

11. See Cohen (1993, 117–121) for a discussion of this story. One of the ground rules for midrashic commentary is that the biblical text must be shown to be without errors. While this expectation no longer governs the explorations of contemporary scholars, it is hard for people to shake off the belief that biblical tales ought to have a homiletic message or exemplify the ethical principles assumed to constitute the Bible's core. By contrast, I deliberately resist the temptation to such readings. To my mind the reward is a gain, not a loss, in meaning. I might, presumptuously, characterize my present book as yet another midrash: one that is not, it is true, bound by any requirement to underwrite the literal truth of the Bible, the teachings of the rabbis, or the prevailing views on the ethics of Judaism but that assumes that hardly a detail is in the text except for some good structural reason—and that meaning is to be discovered by pursuing connections, similarities, differences, and transformations in the narrative itself and in the surrounding text, not by looking outside to some other realm of legitimation or value, even the realm of established morality.

12. I discuss the importance of ritual symbolism in mediating these two extremes in quite another religious and cultural context in Paul 1979. For a full-length investigation of these and related issues in the Jewish tradition, see Biale (1992).

13. I shall not enter into the debates about the meaning of this passage. But it is worth mentioning that Lévi-Strauss's one foray into biblical exegesis (known to me at any rate) is a short paper (1988a) that argues, on the basis of a comparison of the present biblical passage with some Bororo Indian traditions about penis sheaths, that the "thou" addressed in Zipporah's speech "Thou art a bridegroom of blood" is the foreskin itself. This strikes me as being as plausible as any of the other

proposed interpretations, and certainly more interesting. I tend to share Lévi-Strauss's lack of respect for cultural boundaries when it comes to cultural symbolism. Indeed, my interest in the biblical tradition was first aroused when I was engaged in the analysis of Tibetan cultural materials and was repeatedly struck by similarities and parallels underlying their tradition and our own, in spite of the obvious surface differences.

14. I cite here only one of the best and best-known works presenting this thesis, Wellisch (1954); I have encountered it in many widely diverse sources since. For me the most insightful treatment of the story of the Akedah remains that of Bakan (1966), a book that was a major influence on my own thinking. Bakan later explicitly addressed the issue of child abuse in Bakan (1972). Delaney (1989) adds a feminist perspective on the story of the binding of Isaac. Blumenthal (1993) proposes a theology based on the necessity for protest against, as well as acceptance of, the actions of an "abusing God."

15. I return to this subject in Chapter 5.

4
Incest and Its Vicissitudes

1. Of course, it became a part of Judaic tradition that the Torah had actually been in existence since the Creation, or had even prefigured and contributed to it, although before Sinai it had not manifested itself in material form on earth. But this belief is yet another example of the sort of anachronistic imagining of the past that I am talking about: the rabbis could not conceive of something as foundational and of such absolute authority in their own lives as the Torah as not existing at all.

2. This is not empirically true of animals. My point is only that they play this symbolic role in the Western Judeo-Christian conceptual system.

3. For an excellent anthropological study of the story of Dinah see Pitt-Rivers (1977). Other anthropological studies of the patriarchal narratives include Andriolo (1973), Donaldson (1980), and Forsyth (1991).

4. Hopkins (1980) deals specifically with records concerning sibling incest as a widespread practice in Egypt during Roman times. For other sources on pharaonic incest and marriage, see Budge (1904); Černy (1954); Clark (1959); Frankfort (1948); Leach (1976); Middleton (1962); and Robins (1993).

5. According to Robins (1993) there is no evidence in the Egyptian texts themselves supporting the theory that the inheritance system worked by way of the "God's daughter," as described by Leach. Robins argues that this theory was devel-

oped by later observers to make sense of the—to them—puzzling practice of pharaonic incest. Assuming Robins to be right, Leach's argument simply becomes further evidence for my contention (and his own) that what matters is what people thought and think about the pharaohs, not whether what people have supposed is entirely correct.

6. Leach writes: "In our biblical texts the assimilation to the Pharaonic model and hence to the Osiris-Horus schema of positional succession is fairly straightforward. . . . The plain implication of the story [in Gen. 12:10–20] is that Pharaoh and Abraham are virtually interchangeable" (1983, 39–40). It would support my present contention to assert as Leach does that Pharaoh and Abraham are practically the same person for purposes of the myth. But this sort of unwarranted leap and glossing over of inconvenient detail have made it easy for critics to find fault with Leach's structural analyses of biblical material. I try to be more restrained about asserting such intuitively plausible but not necessarily defensible structural connections and equivalences.

<h1 style="text-align:center">5</h1>

Young Man Moses

1. See Lévi-Strauss's *Totemism* (1963). His most extended discussion of kinship and its relation to the general principle of reciprocity is to be found in *The Elementary Structures of Kinship* (1969); see also his article "Social Structure" (1967a).

2. It is not possible, within the compass of this book, to give a fully grounded and convincing demonstration of the importance of the principle of reciprocity in the comparative study of society, where it is as fundamental as Freud found it to be in the operation of the individual psyche. Let me take as an example reciprocity among the Kaluli of Papua New Guinea as reported by Edward Schieffelin (1976). He begins: "The term *wel* means 'exact equivalent' and always implies giving or taking in return for something. When one man strikes another in a fight, someone will try to strike a return blow (*wel*) of equal severity" (109). In situations where wel cannot be provided, *su* or "compensation" is sought: "If another man mistakenly kills my pig, instead of killing one of his in return, my supporters and I may demand a payment in cowrie necklaces and pearlshells" (109). (The Mosaic injunction to exact repayment for injury in Leviticus 24 can, it seems to me, be interpreted as su: if a neighbor inadvertently injures my cow, I do not then kill his cow but seek compensation in an exchange medium such as money, commensurable to the injury done.)

But wel as retaliation for injury is only the negative side of the principle: "In its positive permutation, it is the form for one of the most important vehicles of social relationship: delayed gift exchange. *Wel* in the context of gift exchange refers, not to retaliation for injury, but to a gift given in return for another gift. Again, *wel* means an exact equivalent. If I give you a pig, and you give me a pig of the same size at a later date, that is *wel*" (112). As Schieffelin summarizes the Kaluli ethos: "The Kaluli sense of matching equivalents in resolving situations of grievance or prestation is a fine one. In this they tend to feel that *wel* is a more satisfying outcome to events than *su*" (112).

One could multiply this example with the help of others from around the globe. What is important, however, is that this form of exchange occurs neither in a market economy nor in a situation where a central governing authority—the state—has arisen and introduced a system of obligation between strata of society marked by a permanent status inequality. The principle of wel, like for like, is thus the ruling principle of justice in societies characterized by foraging, horticultural, or pastoral economies.

A good overview of anthropological theory concerning different forms of economic exchange that emphasizes reciprocity is to be found in Sahlins (1972). For an ambitious attempt to establish reciprocity as one of four fundamental types of human relationship, see Fiske (1991). Trivers, in a well-known article (1971), established reciprocity as a fundamental principle in social life on the basis of purely Darwinian considerations. Axelrod (1984) showed, from the point of view of game theory, that repaying like for like is the optimal approach to interpersonal strategizing. I need hardly mention that is also the golden rule at the heart of Judeo-Christian ethos: do as you are done by, or more proactively, do you as you would like to be done by.

3. One should recall here Norman O. Brown's tour de force examination of the concepts of debt, gift, guilt, money, and dirt in his *Life against Death* (1959). That book is usually paired in one's mind with Marcuse's *Eros and Civilization* (1962). Both are central to the critique of civilization in a Freudian mode, and as such I acknowledge my debt to them. On the other hand, both propose optimistic, not to say ecstatic, scenarios that may have fitted the mood of the sixties but now seem to me of dubious plausibility or value.

4. On revenge and gift exchange as reciprocals, see my discussion of the Kaluli concept of wel in note 2, above. For an ethnographic account of revenge as a well-calibrated system of social justice played according to definite rules, see Boehm's *Blood Revenge* (1984), a description and analysis of feuding in Montenegro.

As I have noted elsewhere (1995), the idea of blood revenge epitomizes, for a "civilized" state society, the essence of "barbarity." This is a profoundly ethnocentric view, which fails to take into account what "justice" would be in a society without a centralized state holding a monopoly on legitimate force, including the power to police the populace. For a study of our present society's (ambivalent) feelings about revenge as a motive and principle, see Jacoby (1983).

5. To argue that the Judaic tradition has never viewed the revolt against Pharaoh as a source of guilt is no more valid than was the Rat Man's remark when

Freud interpreted to him the source of his own obsessional conflict: "But I thought nothing of that!" If the obsessional neurotic knew consciously what he was feeling guilty about, he would not be an obsessional neurotic. It is precisely the fact that the fantasy generating the guilt is unrecognized that gives it its compulsory force.

Nor do I assume that a person, neurotic or healthy, needs to be consciously aware of guilt in order to be subject to its dynamic effects. On the contrary, when a successful defensive and/or adaptive system is in place, the person may feel quite untroubled, revealing anxiety or guilt only when the defense—for example, the proper performance of a ritual—is interfered with. In other words, when someone feels guilty about an infraction of a religious law or a failure to mark some observance, I would propose that the subjective feeling of guilt is not a reaction to the lapse but the perception of underlying guilt following upon a breach in the defense against it. This would also help explain the often disproportionate affect experienced in such situations.

6. My analysis here follows ideas put forward by Otto Rank in his classic study of the hero myth (1964).

7. Similar conclusions about Jochabed's actions were reached by Ilana Pardes (1992). There, she also examines the roles of women in various biblical stories, including the tale of Moses's birth, where women often figure as allies who help the junior male outwit the persecuting senior male. A brilliant and extensive analysis of Greek mythology showing how women in those tales bind their sons to them as agents of revenge against their oppressive husbands can be found in Slater (1971).

8. Carroll (1988, 1989) has especially made this point. Leach (1982) goes somewhat overboard in insisting that biblical "history" be regarded purely as "myth," since some parts are clearly more historical than others. Nonetheless his point is valid: the history in the Bible, even when it is relatively realistic, is always to be seen in the larger mythic context in which it is embedded and from which it takes its present significance. Of course, in this regard it does not differ from any other sort of history, which is always told from a certain point of view and from within a certain narrative construct.

9. See Josephus (1978). Freud refers to this legend, and Josephus's mention of it, in Moses and Monotheism (1939, 13n2).

10. See my article "Bettelheim's Contribution to Anthropology" (1990a), a commentary on Bettelheim 1962.

11. My account here follows that in Silver (1982). Silver's book usefully treats the various ways the figure of Moses has been pictured at different moments in cultural history. Thus, in the present story, Moses appears as a warrior-aristocrat, a

characterization designed to appeal to the values of the Hellenistic world. For more on Moses in the Greek setting, see Gager (1972).

Artapanus's propagandistic and apologetic portrayal of Moses, like that of Philo (1935) and other defenders of the Jews to the Greeks, needs to be seen against the backdrop of anti-Jewish views that were already taking shape. In the writings of various non-Jewish authors, Moses is portrayed in highly derogatory ways, no doubt stirring Jews of the time, such as Artapanus, to rise to his defense. The original sources from the Greek and Roman world dealing with the Jews can be found in the extremely valuable work of Stern (1974–84). A positive Hellenistic portrait of Moses appears in Gregory of Nyssa (1978).

12. See my book *The Tibetan Symbolic World* (1982); I also explain some of these ideas in Paul 1980, 1985a, and 1994b. I developed the analytic approach to myth and religious traditions more generally that I employ here while working with ethnographic materials from the Tibetan culture area. It cannot, therefore, be supposed that I have invented my "method" in an ad hoc way to fit the present data. On the contrary, it was only through an engagement with that quite alien symbolic world that I was able to develop the ideas that I now use to help understand our own tradition.

I have since come to regard the Tibetan Buddhist system and the Judeo-Christian tradition as much more similar than I had once thought, despite their obvious surface differences. My analysis reveals that the same paradigm underlies both, though it undergoes different transformations in the two systems. I also think the two civilizations are historically closely related as parallel outgrowths of underlying Middle-Eastern prototypes. I compare Western and Tibetan civilization briefly in Paul 1995.

The voyage toward one's own Judaism by way of a detour through Tibet is, as it turns out, not an uncommon one in our times, for reasons it would be interesting to explore. See, for example, Kamenetz (1994).

13. I do not believe it is a coincidence that Jesus (Yeshua) has the same name as Moses's actual "successor" in the Hebrew Bible, Joshua (Yehoshua, shortened by the Aramaic of Jesus's time to Yeshua). I discuss the significance of this briefly in Paul (1987c). Leach writes: "I . . . take it for granted that when the early Christians described themselves as the New Israel they meant what they said. Their divine lawgiver was called Jesus (Joshua) because, like his Old Testament namesake, he was the successor and replacement of Moses" (1983, 35).

6
Death on the Nile

1. An interesting attempt to determine the historical reality behind the tradition of Moses and his accomplishments has been put forward by Elias Auerbach (1975). Among accounts that treat Moses as a real character, two of the most influ-

ential in recent times have been those of Buber (1988) and Rad (1960). Zeligs (1986) offers an extended psychoanalytic account of Moses, treating the biblical text as his free associations. Zeligs's findings overlap with, and have influenced, my own in many respects, and I here acknowledge my great debt to her work. I do not believe, however, that it is possible to treat a character in a text, especially a mythic one, as if he were a person whose motives and psychodynamics can be explored as one would do in analysis with an actual person. A structural approach that treats the character as a semiotic construct, such as I am conducting here, seems to me a more valid way of applying and/or arriving at psychoanalytic insights—not about the characters or the authors (unknown in any case) but about the fantasy the text represents or embodies. For a discussion of this approach to cultural symbolism by way of the structural analysis of fantasy, see my "Question of Applied Psychoanalysis" (1987c). James Nohrnberg's *Like unto Moses: The Constituting of an Interruption* (Bloomington: Indiana University Press, 1995) appeared after my book was in press.

2. Schafer (1960) has particularly reminded us that there is a loving, benevolent side to the paternal imago and of the superego, a side sometimes forgotten in the analytic emphasis on the dimension of rivalry and hostility. As Blos (1985) has pointed out, the ambivalent relationship of father and son has its own dyadic, preoedipal aspect, which is different from the triadic oedipal conflict.

3. This would be so even if there were any truth to Harold Bloom's highly speculative proposal (1990) that the J writer might have been a woman. Bloom himself notes that the Torah as it now stands reflects the views of the other authors and redactors besides J, who were certainly male. See Friedman (1989) for an authoritative discussion of the authorship of the Torah.

4. Psychoanalytic writers long ago noticed the presence of maternal themes and symbolism in the Bible, often with specific reference to the maternal significance of the promised land of Canaan. See, for example, Barag (1946); Grinberg (1962); Peto (1958); Rosenzweig (1940); and Zeligs (1960).

5. The technique of symbolic analysis I employ here is closely related to that proposed by Dundes (1987), whereby symbolic equivalences in folklore can be demonstrated by finding different images used in a parallel structural way in variants of a tale.

6. Berke and Schneider (1994) explore the range of positive and negative images denoted in Hebrew by words etymologically close to the grapheme *sd*, meaning "breast," arguing for a Kleinian view of splitting that is completely consistent with my analysis. They write: " 'Breast' lies at the very centre of human desire, and hostility. Many languages convey some aspects of the complicated, convoluted and contradictory significance of 'breast,' but to our knowledge none does so better than Hebrew" (492).

7. See M. Klein (1948, 1984).

8. Leach discusses the structural importance of relationships between Israelites and non-Israelites in his essay "The Legitimacy of Solomon," in Leach (1969). One has only to recall that Joseph, Moses, Boaz (David's grandfather), David, and Solomon all took non-Israelite wives to see the fallacy of supposing that non-Israelites are marginal to the biblical history of the Israelites. That the non-Israelites here are all women further supports a maternal reading. The non-Israelite woman Delilah is probably the best-known example of a castrating, bad mother, non-Israelite. For a provocative and insightful study of women in Judges that deals with many of these issues, see Mieke Bal (1988).

9. Wildavsky (1984) uses this passage as the starting point for a systematic examination of different styles of political leadership, with Moses as a prime example.

10. I find convincing the argument of Shapiro and Perry (1976) that for developmental reasons it is only in the immediate postoedipal years that children are able to use symbolic forms effectively to build internal fantasy structures that are stable, complex, and enduring enough to serve as the foundation for adult social and cultural systems. That these fantasies are necessarily "oedipal" does not negate the insight that they derive much of their power over subsequent psychic organization by virtue of being the inheritors of more primordial dyadic preoedipal fantasies. See also Sarnoff (1976), on the importance of the fantasies of early postoedipal latency for the establishment of the socioculturally attuned individual.

11. In Lévi-Strauss's formulation (1967a), social organization comprises the circulation and exchange of three things: women, goods and services, and symbolic communication. Lacan's theories show the strong influence of Lévi-Strauss.

12. In his own fashion, Lacan concerned himself a good deal with Freud's myth of the primal horde. The main discussion of the Name-of-the-Father—the symbolic influence of the dead, or slain, father of the horde—is to be found in his "On a Question Preliminary to Any Possible Treatment of Psychosis" (1977b). Volume 7 of his seminars, *The Ethics of Psychoanalysis* (1992), is pervaded by his response to the Freudian myth translated into his own distinctive terminology. Lacan specifically addresses the figure of the Name-of-the-Father in the context of the symbolism of the biblical tale of the binding of Isaac in 1990; see also 1991. For a recent Lacanian interpretation of *Totem and Taboo,* see Samuels (1990, chap. 6).

13. The theme of the superiority of the younger brother in the Torah is explored by Forsyth (1992) and Goldin (1988b). Moses and Aaron are clearly rivals as well as allies, a fact exacerbated by the later disputes of rival priestly lineages claiming legitimating descent from each of them. Elias Auerbach's analysis (1975)

concludes that Moses and Aaron were originally not brothers but competitors and adversaries, while Miriam was an ally and perhaps even a sister of Aaron. Nonetheless it is one of the accomplishments of the Exodus narrative and the post-Sinaitic portion of the story to have portrayed Moses, Aaron, and Miriam as maintaining a working alliance despite the clear tensions among them. This compromise works because it is always clear that Moses is primus inter pares (as was Joseph in his sibling set). Friedman (1989) demonstrates how much of the text of the Pentateuch can be clarified by seeing it as the ideological battleground for competing claims to priority and legitimacy of different priestly lineages aligning themselves with either Moses or Aaron. Yet the rivalry never becomes explicit or comes to a head, and the superiority of Moses over Aaron is sustained overall.

This relative harmony among the members of a sibling set is, of course, the essential prerequisite to their achieving victory over the primal father and then maintaining a workable social contract without slipping back into the situation of the original horde. Though the new society is a collective achievement, yet it must rest on the imaginative production of a myth and a law embedded in it that is ultimately the work of a single individual, the visionary poet who devises the myth of the hero and uses himself as the model for the main character.

14. Vitz (1983) ingeniously and convincingly argues that a source of Freud's fascination and identification with Moses was the fact that, like Moses, Freud had two beloved "mothers," one Jewish and one Gentile, his birth mother and his Czech nursemaid.

15. The analyses of Carroll (1988, 1989), Grinberg (1962), and Zeligs (1986), for example, all take this oedipal significance for granted. Freud writes in *The Interpretation of Dreams*: "The Emperor and the Empress (or the King and Queen) as a rule really represent the dreamer's parents; and a prince or princess represents the dreamer himself or herself. . . . But the same high authority is attributed to great men as to the Emperor" (1900, 5:353–54).

16. As I showed earlier, a midrash attempts to deny that Joseph's pharaoh died and was succeeded by a different one. By the same token, and with still less textual support, another midrash argues that Exodus 2:23 should be interpreted not to mean that the pharaoh died but that he had leprosy and was thus the same pharaoh who became Moses's adversary during the time of the Exodus (Bialik and Ravnitzky 1992, 62). This interpretive move serves to unite as one man the pharaoh who tried to kill Moses in his youth and the one whom Moses kills at the Red Sea, but it also seems to me to deny the plain meaning of the biblical text.

17. For an excellent treatment of the central importance of the mother's brother, not only in anthropological theory but in the evolution of human society, see Fox (1993). To a classically trained social anthropologist, the fact that Pharaoh is

Moses's mother's brother has deep significance. A glance at Lévi-Strauss's chart of the "atom of kinship" makes clear that the mother's brother is a key figure. Fox points out that the mother's brother is not brought in as a result of the decomposition of the more primary father but the other way around: it is the father who is added to the more elementary structure of the mother, her children, and her adult brother, whose genetic interest in his sister's children is as great as, or greater than, a biological father's investment in them. On the mother's brother in Egypt, see Leach (1976).

18. Sarna (1986, 63–80) devotes considerable attention to the question of whether Moses, Aaron, or God is the actual agent in the ten plagues that lead up to the departure from Egypt and the scene at the Red Sea.

19. See Plaut (1983, 2:152) on the traditions of the later fate of Pharaoh.

20. I give another answer to the question of what the "new weapon" was that emboldened the brothers in Paul 1976.

21. Meissner has been one of the most influential and prolific writers on religious topics from a psychoanalytic viewpoint. His *Psychoanalysis and Religious Experience* (1984b) is a major overview of the field. He has explored the cultic process—whereby groups, in organizing themselves, project hostility outward onto supposed enemies, thus binding themselves in a shared paranoid fantasy—with specific reference to the origins of the Judeo-Christian religious tradition (see 1984a, 1988, 1990).

22. The reference is to the title of an essay by Géza Róheim, recently repub lished in an English translation (1985 [1923]). Róheim's early writings on psychoanalytic anthropology played a formative role in our discipline and had an influence on my own intellectual development.

7
After the Death of the Primal Father

1. For a study of this important figure, see Beidelman (1974).

2. A fine overview of the role of rituals of commemoration in social reproduction and continuity can be found in Connerton (1989).

3. For an excellent contemporary account of the anthropology of pastoralism and its implications for social and interfamilial dynamics, one highly relevant to my present study, see Meeker (1989). Although his book deals mainly with African pastoralism, Meeker concludes with an insightful discussion of the Israelites.

4. I here follow Leach's exposition (1970, 26–31) of Lévi-Strauss's original argument.

5. See also Sahlins (1976), who makes these points in discussing cannibalistic fantasies and symbolism in different culinary cultures.

6. On Israelite monotheism as a reaction against the historical practice of the sacrifice of first-born children, see Bergmann (1992). This is an interesting book, but it also represents the kind of literal, historical approach to the Bible from a psychoanalytic point of view that I am attempting to get away from here.

7. Obviously this passage is written from a "belated" point of view, no doubt having been placed here to ground a present ritual practice in the mythic cosmogonic past. But this is the perspective on the text that I am deliberately not taking here. The historical process by which the text came into being is not my subject; rather, I am examining the product of that process, which stands before us as an already existing cultural object.

8. See Plaut (1983, 2:193).

8
Facing Mount Sinai

1. Let me reiterate that the justice and equality achieved after the rebellion in both the biblical and the Freudian myth are for men only. My analysis of this system should not be confused with an endorsement of it.

2. For a recent history of the construction of the concept of the "primitive" in social anthropology see Kuper (1988). Lévi-Strauss's well-known demolition of the concept of totemism (1963) was anticipated by Goldenweiser (1910).

3. Deuteronomy stands apart from the rest of the Torah both stylistically and historically, having been wholly composed by an author, "D," different from any of the others whose texts are interwoven in the first four books. On the question of biblical authorship, see Friedman (1989). On D, with special attention to the subject of Moses, see the authoritative monograph of Polzin (1980).

4. For a full-length exposition of this widely accepted psychoanalytic view, see Brenner (1982).

5. See Freud (1987 [1915]). The fact that the actual evolutionary scenario Freud sets forth there strikes us today as unconvincing is, to my mind, less important than that he saw the relevance of this kind of interpretive strategy.

6. See Nesse (1990a, 1990b), one of the most original and authoritative contributors to the rapidly growing field of evolutionary psychology.

7. See DSM-IV (1994, 417–423).

8. See DSM-IV (1994, 669–673).

9. There has been debate in the field over whether Obsessive-Compulsive Disorder is just a more severe manifestation of Obsessive-Compulsive Personality Disorder or whether the two are quite different pathological entities. Esman (1989), who has recently surveyed the problem from a psychoanalytic point of view, cites studies showing that a previous history of Obsessive-Compulsive Personality Disorder is not correlated with Obsessive-Compulsive Disorder, which suggests unrelated etiologies. That is, people with the Axis II diagnosis are no more likely to have the Axis I disorder than anyone else. This would not invalidate the psychodynamic view that both derive their phenomenological appearance from the deployment of similar defenses against similar impulses, whether the impulses spring from conflictual or organic substrata.

10. Oldham and Morris (1990, 57).

11. I would venture to say that the understanding of the psychodynamics of the obsessive-compulsive character is one of the areas where psychoanalytic thought and practice has needed to evolve least since Freud's original formulations. No doubt this is partly due to the fact that in this area Freud knew what he was talking about from personal experience. His main works on the subject include Freud (1894, 1895, 1907, 1908a, 1908b, 1909, 1913a, 1913b, 1917, 1918 [1914], and 1926). Other standard sources include Anna Freud (1966), Fenichel (1945), Nagera (1986), Salzman (1980), as well as the various authors to whom I referred in the text of the previous section.

12. A. Kris (1994) writes: "I prefer to speak of punitive, unconscious self-criticism . . . rather than of unconscious guilt alone, because that attitude is common to shame, humiliation, and depressive affects, as well as to guilt" (657). I agree with Kris that "punitive, unconscious self-criticism" is a more accurate descriptive phrase than unconscious guilt, and that one sees it clinically in the other guises to which he refers. On the other hand, I think that in obsessional neurosis self-criticism does generally take the specific form of guilt, as opposed to shame, etc., and that by the same token Western Judeo-Christian civilization has constructed its own ethos using guilt as a linchpin (in contrast to many other sociocultural systems in which shame is more explicitly elaborated). Here, I wish to specify just how that peculiarly Western sense of guilt is constructed and on what fantasies it is based.

13. I do not wish to enter a minefield unnecessarily here. It seems obvious

to me that parental attitudes and actions of seduction, rejection, abuse, narcissistic manipulation, and so on, when they occur, are real determinants of the child's psychology and instigate or provoke the child's emotional responses. But this does not negate the fact that these parental stimuli are experienced by a child with strong feelings, wishes, fears, impulses, and fantasies of its own, and that unconscious "memories" reflect the interaction of these factors in ways that are at once highly idiosyncratic and yet of a certain more general type with a specifiable structure.

14. One respect in which current psychoanalytic understanding of obsessional dynamics has changed since Freud's time is that they are less frequently referred to as "anal." This is not because anal themes are not still central in obsessional-compulsive neurosis and character structure (they are), but rather because the use of the libido theory as the central organizing system of classification has fallen by the wayside in psychoanalytic practice. In the Torah text, specifically anal themes are most prominent in the concern with purity, contamination, and contagion, to which I will devote some attention later in this chapter. (On the Bible as an obsessional document, see Chasseguet-Smirgel [1983]; on anality generally, see Chasseguet-Smirgel [1985] and Shengold [1988].)

If one wished to explore anality in the Torah narrative, one might well begin with the scene in Exodus 33:17–23 in which, as Marx with his mordant wit so nicely put it, God gives Moses a demonstration of his existence a posteriori. I have discussed anal themes in a biblical context in Paul 1985a.

15. I shall not address the issue of whether activity or passivity, sadism or masochism, is "primary." I shall simply speak of "sadomasochism," which implies the necessary interimplication of the two.

16. See Mahler, Pine, and Bergman (1975).

17. While Freud did see religion as a neurosis of civilization, in his original observations about the connection between obsessional rituals and religious practices (1907) he also made a distinction between the individual manifestation, which he deemed pathological, and the social one, which he did not describe as a pathology: "One might venture to regard obsessional neurosis as a pathological counterpart of the formation of a religion" (1907, 126). Spiro's concept of religious institutions as culturally constituted defense mechanisms (1987c) is apposite here.

18. See "The Abominations of Leviticus" in Douglas, Purity and Danger (1966). For critiques by psychoanalytic anthropologists, see Devos (1975) and Spiro (1987d).

19. For the legendary tradition concerning Aaron's death, see Ginzberg (1911, 3:324–328).

20. This passage contains a statement of the principle of mimetic violence, which plays a central role in the influential work of René Girard (1978).

21. This principle is exemplified, for instance, in our injunction to count to ten before acting on an angry impulse.

22. I regard it as probably no accident that the first examples of writing, dating from the early moments of the birth of civilization in the Near East, consist primarily of lists, tabulations, and records of fiscal transactions.

23. Leach (1986) discusses water symbolism in the story of Moses.

9
The Living Myth

1. I am inclined to believe that major generic dimensions of certain unconscious fantasies, especially oedipal ones, have innate genetic foundations. I think this for the same reason Freud thought so: empirically, such fantasies as those associated with castration fears, the primal scene, and seduction scenes appear too commonly, in too stereotyped a way, and with too much strength and centrality in psychic organization, despite widely varied individual experiences, to be explained by ontogenetic process and "real" experience alone. The same considerations apply, perhaps even more so, to the appearance of these themes, albeit in different guises and transformations, in the mythic and ritual symbolism of a wide and possibly universal array of cultural systems. While I do not believe in the historical reality of Freud's primal horde and the myth associated with it, it does seem likely that humans have, as part of their innate mental endowment, fantasies and associated affects, mental representations, and structures that are residues of our evolution from primates living in bands with male hierarchies that may have been related to mating strategies in the group. I shall leave this aspect of the power of myth and mythic symbolism for further exploration elsewhere.

2. Victor Turner, from whom I borrow the term "dominant symbol," writes: "The meaning-context of certain dominant symbols possesses a high degree of constancy and consistency throughout the total symbolic system. . . . Such symbols also possess considerable autonomy with regard to the aims of the rituals in which they appear. . . . They are the relatively fixed points in both the social and cultural structures. . . . They may be regarded . . . as ends in themselves, as representative of the axiomatic values of the widest . . . society" (1967b, 31–32).

3. This theoretical view of the relation between cultural symbols and individual fantasy is to be found also in the work of Spiro (1987b and 1987c for example) and Obeyesekere (1981, 1990).

4. See Paul (1979, 1990b) for other statements and applications of this view.

5. Bateson (1958); Rappaport (1972); Turner (1969). These are just a few representatives of a view in cultural anthropology that ritual corresponds, as it were, to the reproductive organs of society.

6. On the practices of Passover (and other festivals), see also Bokser (1984); Feeley-Harnick (1981); Glatzer (1979); Isaac Klein (1979); Raphael (1990); Segal (1963); and Waskow (1982), which is less scholarly but has an interesting and appealing viewpoint. See Grinberg (1962) for a deeply insightful psychoanalytic study of Passover, one that anticipates and parallels much of my own interpretation, and by which I have been much influenced.

7. Charles Sarnoff (1976) describes the process thus: "Myths characteristic of the culture provide ready-made heroes for fantasies [in latency]. Through such myths, the mechanisms of the structure of latency are adapted to passive identification with tales and legends characteristic of the child's social group. Ethical patterns conveyed by the legends are incorporated into the superego contents" (154).

Peter Brown (1991) also provides a succinct overview of the process through which people identify with stories.

8. I have not even opened here the vast question of the socialization techniques that contribute to the formation of obsessional character traits and defenses. Suffice it to say that I consider "schooling," that is, training in the skills of literacy and mathematics, from the beginning of latency onward, one of the primary devices for inculcating the skills needed for intellectualization, isolation of affect, and the eroticization of thought that, in moderation, lead to mastery of the requisite techniques of civilized bureaucracy. This is a large topic that I must leave to one side here.

9. The classic exposition of the difference between linear history and the cyclical eternal present of mythic time is that of Eliade (1965).

10. See Lacan (1977, 154).

11. I have put forward some of my ideas about cultural symbols as replicators parallel to, and in some kind of complex relation with, genetic replicators, in Paul 1987a, 1994b, and n.d. For another attempt to explain religion in terms of its liability to be replicated in Dawkins's sense, see Boyer (1994).

12. See Roy Wagner's ideas about "symbols that stand for themselves" (1986). See also Stromberg (1993).

13. An intriguing study of such recursive, self-reflexive phenomena is to be found in Hofstadter (1979).

14. Plaut points out that the phrase "this Teaching" refers to the book of Deuteronomy specifically; but that older commentators believed it to refer to the whole Torah and considered it proof that the Torah was the work of Moses (1983, 5:337).

15. For more on this widespread belief see La Barre (1984).

10
Christianity and the Prophet Like Moses

1. My discussion of the relation between images of Moses and Jesus in the Hebrew and Christian Scriptures has been guided by works of Boismard (1988), Chavasse (1954), D'Angelo (1979), Glasson (1963), Saldarini (1984), and most especially the admirable monograph of Marty (1984). As reference works I have consulted the *Anchor Bible* series (1964–94); the *NRSV-NIV Parallel New Testament in Greek and English* (1990); and Léon-Dufour (1980). Citations of the Christian Bible are from the Revised Standard Version.

2. The traditional iconography of the flight into Egypt in Western Christian–inspired art often includes the detail of the Holy Family riding on an ass, thus constituting a further allusion to the description of Moses's return to Egypt in Exodus 4:19–20.

3. For a full-length discussion of the mythic and folkloric significance of the number forty in the Western tradition, see Brandes (1985).

4. I discuss the idea that an intention to commit an act can be distinguished from the act itself in my article "Act and Intention in Sherpa Society and Culture" (1995).

5. It is of course a matter of vital importance that Saint Paul renounced the laws of *kashrut* and the *mitzvah* of circumcision, thereby clearing away major obstacles to the spread of the doctrine beyond the confines of Jewry.

6. I cannot expand on the point here, but this passage certainly points to the Kleinian fantasies of oral incorporation and introjection of the maternal body to which I referred when claiming Moses as the "nursing father" in his role of provider of food for the Israelites in the desert.

7. I am, of course, aware that postbiblical Christian theology usually identifies the original sin as the "fall" of the primal pair, Adam and Eve, when they

disobeyed God in the Garden of Eden. Clearly, I identify it differently. The situation in the garden, however, is also a close replica of the paradigmatic triad of the primal horde, in which God is the senior male, Adam the junior male, and Eve the woman. Adam's "rebellion" and subsequent fall might thus be understood as a symbol or token, serving as a displacement story for the far more elaborate mythic structure I have identified in the narrative, from which it derives its otherwise apparently inappropriate power, and which accounts for its drastic consequences. I have discussed the story of the Garden of Eden in Paul (1977). Reik (1958) interprets the Fall story as a version of the primal-horde scenario.

8. The phrase translated in the RSV as "Author of life" is *archēgon tēs zōēs.* The word *archēgon* appears four times in the Christian Bible, where it variously means "author," "originator," "prince," or "pioneer," in the sense of one who leads the way for others to follow.

9. For that matter, Moses also lied, in claiming that he wished, not to take the Israelites permanently out of Egypt, but to retire to the wilderness to perform a religious ritual.

10. Here, as elsewhere, the application to the present discussion of Alan Fiske's theory of the elementary relational structures, particularly Equality Matching versus Communal Sharing, would be valuable and illuminating (1991).

11. Exactly the same scenario, by the way, is enacted in the story of *Oedipus Rex,* though with fewer characters, thanks to the ingenious way Sophocles fuses several parts into one character. Here, the original ruler of Thebes is Laius. Oedipus, by unwittingly killing him, becomes the usurping bad king, whose unpunished crime causes a plague (thus making him an infanticide, since the women are made barren). But Oedipus is also the avenger of Laius: when he discovers that he himself is the usurper, he castrates (blinds) and deposes himself. In doing so, he also enacts the part of the martyred victim. Finally, in banishing himself, Oedipus leaves the throne vacant for an "innocent" third party, Creon, his mother's brother.

Epilogue

1. I should emphasize that the assertion that the Bible story and the primal horde myth are identical does not imply that the Bible is the only vehicle by means of which the primal horde myth is transmitted, or that this myth is confined to the Judeo-Christian tradition, or that it is purely cultural and has no innate, genetic foundation. On the contrary, I think all these propositions are untrue. Further exploration of them, however, would be beyond the limits of the present book.

Bibliography

Alter, Robert. 1981. *The Art of Biblical Narrative*. New York: Basic.

Anchor Bible. 1964–94. William Foxwell Albright and David Noel Freedman, general eds. Garden City, N.Y.: Doubleday.

Andriolo, Karin R. 1973. A Structural Analysis of Genealogy and Worldview in the Old Testament. *American Anthropologist* 75:1657–1669.

Arlow, Jacob A. 1951. A Psychoanalytic Study of a Religious Rite, Bar Mitzvah. *Psychoanalytic Study of the Child*. New York: International Universities Press, 6:353–374.

———. 1961. Ego Psychology and the Study of Mythology. *Journal of the American Psychoanalytic Association* 9:371–393.

———. 1980. The Revenge Motive in the Primal Scene. *Journal of the American Psychoanalytic Association* 28:519–541.

———. 1995. Stilted Listening: Psychoanalysis as Discourse. *Psychoanalytic Quarterly* 64:215–233.

Ater, M. 1983. A New Look at "Moses and Monotheism." *Israel Journal of Psychiatry and Related Sciences* 20:179–191.

Auerbach, Elias. 1975. *Moses*. Detroit: Wayne State University Press.

Auerbach, Erich. 1974 [1946]. *Mimesis: The Representation of Reality in Western Literature*. Trans. W. Trask. Princeton: Princeton University Press.

Axelrod, Robert. 1984. *The Evolution of Cooperation*. New York: Basic.

Bakan, David. 1958. *Sigmund Freud and the Jewish Mystical Tradition*. Princeton: Van Nostrand.

———. 1966. *The Duality of Human Existence: Isolation and Communion in Western Man*. Boston: Beacon.

———. 1972. *Slaughter of the Innocents*. Boston: Beacon.

———. 1979. *And They Took Themselves Wives: The Emergence of Patriarchy in Western Civilization*. New York: Harper and Row.

Bal, Mieke. 1988. *Death and Dissymmetry: The Politics of Coherence in the Book of Judges*. Chicago: University of Chicago Press.

Barag, G. G. 1946. The Mother in the Religious Concepts of Judaism. *American Imago* 4:32–53.

Baron, Salo W. 1969 [1939]. A Review of Freud. In R. J. Christen and H. E. Hazelton, eds. *Monotheism and Moses*. Lexington, Mass.: D.C. Heath, 39–43.

Barthes, Roland. 1983. *On Racine*. Trans. R. Howard. New York: Performing Arts Journal Publications.

Bateson, Gregory. 1958. *Naven: A Survey of the Problems Suggested by a Composite Picture of the Culture of a New Guinea Tribe Drawn from Three Points of View*. Stanford: Stanford University Press.

Beidelman, T. O. 1974. *W. Robertson Smith and the Sociological Study of Religion*. Chicago: University of Chicago Press.

Benjamin, Jessica. 1988. *The Bonds of Love: Psychoanalysis, Feminism, and the Problem of Domination*. New York: Pantheon.

Bennington, Geoffrey. 1994. Mosaic Fragments: If Derrida Were an Egyptian . . . In G. Bennington, *Legislations: The Politics of Deconstruction*. London: Verso, 207–228.

Bergmann, Martin. 1982. Moses and the Evolution of Freud's Identity. In M. Ostow, ed., *Judaism and Psychoanalysis*. New York: Ktav.

———. 1992. *In the Shadow of Moloch: The Sacrifice of Children and Its Impact on Western Religions*. New York: Columbia University Press.

Berke, Joseph, and Stanley Schneider. 1994. Antithetical Meanings of "the Breast." *International Journal of Psychoanalysis* 75:491–498.

Bettelheim, Bruno. 1962. *Symbolic Wounds*. New York: Collier.

Biale, David. 1992. *Eros and the Jews: From Biblical Israel to Contemporary America*. New York: Basic.

Bialik, Hayim Nahman, and Yehoshua Hana Ravnitzky, eds. 1992. *The Book of Legends: Sefer Ha-Aggadah; Legends from the Talmud and Midrash*. Trans. W. G. Braude. New York: Schocken. (Hebrew edition: *Sefer ha-Aggadah*, 1952. Tel-Aviv: Dvir.)

Bin Gorion, Micha Joseph, ed. 1976. *Mimekor Yisrael: Classical Jewish Folktales*. Trans. I. M. Lask. Vol. 1. Bloomington: Indiana University Press.

Bloom, Harold. 1990. The Author J. In D. Rosenberg and H. Bloom, *The Book of J*. New York: Grove, Weidenfeld, 3–55.

Blos, Peter. 1985. *Son and Father*. New York: Free Press.

Blum, Ernst. 1956. Über Sigmund Freuds: Der Mann Moses und die monotheistische Religion. *Psyche* 10:367–390.

Blum, Harold P. 1991. Freud and the Figure of Moses: The Moses of Freud. *Journal of the American Psychoanalytic Association* 39:513–536.

Blumenthal, David. 1993. *Facing the Abusing God: A Theology of Protest*. Louisville, Ky.: Westminster/John Knox.

Boehm, Christopher. 1984. *Blood Revenge: The Enactment and Management of Conflict in Montenegro and Other Tribal Societies*. Philadelphia: University of Pennsylvania Press.

Boismard, Marie-Emile. 1988. *Moïse ou Jésus: Essai de Christologie Johannique*. Louvain, Belgium: University Press of Leuven.

Bokser, Baruch M. 1984. *The Origins of the Seder: The Passover Rites and Early Rabbinic Judaism*. Berkeley: University of California Press.

Boyarin, Daniel. 1990. *Intertextuality and the Reading of Midrash*. Bloomington: Indiana University Press.

———. 1994. *Carnal Israel: Reading Sex in Talmudic Culture*. Berkeley: University of California Press.

Boyer, Pascal. 1994. *The Naturalness of Religious Ideas: A Cognitive Theory of Religion*. Berkeley: University of California Press.

Brandes, Stanley. 1985. *Forty: The Age and the Symbol*. Knoxville: University of Tennessee Press.

Brenner, Charles. 1982. *The Mind in Conflict.* New York: International Universities Press.

Breuer, Josef, and Sigmund Freud. 1895. *Studies on Hysteria.* In S. Freud, *The Standard Edition of the Complete Psychological Works of Sigmund Freud.* Ed. James Strachey. 24 vols. London: Hogarth, 1953–74, vol. 2.

Brown, Norman O. 1959. *Life against Death: The Psychoanalytical Meaning of History.* Middletown, Conn.: Wesleyan University Press.

———. 1966. *Love's Body.* New York: Viking.

Brown, Peter. 1991. *The Hypnotic Brain: Hypnotherapy and Social Communication.* New Haven: Yale University Press.

Buber, Martin. 1988. *Moses: The Revelation and the Covenant.* Atlantic Highlands, N.J.: Humanities Press.

Budge, E. A. Wallis. 1904. *The Gods of the Egyptians.* London: Methuen.

Calasso, Roberto. 1994. *The Ruin of Kasch.* Trans. W. Weaver and S. Sartarelli. Cambridge, Mass.: Belknap.

Carroll, Michael P. 1988. *Moses and Monotheism* and the Psychoanalytical Study of Early Christian Mythology. *Journal of Psychohistory* 15:295–310.

———. 1989. "Moses and Monotheism" Revisited—Freud's "Personal Myth"? *American Imago* 44:15–35.

Černy, J. 1954. Consanguineous Marriages in Pharaonic Egypt. *Journal of Egyptian Archaeology* 40:23–28.

Certeau, Michel de. 1988. The Fiction of History: The Writing of *Moses and Monotheism.* In M. de Certeau, *The Writing of History.* Trans. T. Conley. New York: Columbia University Press, 308–354.

Chasseguet-Smirgel, Janine. 1983. Perversion and the Universal Law. *International Review of Psycho-Analysis* 10:293–301.

———. 1985. *Creativity and Perversion.* London: Free Association Books.

Chavasse, Claude. 1954. Jesus Christ and Moses. Parts I and II. *Theology* 54:244–250, 289–296.

Christen, Robert J., and Harold E. Hazelton, eds. 1969. *Monotheism and Moses: The Genesis of Judaism.* Lexington, Mass.: D.C. Heath.

Clark, R. T. Rundle. 1959. *Myth and Symbol in Ancient Egypt.* London: Thames and Hudson.

Cohen, Jonathan. 1993. *The Origins and Evolution of the Moses Nativity Story.* Leiden: E. J. Brill.

Cohn, Norman. 1993. *Cosmos, Chaos, and the World to Come: The Ancient Roots of Apocalyptic Faith.* New Haven: Yale University Press.

Connerton, Paul. 1989. *How Societies Remember.* New York: Cambridge University Press.

Dalman, Gustaf. 1928. *Arbeit und Sitte in Palästina.* Volume 6: *Zeltleben, Vieh-und Milchwirtschaft, Jagd, Fischfang.* Gütersloh, Germany: C. Bertelsmann.

D'Angelo, Mary Rose. 1979. *Moses in the Letter to the Hebrews.* Missoula, Mont.: Scholars.

Dawkins, Richard. 1976. *The Selfish Gene.* Oxford: Oxford University Press.

———. 1982. *The Extended Phenotype*. Oxford: Oxford University Press.

Day, Max. 1988. A Psychoanalyst Looks at Moses in 1988. Unpublished.

Delaney, Carol. 1989. The Legacy of Abraham. In M. Bal, ed., *Anti-Covenant: Counter-Reading Women's Lives in the Hebrew Bible*. Sheffield: Almond Press, 27–41.

Desmonde, William H. 1950. The Murder of Moses. *American Imago* 7:351–367.

Devereux, Georges. 1953. Why Oedipus Killed Laius. *International Journal of Psychoanalysis* 34:134–141.

DeVos, George. 1975. The Dangers of Pure Theory in Anthropology. *Ethos* 3:77–91.

Donaldson, Mara. 1980. Kinship Theory in the Patriarchal Narratives: The Case of the Barren Wives. *Journal of the American Academy of Religion* 49:77–87.

Doria-Medina, Roberto. 1991. On Freud and Monotheism. *International Review of Psycho-Analysis* 18:489–500.

Douglas, Ann. 1995. *Terrible Honesty: Mongrel Manhattan in the 1920s*. New York: Farrar, Straus, and Giroux.

Douglas, Mary. 1966. The Abominations of Leviticus. In M. Douglas, *Purity and Danger: An Analysis of Concepts of Pollution and Taboo*. London: Routledge and Kegan Paul, 41–57.

DSM-IV. (*Diagnostic and Statistical Manual of Mental Disorders*.) 1994. 4th ed. Washington, D.C.: American Psychiatric Association.

Dulaney, Siri, and Alan Page Fiske. 1994. Similarities between Rituals and Obsessive-Compulsive Disorder: Is There a Common Neuropsychological Mechanism? *Ethos* 22:243–283.

Dunbar, Robin I. M. 1988. *Primate Social Systems*. Ithaca: Cornell University Press.

Dundes, Alan. 1980. The Hero Pattern and the Life of Jesus. In A. Dundes, *Interpreting Folklore*. Bloomington: Indiana University Press, 223–261.

———. 1987. The Symbolic Equivalence of Allomotifs in the Rabbit-Herd (AT 570). In A. Dundes, *Parsing through Customs: Essays by a Freudian Folklorist*. Madison: University of Wisconsin Press, 167–177.

Durkheim, Emile. 1915. *The Elementary Forms of the Religious Life*. Trans. J. W. Swain. New York: Free Press.

———. 1983. *Pragmatism and Sociology*. Cambridge: Cambridge University Press.

Edmunds, Lowell. 1985. *Oedipus: The Ancient Legend and Its Later Analogues*. Baltimore: Johns Hopkins University Press.

Edmunds, Lowell, and Alan Dundes, eds. 1983. *Oedipus: A Folklore Casebook*. New York: Garland.

Eilberg-Schwartz, Howard. 1990. *The Savage in Judaism: An Anthropology of Israelite Religion and Ancient Judaism*. Bloomington: Indiana University Press.

———. 1994a. *God's Phallus and Other Problems for Men and Monotheism*. Boston: Beacon.

———. 1994b. Homoeroticism and the Father God: An Unthought in Freud's *Moses and Monotheism*. *American Imago* 51:127–159.

Eilberg-Schwartz, Howard, ed. 1992. *People of the Body: Jews and Judaism from an Embodied Perspective*. Albany: State University of New York Press.

Eliade, Mircea. 1965. *The Myth of the Eternal Return: Cosmos and History*. Princeton: Princeton University Press.

Encyclopedia Judaica. 1972. Jerusalem: Keter.

Esman, Arnold H. 1989. Psychoanalysis and General Psychiatry: Obsessive-Compulsive Disorder as a Paradigm. *Journal of the American Psychoanalytic Association* 37:319–336.

Exodus Rabbah. See *Midrash Rabbah*.

Fairbairn, W. Ronald. 1952. *Psychoanalytic Studies of the Personality*. London: Tavistock.

Feeley-Harnick, Gillian. 1981. *The Lord's Table: Eucharist and Passover in Early Christianity*. Philadelphia: University of Pennsylvania Press.

Feldman, A. Bronson. 1955. Mother-country and Fatherland. *Psychoanalysis: Journal of Psychoanalytic Psychology* 3:27–45.

Feldman, Yael S. 1989. Recurrence and Sublimation: Toward a Psychoanalytic Approach to Biblical Narrative. In B. Olshen and Y. S. Feldman, eds., *Approaches to Teaching the Hebrew Bible as Literature*. New York: MLA Publications, 72–82.

————. 1994. "And Rebecca Loved Jacob," but Freud Did Not. In P. L. Rudnytsky and E. H. Spitz, eds., *Freud and Forbidden Knowledge*. New York: New York University Press, 7–25.

Fenichel, Otto. 1945. Obsession and Compulsion. In O. Fenichel, *The Psychoanalytic Theory of Neurosis*. New York: Norton, 268–310.

Fiske, Alan Page. 1991. *Structures of Social Life: The Four Elementary Forms of Human Relations*. New York: Free Press.

Forsyth, Dan W. 1991. Sibling Rivalry, Aesthetic Sensibility, and Social Structure in Genesis. *Ethos* 19:453–510.

Fox, Robin. 1980. *The Red Lamp of Incest*. New York: Dutton.

————. 1993. Sisters' Sons and Monkey's Uncles: Six Theories in Search of an Avunculate. In R. Fox, *Reproduction and Succession. Studies in Anthropology, Law, and Society*. New Brunswick, N.J.: Transaction, 191–232.

Frankel, Ellen. 1989. *The Classic Tales: 4000 Years of Jewish Lore*. Northvale, N.J.: Jason Aronson.

Frankfort, Henri. 1948. *Ancient Egyptian Religion: An Interpretation*. New York: Harper and Row.

————. 1951. *The Birth of Civilization in the Near East*. Bloomington: Indiana University Press.

Fredman, Ruth Gruber. 1981. *The Passover Seder: Afikoman in Exile*. Philadelphia: University of Pennsylvania Press.

Freedman, D. A. 1989. Obsessions and Normality. *Across-Species Comparisons and Psychiatry Newsletter* 2:5–8.

Freud, Anna. 1966. Obsessional Neurosis: A Summary of Psycho-Analytic Views Presented at the Congress. *International Journal of Psycho-Analysis* 47:116–122.

Freud, Sigmund. 1894. The Neuro-Psychoses of Defense. In S. Freud, *The Standard Edition of the Complete Psychological Works of Sigmund Freud*. Ed. James Strachey. (Hereafter *SE*) 24 vols. London: Hogarth, 1953–74, 3:41–61.

————. 1895. Obsessions and Phobias: Their Psychical Mechanisms and Their Aetiology. *SE* 3:69–82.

————. 1896. Further Remarks on the Neuro-Psychoses of Defence. *SE* 3:159–188.

————. 1900. *The Interpretation of Dreams*. *SE* vols. 4–5.

————. 1907. Obsessional Actions and Religious Practices. *SE* 9:115–128.

————. 1908a. Character and Anal Erotism. *SE* 9:167–176.

————. 1908b. "Civilized" Sexual Morality and Modern Nervous Illness. *SE* 9:177–204.

————. 1909. Notes upon a Case of Obsessional Neurosis. *SE* 10:151–318.

————. 1911. Psycho-Analytic Notes on an Autobiographical Account of a Case of Paranoia (Dementia Paranoides). *SE* 12:9–82.

————. 1913a. The Disposition to Obsessional Neurosis. *SE* 12:311–326.

————. 1913b. *Totem and Taboo: Some Points of Agreement between the Mental Lives of Savages and Neurotics*. *SE* 13:1–161.

————. 1914. On Narcissism: An Introduction. *SE* 14:67–104.

————. 1915a. Instincts and Their Vicissitudes. *SE* 14:111–140.

————. 1915b. Thoughts for the Times on War and Death. *SE* 14:273–308.

————. 1916–17. *Introductory Lectures on Psycho-Analysis*. *SE* vols. 15–16.

————. 1917. On Transformations of Instinct as Exemplified in Anal Erotism. *SE* 17:125–134.

————. 1918 [1914]. From the History of an Infantile Neurosis. *SE* 17:1–122.

————. 1919. The Uncanny. *SE* 17:217–252.

————. 1921. Group Psychology and the Analysis of the Ego. *SE* 18:65–144.

————. 1923. The Ego and the Id. *SE* 19:1–59.

————. 1925. An Autobiographical Study. *SE* 20:7–74.

————. 1926 [1925]. Inhibitions, Symptoms, and Anxiety. *SE* 20:75–172.

————. 1927. The Future of an Illusion. *SE* 21:1–56.

————. 1930 [1929]. *Civilization and Its Discontents*. *SE* 21:57–147.

————. 1931. Libidinal Types. *SE* 21:215–220.

————. 1939 [1934–38]. *Moses and Monotheism: Three Essays*. *SE* 23:1–138.

————. 1940 [1938]. Splitting of the Ego in the Process of Defense. *SE* 23:271–278.

————. 1987 [1915]. *A Phylogenetic Fantasy: Overview of the Transference Neuroses*. Ed. I. Grubrich-Simitis. Trans. Axel Hoffer and P. T. Hoffer. Cambridge, Mass.: Belknap.

Frieden, Ken. 1990. *Freud's Dream of Analysis*. Albany: State University of New York Press.

Friedman, Richard E. 1989. *Who Wrote the Bible?* New York: Summit.

Gager, John G. 1972. *Moses in Greco-Roman Paganism*. Nashville, Tenn.: Abington.

Gaster, Theodore H. 1953. *Festivals of the Jewish Year.* New York: Morrow.

Gay, Peter. 1987. *A Godless Jew: Freud, Atheism, and the Making of Psychoanalysis.* New Haven: Yale University Press.

Geertz, Clifford. 1973. Religion as a Cultural System. In C. Geertz, *The Interpretation of Cultures.* New York: Basic, 87–125.

Gilman, Sander. 1993. *Freud, Race and Gender.* Princeton: Princeton University Press.

Ginzberg, Louis. 1911. *The Legends of the Jews.* 7 vols. Philadelphia: Jewish Publication Society of America.

Girard, René. 1978. *Violence and the Sacred.* Trans. P. Gregory. Baltimore: Johns Hopkins University Press.

Glasson, T. F. 1963. *Moses in the Fourth Gospel.* Great Britain: SCM Press.

Glatzer, Nahum N. 1962. *Hammer on the Rock: A Short Midrash Reader.* New York: Schocken.

Glatzer, Nahum N., ed. 1979. *The Passover Haggadah.* New York: Schocken.

Goldberg, Harvey E. 1987. Torah and Children: Some Symbolic Aspects of the Reproduction of Jews and Judaism. In H. E. Goldberg, ed., *Judaism Viewed from Within and from Without.* Albany: State University of New York Press, 107–130.

Goldenweiser, Alexander. 1910. Totemism, an Analytical Study. *Journal of American Folklore* 23:179–293.

Goldin, Judah. 1971. *The Song at the Sea: Being a Commentary on a Commentary in Two Parts.* New Haven: Yale University Press.

———. 1988a. The Death of Moses: An Exercise in Midrashic Transposition. In J. Goldin, *Studies in Midrash and Related Literature.* Philadelphia: Jewish Publication Society, 175–186.

———. 1988b. The Youngest Son, or Where Does Genesis 38 Belong. In J. Goldin, *Studies in Midrash and Related Literature.* Philadelphia: Jewish Publication Society, 121–140.

Goldstein, Bluma. 1992. From Rome to Egypt: Freud's Mosaic Transformations. In B. Goldstein, *Reinscribing Moses. Heine, Kafka, Freud, and Schoenberg in a European Wilderness.* Cambridge: Harvard University Press, 66–126.

Gregory of Nyssa, Saint. 1978. *The Life of Moses.* New York: Paulist.

Griffiths, John Gwyn, ed. and trans. 1970. *Plutarch's De Iside et Osiride.* Cambridge: University of Wales Press.

Grinberg, Léon. 1962. Psychoanalytic Considerations on the Jewish Passover Totemic Sacrifice and Meal. *American Imago* 19:391–424.

Handelman, Susan A. 1987. *The Slayers of Moses: The Emergence of Rabbinic Interpretation in Modern Literary Theory.* Albany: State University of New York Press.

Hegel, Georg. 1967 [1807]. *The Phenomenology of Spirit.* Trans. J. B. Baillie. New York: Harper and Row.

Hinde, Robert A., ed. 1983. *Primate Social Relationships.* Oxford: Blackwell Scientific Publishers.

Hofstadter, Douglas R. 1979. *Gödel, Escher, Bach: An Eternal Golden Braid*. New York: Basic.

Holtz, Barry W., ed. 1984. *Back to the Sources: Reading the Classic Jewish Texts*. New York: Summit.

Hopkins, Keith. 1980. Brother-Sister Marriage in Roman Egypt. *Comparative Studies in Society and History* 22:303–354.

Hunt, Lynn. 1992. *The Family Romance of the French Revolution*. Berkeley: University of California Press.

Ingham, John M. 1992. Freud in a Forest of Symbols: The Religious Background of Psychoanalytic Anthropology. In D. H. Spain, ed., *Psychoanalytic Anthropology after Freud: Essays Marking the Fiftieth Anniversary of Freud's Death*. New York: Psyche, 139–161.

Jacoby, Susan. 1983. *Wild Justice: The Evolution of Revenge*. New York: Harper and Row.

Johnson, Allen W. 1992. Psychoanalysis and Materialism: Do They Mix? In D. H. Spain, ed., *Psychoanalytic Anthropology after Freud: Essays Marking the Fiftieth Anniversary of Freud's Death*. New York: Psyche, 224–249.

Johnson, Allen W., and Douglass Price-Williams. 1995. *Oedipus Ubiquitous: The Family Complex in World Folk Literature*. Stanford: Stanford University Press.

Jones, Ernest. 1953–57. *The Life and Work of Sigmund Freud*. 3 vols. New York: Basic.

Josephus, Flavius. 1978. *Jewish Antiquities*. Trans. St. John Thackeray. Cambridge: Harvard University Press.

JPS Torah Commentary. 1989–91. Nahum Sarna, gen. ed. Philadelphia: Jewish Publication Society.

Kamenetz, Roger. 1994. *The Jew in the Lotus: A Poet's Rediscovery of Jewish Identity in Buddhist India*. San Francisco: Harper.

Kardiner, Abram. 1977. *My Analysis with Freud: Reminiscences*. New York: Norton.

Kernberg, Otto F. 1984. *Object Relations Theory and Clinical Psychoanalysis*. Northvale, N.J.: Jason Aronson.

Klein, Dennis B. 1985. *Jewish Origins of the Psychoanalytic Movement*. Chicago: University of Chicago Press.

Klein, Isaac. 1979. *A Guide to Jewish Religious Practice*. New York: Jewish Theological Seminary of New York.

Klein, Melanie. 1948. *Contributions to Psychoanalysis 1921–1945*. London: Hogarth.

———. 1984. *Envy and Gratitude and Other Works, 1946–63*. New York: Free Press.

Kojève, Alexandre. 1969. *Introduction to the Reading of Hegel*. Ed. R. Queneau. Trans. J. H. Nicholls, Jr. New York: Basic.

Koret, Reuven J. 1986. The Pious Fraud: Freud and Joseph, Mann and Moses. *Response* 15:3–22.

Kris, Anton O. 1994. Freud's Treatment of a Narcissistic Patient. *International Journal of Psycho-Analysis* 75:649–664.

Krüll, Marianne. 1986. *Freud and His Father*. Trans. A. J. Pomerans. New York: Norton.

Kuper, Adam. 1988. *The Invention of Primitive Society: Transformations of an Illusion*. London: Routledge.

———. 1994. *The Chosen Primate: Human Nature and Cultural Diversity*. Cambridge: Harvard University Press.

La Barre, Weston. 1984. *Muelos: A Stone Age Superstition about Sexuality*. New York: Columbia University Press.

Lacan, Jacques. 1970. Radiophonie. *Scilicet* 2/3:55–99.

———. 1977a. *Ecrits: A Selection*. Trans. A. Sheridan. New York: Norton, 146–178.

———. 1977b. *Ecrits: A Selection*. Trans. A. Sheridan. New York: Norton, 179–225.

———. 1990. Introduction to the Names-of-the-Father Seminar. In J. Lacan, *Television*. Trans. D. Hollier et al. Ed. J. Copjec. New York: Norton, 81–97.

———. 1991. Oedipe et Moise et le pere de la horde. In J. Lacan, *Le Seminaire, 18: L'envers de la psychanalyse*. Paris: Seuil, 117–153.

———. 1992. *The Seminars of Jacques Lacan: Book VII, The Ethics of Psychoanalysis, 1959–60*. Ed. J.-A. Miller. Trans. D. Porter. New York: Norton.

Lakoff, George, and Mark Johnson. 1980. *Metaphors We Live By*. Chicago: University of Chicago Press.

Leach, Edmund. 1969. *Genesis as Myth and Other Essays*. London: Jonathan Cape.

———. 1970. *Claude Lévi-Strauss*. New York: Viking.

———. 1976. The Mother's Brother in Ancient Egypt. *Royal Anthropological Institute Newsletter* 15:19–21.

———. 1982. Anthropological Approaches to the Study of the Bible during the Twentieth Century. In G. M. Tucker and D. A. Knight, eds., *Humanizing America's Iconic Book*. Chico, Calif.: Scholars, 73–94.

———. 1983. Why Did Moses Have a Sister? In E. Leach and D. A. Aycock, *The Structural Study of Biblical Myth*. Cambridge: Cambridge University Press, 33–66.

———. 1986. The Big Fish in the Biblical Wilderness. *International Review of Psycho-Analysis* 13.129–111.

Léon-Dufour, Xavier. 1980. *Dictionary of the New Testament*. Trans. T. Prendergast. San Francisco: Harper and Row.

Lévi-Strauss, Claude. 1963. *Totemism*. Boston: Beacon.

———. 1967a. Social Structure. In C. Lévi-Strauss, *Structural Anthropology*. Trans. C. Jacobson and B. Grundfest Schoepf. Garden City, N.Y.: Doubleday Anchor, 269–319.

———. 1967b. Structural Analysis in Linguistics and in Anthropology. In C. Lévi-Strauss, *Structural Anthropology*. Trans. C. Jacobson and B. Grundfest Schoepf. Garden City, N.Y.: Doubleday Anchor, 29–53.

———. 1967c. The Structural Study of Myth. In C. Lévi-Strauss, *Structural Anthropology*. Trans. C. Jacobson and B. Grundfest Schoepf. Garden City, N.Y.: Doubleday Anchor, 202–228.

————. 1969. *The Elementary Structures of Kinship*. Trans. J. H. Bell, J. R. von Sturmer, and R. Needham. Boston: Beacon.

————. 1969–81. *Mythologiques*. Trans. J. Weightman and D. Weightman. 4 vols. New York: Harper and Row.

————. 1988a. Exode sur *Exode*. *L'Homme* 27:13–23.

————. 1988b. *The Jealous Potter*. Trans. B. Chorier. Chicago: University of Chicago Press.

Lévy-Valensi, Eliane Amado. 1984. *Le Moïse de Freud ou la référence occulte*. Monaco: Editions du Rocher.

Loewald, Hans W. 1979. The Waning of the Oedipus Complex. *Journal of the American Psychoanalytic Association* 27:751–775.

Loewenberg, Peter. 1971. Sigmund Freud as a Jew: A Study in Ambivalence and Courage. *Journal of the History of the Behavioral Sciences* 7:363–369.

Lyotard, Jean-François. 1977. Jewish Oedipus. Trans. S. Hanson. *Genre* 10:395–411.

McCloskey, Donald. 1994. Bourgeois Virtue. *American Scholar* 63:177–191.

McGrath, William J. 1986. *Freud's Discovery of Psychoanalysis*. Ithaca: Cornell University Press.

MacKinnon, Roger A., and Robert Michels. 1971. *The Psychiatric Interview in Clinical Practice*. Philadelphia: W. B. Saunders.

Mahler, Margaret, Fred Pine, and Anni Bergmann. 1975. *The Psychological Birth of the Human Infant: Symbiosis and Individuation*. New York: Basic.

Mahony, Patrick J. 1982. *Freud as a Writer*. Rev. ed. New Haven: Yale University Press.

————. 1989. *On Defining Freud's Discourse*. New Haven: Yale University Press.

Marcuse, Herbert. 1962. *Eros and Civilization: A Philosophical Inquiry into Freud*. New York: Viking.

Marty, William Henry. 1984. The New Moses. Ph.D. diss., Dallas Theological Seminary.

Mauss, Marcel. 1967. *The Gift: Forms and Functions of Exchange in Archaic Societies*. Trans. I. Cunnison. New York: Norton.

Meeker, Michael E. 1989. *The Pastoral Son and the Spirit of Patriarchy: Religion, Society, and Person among East African Stock Keepers*. Madison: University of Wisconsin Press.

Meissner, W. W. 1978. *The Paranoid Process*. New York: Jason Aronson.

————. 1984a. The Cult Phenomenon: Psychoanalytic Perspectives. *Psychoanalytic Study of Society*. Hillsdale, N.J.: Analytic, 10:91–111.

————. 1984b. *Psychoanalysis and Religious Experience*. New Haven: Yale University Press.

————. 1988. The Origins of Christianity. *Psychoanalytic Study of Society*. Hillsdale, N.J.: Analytic, 13:29–62.

————. 1990. Jewish Messianism and the Cultic Process. *Psychoanalytic Study of Society*. Hillsdale, N.J.: Analytic, 15:347–370.

Michaels, Joseph J., and Robert T. Porter. 1949. Psychiatric and Social Implications of Contrasts between Psychopathic Personality and Obsessive Compulsion Neurosis. *Journal of Nervous and Mental Disease* 109:122–132.

Middleton, Russell. 1962. Brother-Sister and Father-Daughter Marriage in Ancient Egypt. *American Sociological Review* 27:603–611.

Midrash Rabbah. 1939. Ed. H. Friedman and M. Simon. Trans. S. M. Lehrman. London: Soncino.

Miller, Amos W. 1965. *Understanding the Midrash: Interpretations of the Exodus for Modern Times.* New York: Jonathan David.

Miller, John W. 1983. Psychoanalytic Approaches to Biblical Religion. *Journal of Religion and Health* 22:19–29.

Miller, Justin. 1981. Interpretations of Freud's Jewishness, 1924–74. *Journal of the History of the Behavioral Sciences* 17:357–374.

Moore, Burness E., and Bernard D. Fine, eds. 1990. *Psychoanalytic Terms and Concepts.* New Haven: Yale University Press.

Nagera, Humberto. 1978. *Obsessional Neurosis: Developmental Psychopathology.* New York: Jason Aronson.

Nesse, Randolph M. 1990a. Evolutionary Explanations of Emotion. *Human Nature* 1:261–289.

———. 1990b. The Evolutionary Function of Repression and the Ego Defenses. *Journal of the American Academy of Psychoanalysis* 18:260–285.

NRSV-NIV Parallel New Testament in Greek and English. 1990. Trans. A. Marshall. Grand Rapids: Zondervan.

Numbers Rabbah. See *Midrash Rabbah.*

Obeyesekere, Gananath. 1981. *Medusa's Hair: An Essay on Personal Symbols and Religious Experience.* Chicago: University of Chicago Press.

———. 1990. *The Work of Culture: Symbolic Transformation in Psychoanalysis and Anthropology.* Chicago: University of Chicago Press.

Oelschlegel, Lydia. 1943. Regarding Freud's Book on "Moses": A Religio-Psychoanalytic Study. *Psychoanalytic Review* 30:67–76.

Oldham, John M., and Lois B. Morris. 1990. *The Personality Self-Portrait.* New York: Bantam.

Oring, Elliott. 1984. *The Jokes of Sigmund Freud: A Study in Humor and Jewish Identity.* Philadelphia: University of Pennsylvania Press.

Ostow, Mortimer, ed. 1982. *Judaism and Psychoanalysis.* New York: Ktav.

Pardes, Ilana. 1992. *Countertraditions in the Bible: A Feminist Approach.* Cambridge: Harvard University Press.

Patai, Raphael. 1981. *Gates of the Old City: A Book of Jewish Legends.* Detroit: Wayne State University Press.

Paul, Robert A. 1976. Did the Primal Crime Take Place? *Ethos* 4:311–352.

———. 1977. The First Speech Events: *Genesis* as the Nursery for Consciousness. *Psychocultural Review* 1:179–194.

———. 1979. Dumje: Paradox and Resolution in Sherpa Religious Symbolism. *American Ethnologist* 6:274–304.

———. 1980. Symbolic Interpretation in Psychoanalysis and Anthropology. *Ethos* 8:286–294.

———. 1982. *The Tibetan Symbolic World: Psychoanalytic Explorations.* Chicago: University of Chicago Press.

———. 1985a. David and Saul at En Gedi. *Raritan* 4:110–132.

———. 1985b. The Oedipus Complex in Anthropology Today. *Reviews in Anthropology* 12:353–360.

———. 1987a. The Individual and Society in Cultural and Biological Anthropology. *Cultural Anthropology* 2:80–93.

———. 1987b. Lina Wertmüller's "Seven Beauties": An Analysis and Reevaluation. *Journal of Psychoanalytic Anthropology* 9:7–32.

———. 1987c. The Question of Applied Psychoanalysis and the Interpretation of Cultural Symbolism. *Ethos* 15:82–103.

———. 1989. Psychoanalytic Anthropology. *Annual Review of Anthropology* 18:177–202.

———. 1990a. Bettelheim's Contribution to Anthropology. *Psychoanalytic Study of Society.* Hillsdale, N.J.: Analytic, 15:311–334.

———. 1990b. What Does Anybody Want? Desire, Purpose, and the Acting Subject in the Study of Culture. *Cultural Anthropology* 5:431–451.

———. 1991. Freud's Anthropology: A Reading of the Cultural Books. In J. Neu, ed., *The Cambridge Companion to Freud.* Cambridge: Cambridge University Press, 267–286.

———. 1994a. Freud, Sellin, and the Death of Moses. *International Journal of Psycho-Analysis* 75:825–837.

———. 1994b. My Approach to Psychological Anthropology. In M. M. Suarez-Orozco, G. Spindler, and L. Spindler, eds., *The Making of Psychological Anthropology II.* Fort Worth, Tex.: Harcourt, Brace, 80–102.

———. 1995. Act and Intention in Sherpa Society and Culture. In L. I. Rosen, ed., *Other Intentions.* Santa Fe: SAR Press, 15–46.

———. n.d. Symbolic Reproduction and Sherpa Monasticism. In U. Linke and W. Shapiro, eds., *Denying Biology.* New York: University Press of America, in press.

Peto, A. 1958. The Demonic Mother Imago in the Jewish Religion. *Psychoanalysis and the Social Sciences* 5:280–287.

Philo. 1935. *De Vita Moyesis.* Trans. F. H. Coulson. Cambridge: Harvard University Press.

Pitt-Rivers, Julian. 1977. *The Fate of Shechem or the Politics of Sex.* Cambridge: Cambridge University Press.

Plaut, W. Gunther, ed. and trans. 1983. *The Torah: A Modern Commentary.* 5 vols. New York: Union of American Hebrew Congregations.

Pollock, George H. 1988. Oedipus: The Myth, the Developmental Stage, the Universal Theme, the Conflict and the Complex. In G. H. Pollock and J. M. Ross, eds. *The Oedipus Papers*. Madison, Conn.: International Universities Press.

Pollock, George H., and John Munder Ross, eds. 1988. *The Oedipus Papers*. Madison, Conn.: International Universities Press.

Polzin, Robert. 1980. *Moses and the Deuteronomist: A Literary Study of the Deuteronomic History*. New York: Seabury.

Rad, Gerhard von. 1960. *Moses*. New York: Association Press.

Raglan, Lord (Fitzroy Sommerset). 1936. *The Hero: A Study in Tradition, Myth, and Drama*. New York: Oxford University Press.

Rank, Otto. 1964. The Myth of the Birth of the Hero. In O. Rank, *"The Myth of the Birth of the Hero" and Other Writings*. Trans. F. Robbins and S. E. Jeliffe. New York: Random House, 3–96.

Raphael, Chaim. 1990. *Festival Days: A History of Jewish Celebrations*. New York: Grove Weidenfeld.

Rapaport, Samuel. 1968. *A Treasury of the Midrash*. New York: Ktav.

Rapoport, Judith. 1989. *The Boy Who Couldn't Stop Washing*. New York: Dutton.

Rappaport, Roy A. 1972. The Obvious Aspects of Ritual. In R. A. Rappaport, *Ecology, Meaning, and Religion*. Berkeley: North Atlantic Books, 173–221.

Reid, Stephen. 1972. *Moses and Monotheism*: Guilt and the Murder of the Primal Father. *American Imago* 29:11–34.

Reik, Theodor. 1958. *Myth and Ritual: The Crime and Punishment of Mankind*. London: Hutchinson.

———. 1959. *Mystery on the Mountain: The Drama of the Sinai Revelation*. New York: Harper and Row.

Rice, Emanuel. 1990. *Freud and Moses: The Long Journey Home*. Albany: State University of New York Press.

———. 1993. Freud, Goethe, and Origen: The Duality and Slaying of Moses. *Psychoanalytic Study of Society*. Hillsdale, N.J.: Analytic, 18:361–380.

Ricoeur, Paul. 1970. *Freud and Philosophy: An Essay in Interpretation*. Trans. D. Savage. New Haven: Yale University Press.

Rieff, Philip. 1979. *Freud. The Mind of the Moralist*. Chicago. University of Chicago Press.

Robert, Marthe. 1976. *From Oedipus to Moses: Freud's Jewish Identity*. Trans. R. Manheim. Garden City, N.Y.: Doubleday.

Robertson, Ritchie. 1988. Freud's Testament: *Moses and Monotheism*. In E. Timms and N. Segal, eds., *Freud in Exile: Psychoanalysis and Its Vicissitudes*. New Haven: Yale University Press, 80–89.

———. 1994. On the Sources of *Moses and Monotheism*. In S. L. Gilman et al., eds., *Reading Freud's Reading*. New York: New York University Press, 261–285.

Robins, Gay. 1993. *Women in Ancient Egypt*. London: British Museum Press.

Rodseth, Lars, Richard W. Wrangham, Alisa Harrigan, and Barbara B. Smuts. 1991. The Human Community as a Primate Society. *Current Anthropology* 32:221–254.

Rogers, Robert. 1978. *Metaphor: A Psychoanalytic View*. Berkeley: University of California Press.

Róheim, Géza. 1985 [1923]. After the Death of the Primal Father. *Psychoanalytic Study of Society*. Hillsdale, N.J.: Analytic, 11:33–61.

Roith, Estelle. 1987. *The Riddle of Freud: Jewish Influences on His Theory of Female Sexuality*. London: Tavistock.

Rosenbaum, M., and A. M. Silverman, eds. and trans. 1963. *Pentateuch with Targum, Onkelos, Haphtarah, and Rashi's Commentary*. 5 vols. New York: Hebrew.

Rosenzweig, E. M. 1940. Some Notes, Historical and Psychoanalytical, on the People of Israel and the Land of Israel, with Special Reference to *Deuteronomy*. *American Imago* 1:50–63.

Rubin, Gayle. 1975. The Traffic in Women: Notes of the Political Economy of Sex. In R. Reiter, ed., *Toward an Anthropology of Women*. New York: Monthly Review Press.

Rubinstein, Richard L. 1968. *The Religious Imagination: A Study in Jewish Theology*. New York: Bobbs-Merrill.

Sahlins, Marshall. 1972. *Stone Age Economics*. Chicago: Aldine-Atherton.

———. 1976. *Culture and Practical Reason*. Chicago: University of Chicago Press.

Saldarini, Anthony J. 1984. *Jesus and Passover*. New York: Paulist.

Salzman, Leon. 1980. *Treatment of the Obsessional Personality*. New York: Jason Aronson.

Samuels, Robert. 1994. *Between Philosophy and Psychoanalysis: Lacan's Reconstruction of Freud*. New York: Routledge.

Sandler, Joseph, and A. Hazari. 1960. The Obsessional: On the Psychological Classification of Obsessional Character Traits and Symptoms. *British Journal of Medical Psychology* 33:113–122.

Sarna, Nahum. 1987. *Exploring Exodus: The Heritage of Biblical Israel*. New York: Schocken.

Sarnoff, Charles. 1976. *Latency*. New York: Jason Aronson.

Schafer, Roy. 1960. The Loving and Beloved Super-Ego in Freud's Structural Theory. *Psychoanalytic Study of the Child*. New York: International Universities Press, 15:168–188.

Schieffelin, Edward L. 1976. *The Sorrow of the Lonely and the Burning of the Dancers*. New York: St. Martin's.

Scholem, Gershom, ed. 1949. *Zohar: The Book of Splendor*. New York: Schocken.

Schorske, Carl E. 1993. Freud's Egyptian Dig. *New York Review of Books*, May 27, 35–40.

Schur, Max. 1972. *Freud: Living and Dying*. New York: International Universities Press.

Segal, J. B. 1963. *The Hebrew Passover: From the Earliest Times to AD 70*. London: Oxford University Press.

Sellin, Ernst. 1922. *Mose und seine Bedeutung für die israelitisch-judische Religionsgeschichte*. Leipzig: A. Deichertsche Verlagsbuchhandlung.

Shapiro, David. 1965. *Neurotic Styles*. New York: Basic.

Shapiro, Theodore. 1977. Oedipal Distortions in Severe Character Pathologies: Developmental and Theoretical Considerations. *Psychoanalytic Quarterly* 46:559–579.

Shapiro, Theodore, and R. Perry. 1976. Latency Revisited: The Age 7 Plus or Minus 1. *Psychoanalytic Study of the Child.* New Haven: Yale University Press, 32:79–105.

Shengold, Leonard. 1988. *Halo in the Sky: Observations on Anality and Defense.* New Haven: Yale University Press, 1992.

Silver, Daniel Jeremy. 1982. *Images of Moses.* New York: Basic.

Simon, Bennett. 1991. Is the Oedipus Complex Still the Cornerstone of Psychoanalysis? *Journal of the American Psychoanalytic Association* 39:641–668.

Singer, Milton. 1958. The Great Tradition in a Metropolitan Center: Madras. In M. Singer, ed., *Traditional India.* Philadelphia: American Folklore Society, 140–182.

Slater, Philip. 1971. *The Glory of Hera: Greek Mythology and the Greek Family.* Boston: Beacon.

Smith, William Robertson. 1894. *Lectures on the Religion of the Semites.* London: Adam and Charles Black.

Smuts, Barbara, et al., eds. 1987. *Primate Societies.* Chicago: University of Chicago Press.

Spiro, Melford E. 1982. *Oedipus in the Trobriands.* Chicago: University of Chicago Press.

———. 1987a. *Culture and Human Nature.* Chicago: University of Chicago Press.

———. 1987b. Collective Representations and Mental Representations in Religious Symbol Systems. In M. E. Spiro, *Culture and Human Nature.* Chicago: University of Chicago Press.

———. 1987c. Religious Systems as Culturally Constituted Defense Mechanisms. In M. E. Spiro, *Culture and Human Nature.* Chicago: University of Chicago Press.

———. 1987d. Whatever Happened to the Id? In M. E. Spiro, *Culture and Human Nature.* Chicago: University of Chicago Press.

Steiner, John, ed. 1989. *The Oedipus Complex Today.* London: Karnac.

Stern, Menahem. 1974–84. *Greek and Latin Authors on Jews and Judaism.* 3 vols. Jerusalem: Israel Academy of Sciences and Humanities.

Sternberg, Meir. 1985. *The Poetics of Biblical Narrative.* Bloomington: Indiana University Press.

Stromberg, Peter. 1993. Self Referential Symbols and Identity in a Swedish Church. Paper presented at annual meeting of the American Anthropological Association, San Francisco.

Trivers, Robert. 1971. The Evolution of Reciprocal Altruism. *Quarterly Review of Biology* 46:35–57.

Turner, Victor. 1967a. Ritual Symbolism, Morality, and Social Structure among the Ndembu. In V. Turner, *The Forest of Symbols: Aspects of Ndembu Ritual.* Ithaca: Cornell University Press, 48–58.

———. 1967b. Symbols in Ndembu Ritual. In V. Turner, *The Forest of Symbols: Aspects of Ndembu Ritual*. Ithaca: Cornell University Press, 19–47.

———. 1969. *The Ritual Process: Structure and Anti-Structure*. Chicago: Aldine.

Van Herik, Judith. 1982. Renunciation in the Past: Moses' Monotheism. In J. Van Herik, *Freud on Femininity and Faith*. Berkeley: University of California Press, 170–190.

Vaux, Roland de. 1961. *Ancient Israel: Its Life and Institutions*. Trans. J. McHugh. New York: McGraw-Hill.

Velikovsky, Immanuel. 1941. The Dreams that Freud Dreamed. *Psychoanalytic Review* 28:487–511.

Vitz, Paul. 1988. *Sigmund Freud's Christian Unconscious*. New York: Guilford.

Wagner, Roy. 1986. *Symbols That Stand for Themselves*. Chicago: University of Chicago Press.

Wallace, Edwin R. 1977. The Psychodynamic Determinants of "Moses and Monotheism." *Psychiatry* 40:79–87.

———. 1983. *Freud and Anthropology: A History and Reappraisal*. New York: International Universities Press.

Waskow, Arthur. 1982. *Seasons of Our Joy: A Handbook of Jewish Festivals*. Toronto: Bantam.

Weiner, Annette. 1992. *Inalienable Possessions: The Paradox of Keeping-While-Giving*. Berkeley: University of California Press.

Weiss-Rosmarin, Trude. 1939. *The Hebrew Moses: An Answer to Sigmund Freud*. New York: Jewish Book Club.

Wellisch, Paul. 1954. *Isaac and Oedipus*. London: Routledge and Kegan Paul.

Wildavsky, Aaron. 1984. *The Nursing Father: Moses as a Political Leader*. Tuscaloosa: University of Alabama Press.

Wolfenstein, Eugene V. 1993. *Psychoanalytic-Marxism: Groundwork*. New York: Guilford.

Wulff, M. 1950. An Appreciation of Freud's *Moses and Monotheism*. In M. Wulff, ed., *Max Eitington: In Memoriam*. Jerusalem: Israel Psychoanalytic Society, 125–142.

Yerushalmi, Yosef Hayim. 1982. *Zakhor: Jewish History and Jewish Memory*. Seattle: University of Washington Press.

———. 1989. Freud on the "Historical Novel": From the Manuscript Draft (1934) of *Moses and Monotheism*. *International Journal of Psycho-Analysis* 70:375–395.

———. 1991. *Freud's Moses: Judaism Terminable and Interminable*. New Haven: Yale University Press.

Zeligs, Dorothy F. 1960. The Role of the Mother in the Development of Hebraic Monotheism: As Exemplified in the Life of Abraham. *Psychoanalytic Study of Society*. Hillsdale, N.J.: Analytic, 1:287–310.

———. 1974. *Psychoanalysis and the Bible: A Study in Depth of Seven Leaders*. New York: Bloch.

———. 1986. *Moses: A Psychodynamic Study*. New York: Human Sciences Press.

Index